CELEBRATION
OF
CONTINUITY

CELEBRATION OF CONTINUITY

Themes in Classic East Asian Poetry

PETER H. LEE

HARVARD UNIVERSITY PRESS
CAMBRIDGE, MASSACHUSETTS
AND LONDON, ENGLAND
1979

Printed in the United States of America

Publication of this book has been aided by
a grant from the Harvard-Yenching Institute

Library of Congress Cataloging in Publication Data

Lee, Peter H., 1929–
Celebration of continuity.

Includes bibliographical references and index.
1. Chinese poetry—Themes, motives. 2. Korean poetry—Themes, motives. 3. Japanese poetry—Themes, motives. I. Title.
PL2307.L4 895 78-26145
ISBN 0-674-10457-9

ACKNOWLEDGMENTS

MY INDEBTEDNESS in writing the present book has been cumulative. I am grateful to the John Simon Guggenheim Memorial Foundation for giving me the opportunity to think and travel in several lands.

Parts of several chapters, in a different version, were presented at the conferences on comparative East Asian literature sponsored by the Association for Asian Studies, and I have profited from the comments offered by discussants, especially Richard A. Lanham, Barbara K. Lewalski, Michael C. J. Putnam, and A. Walton Litz. A portion of Chapter One appeared earlier in my *Songs of Flying Dragons: A Critical Reading* (Harvard University Press, 1975), and I am grateful to the Harvard-Yenching Institute for permission to use the material in a modified form.

I am particularly indebted to Hans H. Frankel, Josephine Miles, Earl Miner, and Leonard Nathan for their generous help and encouragement throughout the course of writing; and to James J. Y. Liu for reading my translations of Chinese poetry.

Finally, I wish to acknowledge with thanks permission to quote copyrighted material:

Arion, A Journal of Humanities and Classics, for Peter Whigham's translation of Sappho in *Arion,* IV (1965), 612, by permission of *Arion* and Peter Whigham.

Athlone Press of the University of London, for William Berg, *Early Virgil,* copyright 1974 William Berg.

Cambridge University Press, for H. J. Chaytor, *The Troubadours and England,* copyright 1923 Cambridge University Press; and Ch'u Ta-kao, *Chinese Lyrics,* copyright 1937 Cambridge University Press.

Columbia University Press, for Burton Watson, *Chinese Lyricism,* copyright 1971 Columbia University Press; Burton Watson, *The Complete Works of Chuang Tzu,* copyright 1971 Columbia University Press; *Chinese Rhyme-Prose,* copyright 1968 Columbia University

Press; and *The Manyōshū,* copyright 1965 Columbia University Press; Columbia University Press and Jonathan Cape, Ltd., for Burton Watson, tr., *Cold Mountain: 100 Poems by the T'ang Poet Han Shan,* copyright 1962 Burton Watson.

Constable & Co. Ltd., for Helen Waddell, *Medieval Latin Lyrics,* 1944.

Doubleday & Company, Inc., for *Sunflower Splendor,* edited by Wu-chi Liu and Irving Yucheng Lo, copyright 1975 Wu-chi Liu and Irving Lo, by permission of Doubleday.

George Allen & Unwin, Ltd., and Grove Press, Inc., for Arthur Waley, *The Book of Songs,* copyright 1954; and George Allen & Unwin, Ltd., and Alfred A. Knopf, Inc., for *Translations from the Chinese,* translated by Arthur Waley, copyright 1919 and renewed 1947 Arthur Waley.

Angus C. Graham, for A. C. Graham, tr., *The Book of Lieh-tzu* (London: John Murray, 1966), copyright 1960 A. C. Graham.

Grove Press, Inc., and Penguin Books, Ltd., for *Anthology of Chinese Literature,* I, edited by Cyril Birch, copyright 1965 Grove Press, Inc.; *Anthology of Japanese Literature,* edited by Donald Keene, copyright 1955 Grove Press, Inc., by permission of Grove Press, Inc., and Donald Keene.

Hong Kong University Press, for Shih-shun Liu, *One Hundred and One Chinese Poems,* copyright 1967 Hong Kong University Press.

Indiana University Press, for Rolfe Humphries, *Ovid, Metamorphoses,* copyright 1955 Indiana University Press.

Jonathan Cape Limited, for *Poems of François Villon,* translated by Norman Cameron, by permission of Alan S. Hodge and Jonathan Cape Limited.

James Michie, for *The Odes of Horace* (London: Rupert Hart-Davis, 1964), copyright 1963 James Michie.

Monumenta Serica, for Lois Fusek, "The Kao-T'ang Fu," XXX (1972–73), 417.

Oxford University Press, for C. M. Bowra, *Greek Lyric Poetry* (2nd ed., 1961), copyright 1961 Oxford University Press; Peter Dronke, *Medieval Latin and the Rise of European Love-Lyric* (2 vols., 2nd ed. 1968), vol. I, copyright 1968 Oxford University Press; David Hawkes, *Ch'u Tz'u: The Songs of the South,* copyright 1959 Oxford University Press; David Hawkes, *A Little Primer of Tu Fu,* copyright 1967 Oxford University Press; James Robert Hightower, *The Poetry of T'ao Ch'ien,* copyright 1970 Oxford University Press; and T. F. Higham and C. M. Bowra, *The Oxford Book of Greek Verse in Translation,* copyright 1950 Oxford University Press, by permission of Oxford University Press and Jack Lindsay, from *Theocritus: The Complete Poems,* published by Fanfrolico Press, 1930.

Penguin Books, Ltd., for A. C. Graham, *Poems of the Late T'ang* (Penguin Classics, 1967), copyright 1965 A. C. Graham; Robert Kotewall and Norman L. Smith, *The Penguin Book of Chinese Verse* (Penguin Poets, 1962), copyright 1962 Norman L. Smith and Robert Kotewall; and D. C. Lau, *Lao tzu: Tao Te Ching* (Penguin Classics, 1963), copyright 1963 D. C. Lau.

Princeton University Press, for selections from Wing-tsit Chan, *A Source Book in Chinese Philosophy,* copyright 1963 Princeton University Press (Princeton Paperback, 1969, pp. 7, 8, 104); and James J. Y. Liu, *Major Lyricists of the Northern Sung, A. D. 960–1126,* copyright 1974 Princeton University Press (pp. 56–57, 133, 139).

Stanford University Press, for Helen Craig McCullough, *Tales of Ise: Lyrical Episodes from Tenth-Century Japan,* by permission of Stanford University Press, copyright 1968 The Board of Trustees of the Leland Stanford Junior University.

The Bobbs-Merrill Company and John Warden, for John Warden, *The Poems of Propertius,* copyright 1972 Bobbs-Merrill Company, Inc.

The Macmillan Publishing Co., Inc., and A. P. Watt Ltd., for *The Collected Poems of W. B. Yeats,* 2 lines from "Sailing to Byzantium" (copyright 1928 Macmillan Publishing Co., Inc., renewed 1956 Georgie Yeats); 6 lines from "Lapis Lazuli" (copyright 1940 Georgie Yeats, renewed 1968 Bertha Georgie Yeats, Michael Butler Yeats, and Anne Yeats).

Unesco, for Peter H. Lee, *Poems from Korea: A Historical Anthology.* Published by George Allen & Unwin, Ltd., and the University Press of Hawaii, copyright 1964, 1974, Unesco.

University of California Press, for Wai-lim Yip, *Chinese Poetry: Major Modes and Genres,* copyright 1976 The Regents of the University of California, by permission of University of California Press.

University of Chicago Press, for *Greek Lyrics,* copyright 1949, 1955, 1960 Richmond Lattimore; *The Iliad of Homer,* copyright 1951 University of Chicago; Smith Palmer Bovie, *Virgil's Georgics,* copyright 1956 University of Chicago; and A. C. Graham, "Chuang Tzu's Essay on Seeing Things as Equal," *History of Religion,* IX (1969–1970).

University of Michigan Press, for Frank O. Copley, *Catullus: The Complete Poems,* copyright 1957 University of Michigan.

Vanderbilt University Press, for Alan Ayling and Duncan Mackintosh, *A Collection of Chinese Lyrics,* copyright 1965 Alan Ayling and

Duncan Mackintosh; and *A Further Collection of Chinese Lyrics,* copyright 1969 Alan Ayling and Duncan Mackintosh.

Yale University Press, for *Perspectives on the T'ang,* ed. Arthur F. Wright and Denis Twitchett, copyright 1973 Yale University Press; Hans H. Frankel, *The Flowering Plum and the Palace Lady: Interpretations of Chinese Poetry,* copyright 1976 Yale University Press; and James J. Wilhelm, *The Cruelest Month,* copyright 1965 Yale University Press.

CONTENTS

CELEBRATION
OF
CONTINUITY

INTRODUCTION

THE READER of East Asian poetry is often struck by the frequency of certain phrases, images or image clusters, and themes. We recognize their recurrence and evaluate their functions in the contexts and in the community. Analysis of recurring elements in different forms on the same subject may help to identify a poem as belonging to a certain kind, and not to some other. Such common patterns of imagery and thought have both structural and informational functions; they help the poet to organize his material and provide the reader with readily identifiable modes of orientation. The identification of the common features—I call them topics (topoi)[1]—is even more significant in a society where poetry was an oral as well as communal art; where the spoken word was as important as the written; and where the poet and the singer of poetry had a special social and cultural role. Traditional East Asian poetry assumes an ideal audience with knowledge of principal topics and thematic patterns of a genre. What may now appear to be problematic—rhetorical devices, organizing techniques, and other strategies—were part of a poetic tradition.

The importance of the poet's relationship to his subject and audience may be illustrated by the fact that in East Asia most poetry at one time or another was chanted or sung, often accompanied by music. The "airs" in the *Book of Songs* were folk songs and were supposed to be sung; so were shamanist ritual pieces, "Nine Songs," in the *Ch'u tz'u* anthology, early anonymous ballads (*yüeh-fu*), and early lyrics (*tz'u*). In Korea all poems were meant to be sung. In that society, letters did not destroy but conserved memory. Retentive and creative, memory was a thesaurus of poetry, the receptacle of the living word. The frequency of verbal parallels and formulaic expressions[2] points to the art of creation. Memory reminded the poet of the right movement of thought and sequence of topics, and the poet composed by phrases, motifs, and themes, each theme serving as a mnemonic device for the poet and audience. (Does this mode of composition account for the paratactic nature of East Asian poetry?) The poet's task was to transmit living tradition by a new arrangement of old material, thus lending added significance to the tradition. The poet's (or singer's) countless variations on the same theme were a source of pleasure and a compliment to the memory of listeners, who were quick to recognize allusions to earlier versions, to see the efficacy of the old in the new contexts, and to feel the aesthetic response his invention aroused.

Important images, especially nature images, tend to develop into topics in East Asian poetry. In the *Book of Songs,* which has been proven to be formulaic poetry in an oral tradition,[3] the technique of *hsing* signals a motif or theme by the thematic introduction of nature scenes. The frequence of nature images and of formula phrases, both of Chinese and native origin, in the twenty-one Japanese imperial anthologies (compiled from c. 905 to 1439) or in collections of Korean *sijo* poetry (the latest one lists a total of 3,335 poems) is striking.[4] Japanese poetics insists that the *haiku* contain a season indicator, pointing probably to its thematic orientation. Seasonal, topical, and structural requirements demand certain images; others are required by tradition and convention, serving to establish community of mind and of imagination between poet and audience. Some topoi in Japanese and Korean poetry are of Chinese origin, for example, the sky river (the Milky Way), clouds and rain, the Peach Blossom Spring, the chrysanthemum, and the five willows, the last three from T'ao Ch'ien's poetry.[5] These were first used in writings in Chinese and later in the vernacular. Unlike the difficult metamorphosis of unfamiliar to familiar images in pictorial art (the Castel Sant'Angelo in Rome was transformed into a timbered burg with high-pitched roof by a German woodcut artist [1557]),[6] the verbal reference, the Peach Blossom Spring, for example, could be invoked by a few images—peach blossoms, a fisherman, a stream—or by any combination of these. The use of the topos of *locus amoenus,* an ideal place remote in time or space, could not be adopted without the symbolism it stood for.

Therefore, an inventory of themes, motifs, archetypes, and images or associated images central to the outlook of the East Asian literary mind may offer insight into our understanding of that poetry. Such inquiry will help us comprehend the poet's compositional method and the interplay between tradition and individuality, the vital exchange between the old and the new, "a change in sensibility and views of life and the world, and the individual variation on the traditional theme."[7] Such study should not only discover and classify the conscious use of literary "constants," but try to account for the contextual functions, the qualitative distinctions, and the individual use to which these constants are put.[8] It should attempt, whenever possible, to trace not only variations and innovations in a theme and convention, but stages of their development, the interplay between the typical and the individual.

Certain preferred subjects are derived from universal and timeless themes; but they also reflect the philosophical, political, and aesthetic concerns of the times, the encounter of poetry with history. The truncated propositions of much nature poetry in China, and especially in Yi dynasty Korea, when Confucianism was an official political ideology and society placed so much premium on public service, include: the relative merits of engagement and withdrawal, the preference of country life to city life, the nature of fame. The relative absence in Japan of certain preferred subjects and topoi so prominent in China and Korea points to differences in that country's institutions, beliefs, and literary tastes. Largely missing, for example, are such types of praise poetry as country-house poems and the "not finding him in" topos; retirement poetry built upon the Confucian-Taoist double vision, especially the topos of the fisherman as sage; friendship poetry—send-off poems, poems of parting, on wine, and *carpe diem;* and such Taoist views of time as nondiscrimination. There the priority rests on the poetry of the seasons and of love, as the imperial anthologies seem to indicate.

Whatever the preferred subject, it is shaped and exemplified in the literary heritage and offers us "an array of ways to look at the real world," "a special way to make of culture a common place."[9] The poet creates an artifact by combining topics, which are changed by precedents, and his invention consists in assimilating, managing, and manipulating the material, a complex of allusions and effects. By assimilating the techniques of precedents and by managing topics, he creates his own thematic pattern and makes traditional images newly perceptual. By the creative use of the past, he constantly asserts his relation with tradition and renews cultural contacts between himself and audience. Whatever stance the poet or singer assumes, he is aware of the function of poetry in the education of society and in the development of the imagination.

My study is devoted to the identification and analysis of major topics arranged according to preferred subjects—praise, nature, love, friendship, and time. Although my point of departure is Korean poetry, I have tried not to lose sight of examples in other East Asian and in Western languages, stressing the "differences at the points of maximum resemblance."[10] The poem as poem seeks other poems of a similar kind for recognition and evaluation. East Asian poetry is a field in which the structural diachronist, Guillén's ideal literary critic,[11] would feel at home. The literary value cannot be equated with techniques alone, and I will try to avoid such pitfalls as "ideological appropriation and formalistic devaluation."[12] My discrimination must return the poem, with due consideration of its status in the community, to its right place.

Because my study does not attempt to be historical, such perennial critical issues as spontaneity and artistry, inspiration and art, originality and imitation, are outside its scope. Spontaneous expression often implies, however, the internalization of techniques, and unlabored lines that seem to be produced effortlessly are, like Castiglione's *sprezzatura* (nonchalance), as much a product of inspiration as of art. The author of a recent book on Robert Frost has proposed calling the individual poem "a linguistic preservation of a landscape-engaging act of consciousness."[13] Some critics of the phenomenological school, who emphasize the modes and contents of the poet's consciousness and a system of experiential patterns, seem to feel that topoi studies are less important.[14] But the poet's medium is language, which embodies topoi and other cultural values, and he has to work with the inherited material. An analysis of the function of East Asian poetic topoi may be of value to a phenomenological inquiry, a topoi research with a difference.

My selections and interpretations are subjective. Most Chinese and Japanese poems are chosen from available translations: when there are standard versions, I have used them; when there are not, I have tried to choose the ones that are faithful and readable. Had I but world enough and time, I might have offered all poems in my English; but because most poems from the Korean are my own, I feel that the variety and diversity of styles in the material warrant more than one hand. The book is intended for the general reader with some background in English poetry, who wishes to know something about the topics in East Asian poetry. A discussion of such technical matters as forms, sound patterns, and syntax without the original has little meaning and is omitted.[15]

1 PRAISE

Do not exceed four attacks, five attacks, six attacks, seven attacks, then stop and adjust your ranks. Exert yourselves, officers! May you be martial. Be like tigers, like leopards, like black bears, like brown-and-white bears. In the suburbs of Shang, do not stop and [do not] crush those who flee, so that they can do service in the Western land. Exert yourselves, officers! In so far as you do not exert yourselves, on your persons there will be capital punishment.[1]

WIELDING the yellow battle-ax in the left hand and waving high the white oxtail flag with the right, King Wu marshaled his hosts and uttered this harangue one winter morning at the suburbs of the Shang capital. In his emphasis on heroic prowess and in his comparison of warriors to beasts of prey, we glimpse fragments or, more correctly, the aftermath of the Chinese heroic age. Here, as elsewhere in Chinese literature, the emphasis is not on individual glory and honor but on the effect of one's acts on later generations, the profound, permanent change the event has brought to the Chinese people.

I

The dynastic hymns in the *Book of Songs,* the earliest extant anthology in East Asia, compiled around 600 B.C., present the Chou founders Kings Wen (c. 1122 B.C.) and Wu for their heroic prowess and above all for their fusion of valor and virtue, *fortitudo et sapientia.* In creating the exemplary images of the perfect prince, the poems made use of the technique of praise, especially the praise of a ruler. The praise of dynastic founders—and, later, of ideal Confucian rulers—represents the highest kind of epideictic poetry, with the fullest exploration of encomiastic topics, stylistic devices, special vocabulary and formulas, and elaborate hyperbole. With a stress on the moral utility of praise—reminiscent of the Greek ideal of *paideia* and the classical and Renaissance conception of poetry and history—the end of praise was considered to be chiefly didactic, the creation of patterns of virtue and vice, models of emulation and exhortation. The principal function of the poet (and historian) was therefore to create what Sidney called the "lively images of the virtues and vices," to present the traditionally typical and exemplary as enduring norms for conduct.

Confucian classics and histories say that King Wu's military conquest of the Shang was preceded by the cultural preparation and garnering of the moral power of his father King Wen. The *Book of Songs* mentions Wen's military conquest of Mi and Ch'ung:

241.5 The king blazed forth his anger;
He marshaled his armies,
To check the foe he marched to Lu . . .

241.8 He attacked, he harried,
He cut off, he destroyed.
None anywhere dared oppose him.[2]

In these poems the reader is struck by the lack of such common war topoi in Western heroic poetry as the council of war, the speech before the battle, the review of armies, the movement of the hero, the description of arms.[3] The formulaic language dispenses with most of the descriptive topics essential to the narrative requirements of Western counterparts. King Wen is said to have "blazed forth his anger," as later King Wu's wrath is held responsible for giving repose to the people (*Mencius,* IB, 3) . But culture did not confer a heroic or tragic meaning on wrath or destruction. The four verbs, "attacked," "harried," "cut off," and "destroyed," convey some sense of action and glory. Contextually, however, they stand out and may be a device to question the assumptions of righteous war (as was the case here) or any war often held to be inevitable in reasserting order. The suppression of battles and the concealment of arms had a lasting effect on later poetry.[4]

Therefore, by far the most common topic of praise portrays King Wen as an examplar of the Confucian ideal of virtue. He was "diligent,"[5] "a strong toiler,"[6] "circumspect and reverent."[7] His inward power was "bright" and "without flaw."[8] With "clear and glittering ordinances," he established the sacrifices and toiled to serve God on High, which in the end gave victory to the Chou.[9]

244.3 He did not fulfill his own desires,
But worked in pious obedience to the dead.[10]

God praises him for his modesty and piety, constancy and prudence, which help him to attain Heaven's blessings:

241.7 "I cherish your brilliant virtue,
Which makes no great display in sound or appearance,
Nor is changed with age.

> Without any manipulation or deliberation,
> You follow the principles of the Lord."[11]

A model to myriad lands, he wins the allegiance of his knights and people and spreads his bounties and secures the continuity of his house.

The poems present not a chronological survey of the subject's life, but a catalogue of his virtues. The compilers minimize the king's military heroism and emphasize instead his public moral virtues, especially his love of Heaven and ancestors. It is piety that entitles him to rule. Through his virtuous rule, the dynasty's preservation is secured. As a ritual confirmation of the highest values of society and culture, the poems subtly imply that the king has authority as well as responsibility to Heaven, ancestors, and people. It is no accident, then, that when Chinese and Korean poets of later times attempt to create an image of the ideal Confucian prince, they turn to the examples of Kings Wen and Wu, held responsible for their completion of difficult royal works began by Tan-fu (King Wen's grandfather) in adverse circumstances ("Of old Tan-fu the duke/ Scraped shelters, scraped holes;/ As yet they had no houses."[12]

As inheritor of the mandate bestowed on his father, King Wu (Wu meaning warrior or martial) "swiftly fell upon Great Shang"[13] and

> 285 Conquered the Yin, utterly destroyed them.
> Firmly founded were his works.[14]

Leading gloriously and valiantly, he swiftly pursued the enemy and returned victoriously.[15] Although the *Book of Documents* praises him for the feat of "killing all his enemies," the dynastic hymns transform mere prowess, present him as a possessor of valor and wisdom, and praise his deeds in peace. The bloodshed necessary for founding the new kingdom is justified as a chastisement of the betrayal of Heaven's trust. As the new bearer of hope, peace, and justice, King Wu's deeds are aureoled with providential rightness and explained in moral terms. Mindful of Heaven's bidding[16] he was obedient to clan ancestors, a model to his brothers. He was affable, reverent, and protected by Heaven; no calamities disturbed the country,[17] a recompense for his obedience to Heaven's commands. Guarded and aided by his knights, he brought peace to myriad lands and bequeathed teachings that would give peace and protection to his heirs.[18] Poem 273 praises King Wu for his power to inspire awe in his subjects, among rivers and hills, and all the lands under his control. He is portrayed almost as a mythic figure—able to command rivers and hills. Implied, perhaps, is the moral regeneration of the country symbolized by the rejuvenation of nature, for the restoration of order has cosmic reverberations, although the point here is King Wu's moral power *(yi te)*. Military conquest over, it is time to rule by rites and music, as the king's command seems to indicate:

> 273.3 Then put away your shields and axes,
> Then case your arrows and bows . . .[19]

He will rule by moral power and by example, not by personal heroism. Political and moral stability cannot be maintained by the sword, and panegyric, if it is to fulfil its traditional function, cannot celebrate brute force, military heroism. A dynasty that exists by divine will must safeguard civilization.

As the repository of appropriate princely virtues, Wen and Wu are presented as symbols of Chou expansion, who won Heaven's alliance and the people's allegiance, and are worshiped as a "counterpart of Heaven." Both are praised for their unwavering allegiance to their mission and firmness of purpose. Heaven exacts from them *constantia* and *pietas* and rewards them with constant manifestation of companionship and encouragement. Their virtuous acts, especially their piety and wisdom, are typical examples for future princes to recall.

> 294 Bright he [King Wu] shines in heaven,
> Helping those that succeed him.[20]

The austere language restricts development of such topics as ancestry, birth, youth, and education, but concentrates on preeminent public virtues. The formulaic style facilitates memory and ensures preservation of examples of mores and ethos. As instruments for the preservation and perpetuation of tradition so vital to the survival of culture, the hymns, like the classics, prescribed "a community of forms and ideals."[21]

The composite formula of action and contemplation, valor and wisdom, is usually reserved for the dynastic founder, because the ultimate end of martial valor is to found a state, which restores and safeguards order on all planes—cosmic, political, and moral.[22] Like Aeneas or Christ, so the sage emperors, culture heroes, and virtuous founders and rulers were looked upon as paradigms of moral virtue. Awareness of the inadequacy of the heroic code probably led to the reassessment and redefinition of the heroic ethos. The emergence of a great man in history is often a product of the happy conjunction of virtue and fortune, but the ideals and needs of the time require the transformation of Machiavellian virtù into classical and Christian virtue in the West,[23] and into Confucian virtue in the East. The mere energies of the hero, without the sanction of Heaven, would finally lead to his downfall and self-destruction. A plaything of Fortune, the embodiment of overweening ambition and lust for domination, is usually reserved for the loser, the overreacher mercilessly felled, the unheroic hero. By the inevitable requirements of the heroic–panegyric tradition, the victor must be portrayed differently. He must possess Heaven's blessing and moral virtue; these alone entitle him to establish his own rule. The conferment of the right to rule, the supreme reward for the victor, is generally known as the winning of the mandate of Heaven, the vindication of the morality of revolution, the supreme myth of Confucian political rhetoric.

The Shang incurred the wrath of Heaven because of their impiety and wickedness. King Wen enumerates the crimes in poem 255: giving high positions to brigands and robbers who oppress people; exalting violence and supporting slanders; turning resentment into virtue; disorderly manners; flouting the old ways, statutes, and laws.[24] Indeed, the revilement of the Shang king's wanton perversion of justice and his other vices—the opposite pole from the wise and pious King Wen—is a fit topic for vituperation. Carried out in the name of Heaven and the people to restore a sacred moral order, the Chou's chastisement was the inevitable consequence of vile offenses against Heaven, Earth, and Man. Heaven can destroy a dynasty as easily as it sets it up, hence the recurrent sententiae that affirm communal wisdom.

> 236.1 Heaven cannot be trusted;
> Kingship is easily lost.[25]

> 235.5 Heaven's charge is not forever.

> 235.7 High Heaven does its business
> Without sound, without smell.[26]

> 288.1 Heaven's charge is not easy to hold.[27]

The past is a prototype, a guide, and a mirror:

> 235.6 Don't you mind your ancestors!
> Cultivate your virtue.
> Always strive to be in harmony with Heaven's Mandate.
> Seek for yourselves the many blessings.
> Before Yin lost its army,
> Its kings were able to be counterparts to the Lord on High.
> In Yin you should see as in a mirror
> That the great mandate is not easy [to keep].[28]

History, sister of epic, is a collection of examples, for lessons are best taught by historical parallels. In the accounts of the rise and fall of dynasties and great men, one must discern history's inexorable pattern, the principles that control the destinies of states and men. The use of analogy, the standard medium of presenting moral lessons, was based on the concept of universal parallelism, a correspondence of macrocosm and miscrocosm. This concept stressed the interdependence of Heaven, Earth, and Man, the order and degree in the natural, human, and political planes. The rupture of order in one plane reflects rupture in another. Like the humanist poets and historians of the Renaissance, who emphasized order and degree, the encomiasts (and historians) of East Asia used epideictic rhetoric for moral and political reasons. Therefore poem 235 urges:

> Make King Wen your example,
> In whom all the people put their trust.[29]

These poems not only establish the Confucian heroic ethos, which was seen to comprise valor and wisdom, but provide principal topoi of praise, which were to become the sine qua non of similar epideictic poetry in East Asia. Kings Wen and Wu are described as deputies of Heaven and leaders of people, stressing the importance of divine and earthly testimony. The winning of the mandate is a supreme reward for their reliance on Heaven's will. The hero's vigorous, virtuous rule reasserts order and harmony, for he alone is charged with the safety of state. Only virtue is immortal. The exemplary patterns of virtue are contrasted with those of vice, as in Wen's catalogue of the last Shang king's moral depravity and misrule (255). Praise and satire are related, if the panegyric is to perform its function. A wicked destroyer of order and degree, the Shang's defeat is a proof of its ruler's opposition to Heaven's will and his abuse of regal power. Herein lies the pattern of change: a despot will be overwhelmed and replaced by a just ruler, elected by Heaven and people.

Earlier I mentioned the ellipsis of battle as characteristic of Chinese and, later, Korean poems of praise. This preference for a "cultural heroism,"[30] with emphasis on rites and arts, recalls Western parallels. Already Homer in the *Odyssey* and Virgil in the *Aeneid* showed the inadequacy of the heroic code, how it "destroys more than it creates," and how heroic deeds are often "motivated by greed, accomplished with terror, and indistinguishable from piracy."[31] Most Christian epics of later times tend to subordinate war to peace, as in French historical epics. But perhaps nowhere is the rejection of the traditional ideal of epic enunciated more memorably than in the invocation to Book IX of *Paradise Lost:*

Warrs, hitherto the onely Argument
Heroic deemed, chief maistrie to dissect
With long and tedious havoc fabl'd Knights
In Battles feigned . . .

Milton repudiates "false ethic of military heroism,"[32] and sings instead the new heroism, "the better fortitude/ Of Patience and Heroic Martyrdom" in Christ and Adam. Because the heroic is not a kind of person or action, but a way of looking at persons and actions,[33] the heroic conception of man and history can mean many things to many peoples. The panegyrics in the *Book of Songs*—as later in *Songs of Flying Dragons*—espouse a heroic idea of man rising to preeminence through the "better fortitude" of patience and trials (so eloquently formulated in the *Mencius*) and a belief in his lasting accomplishments. The elimination of *furor impius*,[34] individual glory, senseless slaughter, and military tyranny is a persistent concern in epideictic poetry in East Asia; and nowhere has this Confucian view of heroism received a more sustained poetic treatment than in *Songs of Flying Dragons*.

II

The *Songs of Flying Dragons*,[35] a Korean eulogy cycle in 125 cantos comprising 248 poems, was compiled in 1445–1447 to praise the founding of the Yi dynasty by General Yi Sŏng-gye (1335–1408). Written by the foremost philologists and literary men in the Academy of Worthies, the *Songs* combine poetry and historiography to express the orthodox view of recent history. The compilers acknowledged their indebtedness to the dynastic hymns in the *Book of Songs* in praise of the Chou founders, notably poems 154 (agriculture), 237, 241, 245 (on Hou Chi and agriculture), 270, and 303 (on Shang's genesis). The *Songs* use mostly themes of praise in the classics and histories—stylistic devices of comparison and amplification, the fullest exploration of the device of parallelism, the hysteron-proteron arrangement of cantos, and formulas.

The account of the heroic virtues of Yi Sŏng-gye follows the techniques evolved in the Chinese classics and histories (especially the biographical patterns in moral lives and eulogies of eminent men) that use praise (or blame) to create an exemplum of virtue (or vice). Such a portrait was usually created through chronological narration of the subject's parentage and childhood and idealized accounts of his heroic *facta*, especially military victories. If he was renowned for martial prowess, each episode was carefully constructed to exemplify a specific martial virtue such as fortitude, magnanimity, or constancy.

If he was a universal genius, a flower of valor and virtue, like Yi Sŏng-gye, his qualities as a leader of people followed, again with a series of episodes illustrating diverse aspects of civil virtues in action. These topics of ancestry, nature, and character are the familiar topics of epideictic oratory and rhetoric.[36]

The Iliadic cantos of the *Songs* present Yi Sŏng-gye as possessing unusual gifts of body and character. Set apart from ordinary men in childhood, he possessed splendid appearance and superhuman strength, and wielded huge bows and arrows. He was a supreme archer, a master horseman, and a divine tactician. With these unusual qualities, he pacified the Red Turbans, the Jürched, and the Mongols, and subjugated the Japanese pirates. Commending his selfless deeds for the country and the people, Heaven not only sends auspicious omens and portents, but comes to his succor. He was kind to his men, magnanimous, humble, and consistent. He is compared to a number of Chinese paragons, only to emerge as surpassing them in moral excellence. Admiration and emulation are further stimulated by elements of the marvelous, with Heaven as ally and with omens and portents to underscore the inevitability of the divine plan.

Eminence in arms, however, is not enough if Yi Sŏng-gye is to be portrayed as the prototype of a leader of nation and people, as a possessor of higher civil virtues for the good of society. His heroic prowess must have meaning in terms of Confucian ethical and political tradition. Thus Yi emerges as the embodiment of both martial and moral virtues, the former tempered and finally transformed by reason and piety, wisdom and love. The cheering people rush to him like those hastening to market, claim him as champion of their rights, and show their consent and obedience. Aware of the heavy duties of the ruler, he declines to answer the people's wishes. Heaven finally intervenes and sends him a dream—as it did to King Wu before—urging him to respond to its charge. Discerning the will of Heaven, he at last ascends the throne, founds the House of Yi, and reasserts order and harmony.

The device of emphasizing valor and prowess as essential parts of the founder's deeds, almost an identification of the soldier with the statesman, is striking. Its purpose was to create a universal genius who is proficient in both arms and letters, a synthesis of prowess and virtue, courage and wisdom. Such was the figure of the hero portrayed in histories of China and Korea, especially dynastic founders or restorers of dwindling imperial power, whose posthumous epithets often carry the graph *wu* (warrior, martial) as if to highlight the heroic deeds necessary for a successful revolution or restoration of imperial power.

Yi Sŏng-gye was such a man. His posthumous epithets contain the formula *shen-wu* (august warrior or divine hero), which was adopted by the Japanese as the epithet for their mythical first emperor, a symbol of royal greatness, of soldierly valor. Looked upon as an embodiment of a long native military tradition, Yi deserves such resplendent majesty. The bow is Yi's characteristic weapon, and a number of cantos celebrate his marksmanship.

32 Heaven sent the genius
In order to save the people.
Hence he shot with twenty arrows
Twenty sables in the bush.

43 On Mount Chorae he struck two roebucks
With a single arrow.
Must one paint
This natural genius?

86 He shot six roebucks,
He shot six crows,
He flew across
The slanting tree.

88 He hit the back of forty tailed deer,
He shot the mouths and eyes of the rebels,
He shot down three mice from the eaves,
Were there any like him in the past?

89 Seven pine cones,
The trunk of a dead tree,
Three arrows piercing the helmet—
None like him in the past.

Like Achilles' ashen spear, Odysseus' huge bow, or Beowulf's victory-blessed blade (*sigeeadig bil*), Yi Sŏng-gye's bow was characterized by its unusual size. He cut his own arrows made of the *hu* tree, instead of the usual bamboo, which, like whistling-head arrows, made a whirring noise as they flew through the air. Upon seeing the size of the bow and arrow, his own father remarked that they were not only impractical but, in fact, incapable of being used by man. But Yi Sŏng-gye startled his father by skillfully manipulating the superhuman weapon and killed seven roebucks.

27 His arrow was huge beyond compare—
His father saw it and abandoned it.
On the same day he rejoiced
In him whose genius astounded the day.

Like that of so many heroes, the general's animal in peace and war was the horse. "No animal invites," Bowra comments, "so technical or so discriminating a knowledge or excites stronger affection and admiration" than the horse.[37] It is the hero's trusted friend to whom he usually appeals for help. The immortal steeds of Achilles mourned the impending doom of their master and were pitied by Zeus for serving the mortal man (*Iliad,* XVII.424–450). Like King Mu's eight bayards or Li Shih-min's six bayards that came at the appropriate time to render service, Yi Sŏng-gye had eight stalwart steeds, all of which performed miracles of one sort or another (canto 70):

Heaven gave him courage and wisdom
Who was to bring order to the country.
Hence eight steeds
Appeared at the proper time.

In peacetime, hunting trips, contests, or games provided him with occasions to perfect his horsemanship. In a polo match and archery contests he displayed superhuman feats of marksmanship.

44 It was a polo match played by royal order—
He hit the ball by "sideway block."[38]
People on the nine state roads
All admired his skill.

46 Wishing to display his august power,
Heaven induced him to have a game
And caused him to place
Ten silver mirrors.

63 He shot pears from a hundred paces away,
Displaying his prowess to the guests.
They therefore
Drank toast.

The general's huge bow was the sign of a man "who was to save the world" (canto 27). The contests were actually provided by Heaven, or Heaven induced someone to provide them in order to manifest "his august power" (canto 46) as well as to convince the king and the people and to inspire awe (cantos 31–32, 46). Indeed,

45 Many could shoot an arrow:
But he was aware of his heroic virtue.
With this heroic virtue
He saved many.

Marksmanship alone, therefore, is not the subject of these poems: they are cited as evidence of the general's heroic virtue, indispensable for the mission he was to perform. The contests were occasions for the clarification of his destiny, his awareness of the heavy burden the nation had laid on him. As instances of the hero's trials on a small scale, they mark the points of self-knowledge and progress he has to make for a clear understanding of Heaven's plan.

With his supreme physical and spiritual qualities, Yi Sŏng-gye responded to a call to bring order and peace to a nation harassed by foreign invaders. When, in 1361, the Red Turbans crossed the Yalu and seized the Koryŏ capital, he rallied his men and drove back the enemy (cantos 33–34). In 1362, as Commander of the Northeast, the general was in charge of a campaign against the Mongol minister Naγaču (cantos 35–36, 88); and in 1370 he subjugated the stronghold of the Northern Yüan in Northwest Manchuria (cantos 39–41). A final series of campaigns that brought lasting fame to Yi was against the Japanese pirates in 1377, 1380, and 1382 (cantos 47–52, 58–62).

He gave such service to his country when its safety and survival were at stake. He was not only the image of military prowess, but an epitome of generosity, courage, mercy, and sagacity. He did not parade his valorous deeds before his people; rather, he enjoyed a warm friendship with them. Attentive to the army's safety and morale, he always tried to inspire courage and confidence in his men. The strength and cruelty of the enemy were the measure of his heroism. The terror or grandeur of the events is augmented by strange eruptions that portend victory to Korea and disaster to the enemy, such as a red halo, a mist, or a white rainbow that suddenly fills the sky. These signs of supernatural companionship not only inspire his deeds but reinforce the consciously ethical heroic standard that he stands for. But he is a creature of flesh and blood after all, and he is painfully aware of the cost of human achievements, inseparable from suffering and loss—an enormous cost historical fulfillment exacts. He has mastered the fear of death, but as he contemplates the horror of war, he at once comprehends the limitations and finality of man's deeds. On his way to a decisive battle on Mount Hwang in 1380, he was overwhelmed by compassion and pity for the dead. As he passes the dead bodies that cover the hills and plains, he comprehends the timeless truth:

50 Pitying his own people
He passed by Changdan.
At that time a white rainbow
Cut across the sun.

The implied contrasts of the episode are rich: a just war for the love and pity of people versus outrageous banditry in defiance of all accepted norms; a patriotic hero, an image of virtue and humanity versus unsophisticated villains, exempla of violence and cupidity. One is the embodiment of present and past as well as a hope for future; the other has no past, no future. From the divine viewpoint, therefore, the outcome of the battle has already been decided, for fate (Heaven) is always on the moral side. The enemy, in the poet's eye, is doomed; this is the meaning of the strange cosmic manifestation that the bandits will certainly misread, another cause of their imminent destruction. Here free will and fate are inextricably interwoven, for the general's response to a call in defense of the just cause tallies with divine plan. In this lies the general's preeminence. To one it is a necessary war, an instrument of peace; to the other, a game for the lust of murder and plunder. Hence, his trials and sufferings have moral and symbolic meanings. Canto 50 is the scene of recognition by the hero of his own mortality.

As an embodiment of the struggles of his nation and people, Yi's heroic career is at once authentic and of profound significance. In this national and patriotic meaning lies the unity of his struggles. The trials of Yi Sŏng-gye as a suffering hero should therefore be viewed as the incarnation of his people.[39] And as such it was fully sanctioned by Confucian orthodoxy. "When Heaven is about to confer a great responsibility on any man," Mencius said, "it will exercise his mind with suffering, subject his sinews and bones to hard work, expose his body to hunger, put him to poverty, place obstacles in the paths of his deeds, so as to stimulate his mind, harden his nature, and improve wherever he is incompetent" (6B.15).[40] This is how Heaven prepares man for great tasks, as was the case of Shun, Fu Yüeh, Chiao-ko, Kuan I-wu, and other ideal figures of Confucian tradition. And they succeeded because they were able to take obstacles as a challenge, a necessary step for their development. And Heaven, through signs and portents, constantly reminds them of the moral significance of their deeds. The scope of the trials—which corresponds to the adventures of the hero in the mythological cycle—is the measure of their greatness. The bestowal of service on their fellow men as the hero of tried virtue corresponds to the return of the mythological hero, the only justification of such trials.[41] This, then, is a process in which the hero recognizes not only his limitations, but his true mission in society. And the recognition has to be an achievement, the fruit of his heroic ordeals. In accord with the Confucian conception of a man who, by great endurance and action, raises himself to heroic status, the compilers were able to confer on the general's *facta* a moral and political significance that rendered them ecumenical.

Canto 41, therefore, presents Yi Sŏng-gye as an emblem of humanity and justice whose purpose in war was not spoil or pillage but the restoration of order and peace. Also, wishing to save the dauntless Mongol general Chao Wu, Yi did not use arrowheads (canto 54), but awed him into surrender (1364). Like the English *curtana* (or *curteyn*),[42] the blunted sword of mercy and peace, Yi Sŏng-gye's "wooden arrowhead" (*paktu*), a substitute for the deadly arrowhead, manifests his refusal to wound and destroy. Again, following the thesis of Hsün Tzu, the righteous army was followed by a mass of people in adoration of the commander's virtue, a crowd large enough to serve as a tribute to his prestige and magnificence. He was not only a dispenser of justice and mercy but an epitome of magnetism and majesty. Thus he won the allegiance of the Jürched, of the southern barbarians, and of his people.

The general's return from Wihwa Island in 1388 opposing the planned Liaotung expedition is also singled out as instance of chastisement in Heaven's name of the crimes of the wicked Koryŏ king:

> 10 A mad fellow was reckless and oppressive;
> They therefore awaited his banner of justice.
> With rice in baskets, wine in bottles,
> They welcomed him along the roadside.

This recent historical event is subtly compared to a similar act of King Wu of Chou to legitimate Yi's decision—interpreted not as an act of insurrection or rebellion but as a response to Heaven's charge—and to transform him into an idealized figure, such as King Wu, who had been accepted by orthodox Confucian tradition as the archetype of Heaven's agent and the representative of his people. This epideictic scheme enabled the compilers to give shape and meaning to Yi's decision. He is a man with a destiny, the living representative of the cosmic, moral, and political processes that his career reflects. As Heaven's agent, he reasserts order and transforms the waste land into a harmonious golden world. His every deed is in pursuit of his destiny and affects the welfare of people and nation. His allegiance to Heaven's design elevates him to the level of the ideal examplars in the tradition, the figure of the Confucian hero with a ritualistic function consistently portrayed in the literature of praise. In spite of "a wicked plan" against him, Yi Sŏng-gye, like Kings Wen and Wu, doubted Heaven's bidding and continued to serve the inadequate sovereign.[43] Only when Heaven manifested its will through an auspicious dream (canto 13) and the willing allegiance of the people did he initiate a coup. Thus, the fact that his revolution was not an act of usurpation but "a gift of Heaven" had finally been expounded.

The heroic achievements of the Confucian soldier do not lie so much in his great feats on the battlefield as in his correct interpretation of his duty by setting a new standard of moral excellence. The end of the righteous war, reminds Hsün Tzu, is "to put an end to violence."[44] War should never be undertaken for envy of power and lust of conquest. The Confucian soldier is the upholder of justice and humanity, one who scorns violence and irrationality by subordinating his passions and desires to a higher purpose. What endows him with his strength and purpose is his sense of duty, his trust in his mission as a carrier of civilization, his ability to discharge the mandate in the restoration of harmony and order. "A drowning empire," Mencius expounds, "must be rescued with moral principles."[45] He must be able to look forward to the future, the unified nation and the willing people, and the dynasty that will stand as a symbol of peace and stability. In the sixth book of the *Aeneid,* Aeneas and his father Anchises meet in the underworld; and as they proceed to the upper world, Anchises points out to his son the long line of his descendants, foretells the greatness of Roman rule, and expounds Rome's great mission:

> tu regere imperio populos, Romane, memento
> (hae tibi erunt artes), pacisque imponere morem,
> parcere subiectis et debellare superbos. (VI.851–853)

> You, o Romans, remember to rule nations with your sway—
> these will be your arts—and to impose the tradition of peace,
> to spare the humbled and crush the proud.[46]

In such terms, the Yi dynasty is the triumph of moderation over hatred, of order over disintegration, and of history and culture over human frailty. It must be able to embrace the humbled and defeated under a single society, imposing on them the virtues of order so vital to the establishment and maintenance of the dynasty.[47]

Yi Sŏng-gye fulfilled the function of a Confucian soldier by withstanding the trials and by responding to the demands of destiny willed by Heaven. He distinguished himself not by personal prowess or glory, but by identification of his own destiny with that of the nation. The ultimate justification is the maintenance and preservation of order, best manifested in good government. The cantos that celebrate the statesmanship of Yi Sŏng-gye and Yi Pang-wŏn, therefore, explore the nature and function of kingship, the relations of power and justice, the role of mercy and remonstrance, the importance of learning and orthodoxy, and culminate in the admonitory cantos that conclude the cycle (110–125).

The rhetorical and dramatic devices are the same as those employed in the "arms" cantos. Each canto comprises, as in the "arms" section, parallel studies, the subjects of which are known examples from Chinese history, a universal history in the Confucian ecumene, much in the same manner as seventeenth-century English poetry turned to sacred history for metaphorical amplification. The episodic structure and austere form demanded concision, and the compression of the subject's career into a few lines enabled the compilers to achieve economy and objectivity. The use of stylistic devices for the political-moral purposes of the work was possible because the communal values to which the poems refer were familiar to every schoolboy read in the Confucian mirror for princes literature. In the cantos devoted to Yi Sŏng-gye, the subjects of twin studies include in chronological order Liu Pang (founder of the Han), Liu Pei of Shu Han, Li Shih-min, Kuo Jung (Shih-tsung of the later Chou), Chao K'uang-yin (founder of the Sung), and Qubilai. They are brought in to aggrandize Yi Sŏng-gye with historical sanction or to demonstrate his superiority over the Chinese counterpart, as in a sustained contrast between Yi and Liu Pang (cantos 66, 79). And by virtue of their repetition, some of these exempla acquired the status of topics.

In addition to recurrent rhetorical questions ("Who would not/ Adore him?" canto 78), which proffer praise and elicit the desired response from the reader in a given context, there are the topics of: inexpressibility ("How could we relate all/ The divine power of the inspired man?" canto 87); the interrogative outdoing ("Was there any like him in the past?" canto 88); outdoing, constantly implied throughout the cycle (for example in canto 44); and the Korean equivalent of the India topic to underscore the extent of the hero's renown, usually described as reaching as far as China (canto 72) and occasionally elsewhere. Rhetorical questions, together with apostrophe, underscore the public and affective nature of poetry, an affirmation of a close relationship between the compilers and audiences.

The sovereign qualities of a Confucian king enumerated in the *Songs* recall the cardinal virtues of a Christian prince treated in books *de regimine principum.* Yi Sŏng-gye possessed most of the "king-becoming graces" of Malcolm: benevolence, justice tempered with mercy, learning, wisdom, temperance, compassion (he protected the felicity of his people and aroused awe and love in them), modesty, and brotherly love. It is no accident that the great moral qualities associated with a Confucian ruler are the same as those of a Renaissance king serving as God's steward on earth. Both are asked to conform to a prototype and to perform sanctioned roles, whatever human limitations the traditional ideology entails. As a defender of the moral order in the universe and a representative of his culture, the ruler's conduct is a cause of public order or disorder. The compilers are, therefore, eager to illustrate public doctrine—the special qualifications required of a ruler and the particular functions he is expected to discharge for the good of the human community. Their duty as encomiasts is to raise the real to the ideal, and their allegiance to the tradition required of them is that they reaffirm the public values of order, harmony, and mutuality upon which depend the health and destiny of the realm.

The dominant topic here, so characteristically Confucian, is *jen,* benevolence, goodness, or love. Yi Sŏng-gye's love, in its various forms, finds expression in his dealings with his subordinates, his stepbrother, and his rivals and enemies. He was "polite with his men, kind in words," and therefore able to stabilize the hearts of his subordinates (canto 66). He loved his stepbrother, who once rose in revolt (canto 76):

> Kind and selfless to his brothers,
> He covered their past misdeeds.
> Thus today we enjoy
> Humane manners and customs.

How regulation of the family is necessary to public order is reiterated in canto 119, for one who cannot set his household in order is hardly expected to act as defender of national mores and custodian of the way of the former kings. Yi Sŏng-gye also forgave his former rivals and enemies (canto 77) and restored them to their former ranks. He also showed a consistent concern for the welfare of meritorious subjects, thus winning their lasting loyalty.

> 78 From the start he treated them with true heart,
> To the end his heart was true.
> Who would not
> Adore him?
>
> 79 He was consistent from beginning to end,
> Meritorious subjects were truly loyal to him.
> He secured the throne for myriad years.
> Would his royal work ever discontinue?

Unselfish magnanimity, the impartial administration of justice, is the sine qua non of a humane government. Clemency is sovereignty's ornament and higher safety.[48] To save innocent life is the prerogative of high estate,[49] for clemency succors not only innocence but also virtue. With clemency, spontaneous and unprodded innocence becomes a rule, a public good.[50]

That learning is indispensable to a prince or a gentleman is a commonplace in the tradition. The master said to Tzu-lu, "One who loves humanity but not learning will be obscured by ignorance. One who loves wisdom but not learning will be obscured by lack of principle" (XVII.9).[51] Wisdom proceeds from learning, learning the classics and histories as in the traditional educational system in East Asia. Classics arm man with precepts against every contingency, while history, which embodies the past and teaches by example, provides suitable examples for suitable occasions. Both are a storehouse of exempla, a political and moral mirror in which man finds truth and can know himself. Emphasis on learning is also an affirmation of loyalty to culture, a status symbol of the ruling class which, through the civil service examination in China and Korea, manned the government. Therefore, Yi Sŏng-gye, like Caesar and Augustus in the West, fully accoutered in armor, read books between battles in order to learn the art of government. Regretting that his family had not yet produced a scholar, Yi Sŏng-gye also urged his son to pursue classical learning.[52] Yi Sŏng-gye's respect for scholarship is also evidenced in his courteous reception of Yi Saek when the latter returned from his banishment in 1391:

> 82 Upon receiving an old scholar
> He knelt down with due politeness.

Indeed, "love of learning is akin to wisdom" (*The Mean,* 20; canto 122). Wisdom is among the most important qualities required of the perfect prince. Plato's philosopher-ruler is able to penetrate the shadow into the realities;[53] Synesius recommended study of philosophy as a means to regulate the prince's life;[54] and Sir Thomas Elyot defined wisdom as "that parte of Sapience that of necessitie must be in euery gouernour of a juste or perfeyte publike weale" (III.23). The superior man is watchful over himself when he is alone, examining his own heart (*The Mean,* 1.20).[55] One who is able to bring man and Nature into harmony is an embodiment of the Way of Heaven, sincerity, and such a ruler is one with Heaven. The compilers therefore went to *The Mean* for inspiration, and by identifying the dynastic founder as a "counterpart of Heaven,"[56] he who "hits upon what is right without effort and apprehends without thinking,"[57] they were able to elevate Yi Sŏng-gye to the level of a sage, the elevation sanctioned by the tradition, the ultimate of hyperbolic stance.

In the final section of the *Songs,* the compilers directly address King

Sejong, their patron, the great fount of their inspiration. The principal concern in the earlier part, we recall, was the celebration of paradigmatic acts of the dynastic founder, or the celebration of the virtues he exemplifies, and the source of resonance was the juxtaposition—and often integration—of native and classical material. With the final section, which consists of a series of earnest pleas to the reigning monarch in the form of gracious exhortations, we notice a shift of tone and focus, from more controlled expression in the earlier parts to more poignantly personal utterance, which effects the shifting of the focus from the comparatively distant and normative to the immediate and real. This effective variation of the compilers' strategy evinces how central to their concern, by the nature and tradition of their art, was the impulse to persuade.

Stylistically and thematically, therefore, this section contains the largest occurence of sententiae. As the "familiar, inherited formulas for experience,"[58] these traditional commonplaces are the "vehicles for the wisdom of the ages,"[59] easily learned and memorized. The poets discharge their legitimate function as representatives of "rationality and communal wisdom"[60] in a society conceived as an intricate moral network.

116 If you are unaware of people's sorrows,
Heaven will abandon you.

118 If a king loses his inward power,
Even his kin will rebel.

119 If brothers are split,
A villain will enter and sow discord.

120 If a ruler taxes his people without measure,
The basis of the state will crumble.

122 . . . learning surpasses mere thinking.

125 . . . you can secure the dynasty only
When you worship heaven and benefit the people.

These and similar "sentences," favorite topics of political and moral treatises and handbooks, engage the audience's sympathies; they are precepts tested by history and of vital importance to the Confucian prince. As spokesmen and guardians of Confucian mores and ethos, the compilers' sententiousness in the final section of *Songs* is another way of affirming their faith in the tradition that taught that a ruler is a vital link in the universal order, that the cultivation of moral standards is the root of cosmic and social harmony, that the health of a nation depends on the moral health of a ruler, and that his every act has far-reaching political and moral reverberations.

The theme of cantos 110–113 is the evil of ease and luxury. Some royal ancestors, persecuted and humiliated, had to move from place to place, seeking safety. Ikcho, for example, suffered the treachery of the Jürched chiefs and bore hardships in a clay hut, reminiscent of Tan-fu.[61] In halcyon days, one who is freighted with the full panoply of resplendence is likely to forget the toils of his ancestors and his people. Yi Sŏng-gye met the demands of his society and spent much of his life repulsing invaders and subjugating rebels. He had no time to doff his armor or to have food and drink. Wrapped in royal robes and girt with a belt of precious gems, when you sup "northern viands and southern dainties" or "when you drink superb wine," think twice, our king, the compilers plead.

Peace is "a quiet Nurse of Idleness,"[62] and that decadence and excessive civilization eventually lead to decline has been amply attested by historians, East and West. Peace should not breed evil but heroic courage and resolve. Cantos 114 and 115 amplify the theme from differing viewpoints with differing meanings. When the "wolves," the Red Turbans, and the Japanese pirates, wrought havoc, Yi Sŏng-gye suffered wounds and scars. When a ruler, protected by stately guards, rules the kingdom effortlessly with "dangling robes and folded hands," he should ask himself whether he truly deserves his royal vocation and divine sanction.

> 115 When you have men at your beck and call,
> When you punish men and sentence men,
> Remember, my Lord,
> His mercy and temperance.

The statutes of a benevolent ruler tally with the will of Heaven and of the people, and if a ruler is truly virtuous, there is no need for the statutes at all. "Under a true king, the people feel magnificent and at ease with themselves," Mencius expounded. "Though he punishes them by death, they do not complain" (7A.13).[63] History showed the fate of one who usurped order, ruled by whims and decrees, power and terror, and, posing as the lord of men's destinies, abused royal privilege to permit or destroy life with a mere gesture. Punishment should therefore be graded to the offense, like a physician who applies simple remedies first and grave measures only as a last resort,[64] for a benevolent king is a shepherd and a cruel master is a butcher.[65]

The perfect king is compassionate. Upon seeing the dead bodies that covered the hills and plains during the 1380 campaign against the

Japanese, Yi Sŏng-gye could neither sleep nor eat. He saw as the compassionate Heaven saw, for "a government that cannot bear to see the suffering of the people is conducted [by] a mind that cannot bear to see the suffering of others" (*Mencius*, 2A.6).[66]

> 116 If you are unaware of people's sorrow,
> Heaven will abandon you.
> Remember, my Lord,
> His labor and love.

One such burden is taxation and canto 73 singles out Yi Sŏng-gye's land reform in 1391, for

> 120 If a ruler taxes his people without measure,
> The basis of the state will crumble.

The next topic is modesty and its counterpart, pride, which leads to blindness and bigotry. The compilers have correctly seen the evil of flattery, common to all historical and political literature. Asked what animal was the most dangerous of all, Plutarch, in *How to Tell a Flatterer from a Friend* (19), answered: "If you mean among the wild beast, I will say the tyrant; if among the tamed ones, the flatterer."[67] Plutarch's similes brilliantly characterize the flatterer: a bore-worm, vermin, cuttle-fish, gadfly, ape, and a crab,

> Whose body is all belly; eyes that look
> All ways; a beast that travels on its teeth.[68]

We can best protect ourselves against him when we remember that our soul has two sides: truthfulness and irrationality, love of the honorable and of falsehood.[69]

Flatterers are also slanderers. These artisans of intrigue are at work to unleash the strong passions and irrational forces in man which threaten traditional social forms and relationships. The *Book of Songs* already compared them to "shell-brocades"[70] for their fabrication, and their pretensions and artful words to a "reed organ."[71]

> 200.3 Jibber-jabber, blither-blather!
> Their idea of 'counsel' is to slander men.[72]

They are best served as offerings to "jackals and tigers." These ancient songs anticipated Plutarch's description of the flatterer (and slanderer) when he compared him to "an extravagant wrought picture, which by means of gaudy pigments, irregular folds in the garments, wrinkles, and sharp angles, strives to produce an impression of vividness."[73] Canto 123, therefore, emphasizes the saving of the innocent, the victims of the acrid tongue and treacherous design, with a warning:

When slanderers craftily make mischief,
When they grossly exaggerate small mistakes,
Remember, my Lord,
His wisdom and justice.

Canto 118 celebrates the transforming power of virtue as the bulwark of order, the only means to conquer separatism. Transformed by Yi Sŏng-gye's good government, Jürched chiefs stopped their dispute and composed their differences, just as King Wen's bright virtue caused the rulers of Yü and Jui to feel shame for their petty squabbling. We should also recall the topic that characterizes a hero: the willing allegiance of the people, as when the people willingly followed the course of Ikcho's migration. Hence, Yi Sŏng-gye is praised here as having "won the support of everyone under Heaven," an unmistakable sign of a great man according to Mencius (2B.1).[74] When the virtuous king reigns, even the Tundra comes under census.

53 He opened the four borders,
Men on islands had no more fear of pirates.
Southern barbarians beyond our waters,
How could they not come to him?

Indeed, his moral virtues prevailed to the extremity of the world, here reaching as far as Siam and Liu-ch'iu, as earlier they did among the Mongols and Jürcheds, the Korean equivalent of the India (or Ganges) topic, to which sometimes Thule was added. The first verse of the same canto sings the authority and prestige of Li Shih-min:

He pacified the four seas,
Travelers need not take packed rice.

At the christening of Princess Elizabeth in *Henry VIII,* Cranmer, Archbishop of Canterbury, utters an eloquent prophecy of the glory the infant will bring to England:

In her days every man shall eat in safety,
Under his own vine, what he plants, and sing
The merry songs of peace to all his neighbors.
(V.v.34–36)

Horace, who compared Augustus's rule on earth to Jupiter's in heaven (*Odes,* III.3), depicts the traditional effects of the Augustan peace on the farm, the seas, the vineyard, and the dinner table (IV.5): the ox roams the pastures safely; Ceres fructifies the earth; the seas are safe for travelers; the farmer on his own hillside spends the day and weds his vines to trees; and at the supper table he invokes Augustus's blessings and worships him as a god.[75]

The final canto ends not only with a prophecy of national greatness but with an allusive rhetorical question. The compilers assert again that the security of the throne depends entirely upon the ruler's worship of Heaven and toil for the people.

> A millennium ago,
> Heaven chose the north of the Han.
> There they accumulated goodness and founded the state.
> Oracles foretold: myriad years;
> May your sons and grandsons reign unbroken.
> But you can secure the dynasty only
> When you worship heaven and benefit the people.

They then bring in the figure of T'ai K'ang of Hsia, whose remoteness is enough to protect them from the displeasure of the authorities, and ask:

> Ah, you who will wear the crown, beware,
> Could you depend upon your ancestors
> When you go hunting by the waters of Lo?

On his way from a hunting trip to the south of the Lo River, T'ai K'ang is said to have been ambushed by I, who subsequently seized the throne. T'ai K'ang's loss of the crown by his indulging in pleasure shows how his personal conduct was the immediate source of public disorder. Probably more important in terms of the total symbolic structure is the significance of the hunt, a "political metaphor for tyranny."[76] The traditional associations of the hunt with war and game are familiar enough, but here is emphasized the rapacity of the sportive tyrant, whose prey was not only beast but man. The love of the chase was often an attribute of the evil ruler. History reveals the fate of the tyrannous hunter after men: he is in turn hunted, deposed, banished, and often killed, condign punishment for the transgressor against Heaven, Earth, and Man. Except for the ritualistic game in accord with the law of Nature or the pursuit of the nation's enemy to restore order, the hunt is a metaphor for the unbound energy of the tyrant in disregard of the ideal political and moral order. This is probably the meaning of the final canto, for upon the ruler depend the survival of society and the maintenance of harmony. Such was the figure of the ideal Confucian prince, whose lasting virtues were vital to the future of the dynasty. Thus was created a handbook of education, a *summa* of the topics of Confucian humanism.

Canto 2 invokes tree and water, the static and the dynamic, as the emblems of the new dynasty.

> The tree that strikes deep root
> Is firm amidst the winds.
> Its flowers are good,
> Its fruit abundant.

"Rooted in earth and flowering in heaven,"[77] the tree is a symbol of many things to many people. It is a witness of man's deeds, historical process; it is a guardian of timeless values, moral, cultural, and religious. The pine, cypress, chestnut, catalpa, and acacia at the sacred grove or the altar of soil and grain in ancient China—and later in Korea—stood for a ruling dynasty. As a symbol of rule[78] it inspired awe and reverence, reinforcing the correspondence between man and Nature. The tree that sprouts from a single seed to many roots, a sturdy trunk, manifold branches, and finally to multitudinous leaves served as a symbol of life for individual, generation, and race. The poems of dynastic legends in the *Book of Songs* (154, 237, 239), for example, show the intended symbolism—family descent, its unbroken line and future continuity, in short, the source of greatness of royal works: the spreading young gourd stems and its long vines, the thick oak clumps, or the extended boughs. "Like the generation of leaves," Homer said, "so is the generation of men" (*Iliad,* VI.146–150).[79] Later, certain Confucian and Taoist virtues tinged the symbolism of tree: endurance, fidelity, integrity, order, continuity, freedom, fulfillment, destiny. Analogy between man and tree is very old: heroic warriors are often compared to stalwart oaks, upright ministers to towering pines, and unsullied recluses to a variety of trees and plants.

The growth and decay of the tree of a royal house whose members are boughs, leaves, and fruits—like Edmund Dudley's *The Tree of Commonwealth*[80] and Shakespeare's use of the tree as a royal house in the garden of commonwealth—are elaborated in canto 84:

> The emperor was wise,
> But his heir was not yet born.
> Then the dead willow
> Grew again.

During the reign of the Han emperor Chao, a large stone in Mount T'ai stood up, and in Shang-lin Park a dead willow grew again. The stone and the willow, Kuei Hung interpreted, alluded to the people, portending the rise of a commoner. As was expected, since the emperor had no heir, Liu Hsün (Emperor Hsüan), a commoner, became successor. The second verse, which traces its pedigree to the first, echoes the same theme:

> The country had a long history,
> But it was about to lose Heaven's charge.
> Then a withered tree
> Put forth green leaves.

The dead willow in the Shang-lin Park and the withered tree in Tŏgwŏn stand for the royal house, the Liu family in the first, and in the second the Wang house of the Koryŏ dynasty. The dead tree symbolizes the impending discontinuity of the Han dynasty caused by the barrenness of the emperor and the Koryŏ loss of mandate. Nature rallies against its destroyer, the last Koryŏ kings whose misrule disrupted cosmic harmony, but equally rallies with a providential sign for its restorer. The miraculous flowering of the dead tree intimates Heaven's plan, the imminent reestablishment of cosmic and moral order, a ray of hope in the midst of darkness, an emblem of the victory of life over death.

In addition to the allegory of the tree of dynasty, tree imagery is often used in the poetry of praise and dispraise. The "Ode to Knight Kilbo" dates from the mid-eighth century and was written by a Buddhist monk to praise his friend, the flower of an elite corps in the ancient kingdom of Silla.

> The moon that pushes her way
> Through the thickets of clouds,
> Is she not pursuing
> The white clouds?
>
> Knight Kilbo once stood by the water,
> Reflecting his face in the blue.
> Henceforth I shall seek and gather
> Among pebbles the depth of his mind.
>
> Knight, you are the towering pine,
> That scorns frost, ignores snow.

The first and second stanzas present a thematic comparison, a symbolic equation. The comparison here is between the moon that pursues white clouds and the speaker seeking among pebbles the depth of his friend's mind. But the pebbles themselves are unstable objects, symbols of insecurity and the brevity of existence. Knight Kilbo is no more. He was a prey to mutability, as the pebbles are. The knight once stood by the water, the river of time, a continuous and irreversible flow toward death. The speaker has not denied time as illusory; rather, he has accepted it on its own terms—hence the concluding stanza that introduces a correspondence between the knight and the pine. The knight is dead, but his moral beauties endure. His integrity not only scorns mutability, but imposes a sense of order on the landscape. His nobility is of the mind. The knight represents the principle of growth and order; he is an emblem of an enduring culture.

This ode recalls poem 16 in the *Book of Songs,* which celebrates the unusual merits and exemplary services of the Lord of Shao, a minister under King Ch'eng of Chou, who is said to have judged cases and to have taken shelter under the pear tree. It is invoked for its association with the wise and benevolent governor, though not quite equated with him.

> Young and tender is this sweet pear-tree;
> Do not lop it or knock it,
> For the Lord of Shao took shelter under it.
>
> Young and tender is this sweet pear-tree;
> Do not lop or harm it,
> For the Lord of Shao rested under it.
>
> Young and tender is this sweet pear-tree;
> Do not lop it or uproot it,
> For the Lord of Shao reposed beneath it.[81]

His teaching and his rule by example will continue, and his bounties are bestowed upon all who recognize polysemous meanings of his deeds. The poem extols the benefactor as the representative of the virtuous ruler, and the tree seems to propagate his rule by love, the cause of his enduring fame.

In "Ballad of the Old Cypress," a 24-line heptasyllabic poem, Tu Fu compares Chu-ko Liang (181–234), a great strategist of the Shu Han, to the mighty cypress. Supposed to have been planted by the warrior himself, the tree is said to have started sprouting again in the spring of 967.

> In front of the K'ung-ming Temple stands an old cypress,
> Branches like bronze and roots like rock.
> The girth of its frosty bark, rain-washed, is forty spans,
> Its black top rises two thousand feet to the sky.
> The ruler and his minister in time had their meeting,
> The tree is still loved by the people:
> Joined when clouds come by the mists of the long Wu Gorge,
> Sharing, when the moon shines, the chilly whiteness of the snowy
> mountains.[82]

Like the towering pine in the "Ode to Knight Kilbo," the cypress is depicted first as "a cosmic tree," then as a symbol of afflicted genius, and finally as a symbol of neglected greatness. In spite of its lonely height rising into the gloom of the sky, the tree has withstood "the wind's fierce blast." "Nothing but the power of Divine Providence could have kept it standing for so long," the poet says. "Its straightness must be the work of the Creator himself." If the tree is felled to make beams and rafters, the oxen cannot haul them away, which recalls Marvell's "A Poem on the Death of O.C.": "The tree ere while foreshortened to our view,/ When fall'n shows taller yet than as it grew." The timber may be riddled by termites, but the phoenixes, the birds of auspice, roost in its scented leaves. The last line clinches the message: "From of old the really great has never been found a use for."

In Jonson's "To Penshurst" (*The Forest* [1612]), Sir Philip Sidney is compared to that "taller tree" (the Bear's Oak), emblematic of the enduring virtues of his poetry.[83]

> Thy *Mount,* to which the *Dryads* doe resort,
> Where *Pan,* and *Bacchus* their high feasts have made,
> Beneath the broad beech, and the chest-nut shade;
> That taller tree, which of a nut was set,
> At his great birth, where all the *Muses* met.
> There, in the writhes barke, are cut the names
> Of many a *Sylvane,* taken with his flames. (II.10–16) [84]

So, according to Martial (*Epigrams,* IX.lxi), was the plane-tree planted by Julius Caesar at Cordova, "with its boughs climbing high heaven" (*sic viret et ramis sidera celsa petit,* 10), for it may hope that its "leafy honors shall endure for ever" (*perpetuos sperare licet tibi frondis honores,* 21).[85]

As the simile of tree highlights heroic ideal and behavior in western epic poetry, so the tree imagery in Korean poetry highlights the Confucian pattern and ideal behavior. Confucius singled out the trees of integrity when he declared, "Only when the year grows cold do we see that the pine and cypress are the last to fade" (*Analects,* IX.27). The moral and poetic possibilities of the tree as symbol of fidelity and as emblem of fortitude under affliction are used dramatically during the Yi dynasty's period of factional struggles. Sŏng Sam-mun (1418–1456), one of the six martyred ministers of King Tanjong, expresses his undying loyalty and determination in the following testament:

> Were you to ask me what I'd wish to be
> In the world beyond this world,
> I would answer, a pine tree, tall and hardy

On the highest peaks of Mount Pongnae,
And to be green, alone, green
When snow fills heaven and earth.

Sŏng still remembers his beloved sovereign King Sejong's injunction to protect his royal grandson, Tanjong, upon his death. A victim of a power struggle launched by an ambitious usurper, he is willing to sacrifice his life for the cause of the dynasty. But after his martyrdom he wishes to be the pine that stands firm and tall, with promises of continuity and fulfillment which are denied him. Destiny requires his heroic steadfastness, but he affirms history's inexorable pattern, continuity through change. He wishes to be a living memorial, a guardian of the dynasty, the stalwart pine that accepts suffering, loss, and sacrifice and that stands for hope, victory won through death.

Kim In-hu (1510–1560) and Chŏng Ch'ŏl (1537–1595) handle the topic with even richer insight.

The great pine we felled yesterday
With its high long branches–
Had we left it longer, it would
Have yielded beams, lesser and greater.
When the Royal Hall declines, alas,
What tree will serve to uphold the state?

How could you leave it to rot,
The lumber fit for beams and rafters?
Small men indulge in hot debate
In the torn and tumble-down house.
O carpenters with ink cup and measure,
You rush about to no purpose.

The Royal Hall, metonymy for the reigning dynasty, is built and sustained by a number of beams; but once a great minister is senselessly felled because of his outspoken loyalty, where, Kim asks, can we find a tree that "will serve to uphold the state?" The imminent fall of the Royal Hall mirrors the moral decadence of its dweller. The outrage of innocence is a breach of moral and cosmic order, a refusal on the part of the king to accept his symbolic significance as the center of society and to guarantee justice. Likewise, "small men" in line three in Chŏng's poem are qualified as "carpenters" who ought to strengthen the royal edifice. Instead, these flatterers and calumniators drag the court into their darkness, turning the structure into a "torn and tumble-down house." Hence good and worthy people are left abandoned, the promise of their fulfillment impeded. The imagery of carpentry draws on the Confucian paedeutic tradition where the acceptance of honest admonition is a requisite of a good ruler on his way to becoming a sage. As wood is made straight by the use of the plumb line, so a ruler must emulate the right rule of the former kings. Broad learning and daily examination of his conduct are therefore likened to the application of the plumb line, measure, square, and compass. Hence the poem's oblique censure of royal folly which culminated in destroying the true order. The poet blames the king for having neglected his responsibility to educate and guide the people, opening the way to chaos and anarchy.

We have seen how the Confucian classics emphasize through analogy the place and function of a ruler. He is a polestar to lesser stars in orbit around him (*Analects,* II.1).[86] His brilliance like that of the sun and the moon, and his order like that of the four seasons.[87] His virtue's transforming power is a wind, bringing a metaphorical rain, or rain and dew quickening the maturity of man. Hence one satiated with virtue (humanity and righteousness) does not wish for the flavor of fat meat (*Mencius,* 6A.17).[88] A rich stock of astronomical and natural images, invested with the values and ideals of the tradition, demonstrates not only the metaphorizing tendency of the tradition but also the belief in the correspondence between all realms in the universe. The *Great Learning* says: "From the Son of Heaven down to the common people, all must regard cultivation of the personal life as the root of foundation. There is never a case when the root is in disorder and yet the branches are in order."[89] Divine donation of the mandate to the possessor of great virtue, *The Mean* asserts, is analogous to the nourishment of a "tree that is well taken care of" (17).[90] Later, the same text (20) states the comparison more explicitly:

> When the right principles of man operate, the growth of good government is rapid, and when the right principles of soil operate, the growth of vegetables is rapid. Indeed, government is comparable to a fast-growing plant.[91]

The use of the polysemous imagery of tree is an eloquent reaffirmation of the bond between man and Nature. The Confucian system was based on the correspondence of microcosm and macrocosm, society to Nature. The function of the institutions was therefore to bring man into harmony with Nature, whose pattern man must heed in order to fulfil his own humanity. The requirements for kingship, the concept of the mandate, and moral virtues were all part of political ethics. The ruler is the earthly guardian of universal harmony, and the state, in itself a reflection of that harmony at least in its structure, is a moral and paedeutic institution to safeguard the continuity of society. Man's role in that scheme is to fulfill his appointed place in the moral order of the universe. Contemplation of the eternal pattern, the source of human mores, will lead man to occupy his cosmic place and perform his proper function, as defined by the concept of the five relations. Contrariwise, rebellion against the pattern is a rebellion against his nature, a rupture of natural relations unleashing division and chaos. "Weird occurrences arise from men," says the *Tso Commentary*. "If men have no offense, then weird things will not occur of their own. It is when men abandon their constant ways that weird things occur."[92] It is man who causes Nature to reflect his hubristic act. The real hero of *Songs of Flying Dragons,* therefore, is the dynasty. The unnamed hero, then, is Korea, *res publica,* the first word of the cycle.

III

The *adynaton,* as a hyperbole, represents nature functioning in reverse or contrary to her laws, by a juxtaposition of "the thing regarded as impossible with one or more natural impossibilities."[93] Usually regarded as a trope, it appears in proverbs, vows, and oracles (for example, the sun will set in the East, seaweed will grow on mountain top, honey will flow from yew trees, lambs will mate with tigers or wolves, oaks will bear golden apples, winter will produce crops),[94] and in an affirmation of eternal love and friendship:

> As there are no trustworthy oaths between men and lions,
> nor wolves and lambs have spirit that can be brought to
> agreement
> but forever these hold feelings of hate for each other,
> so there can be no love between you and me.[95]
>
> *Iliad,* XXII.262–265

> No time shall break this peace and truce for Italy, howsoever things shall issue; nor shall any force turn aside my will, not though, commingling all in deluge, it should plunge land into water, and dissolve Heaven into Hell.[96]
>
> *Aeneid,* XII.203–206

> But, number will not tell the many kinds
> Or all their names; nor does the total count;
> Whoever wants to know this should inquire
> To learn how many particles of sand
> The West Wind swirls in Libya's desert plain,
> Or how many waves the Ionian Sea hurls shoreward . . .[97]
>
> *Georgics,* II.104–108

> Who loves you, Pollio, may he come where you too make him
> glad,
> may honey flow for him, harsh brambles bear amomum's spice.

Who hates not Bavius, may he love your songs, O Maevius,
and may he harness foxes, may he milk he-goats.[98]
Eclogues, III.88–91

And sooner will the earth
fool the farmer with unnatural fruits
the sun spur jet-black horses across the sky
the rivers call off their waters
and lead them back to the spring
and fishes lie parched and gasping
on a dry ocean bed
than I should look for someone else to suffer for.[99]
Propertius, II.15. 31–35

The above examples from Greek and Latin poetry illustrate some of the more recurrent types of the topos.

In East Asia, varieties of the *adynaton* are used as a rhetorical device in the poetry of praise. The following anonymous Middle Korean song, a popular version of political rhetoric surviving as "Song of the Gong," approximates "the myth of the impossible":

The king reigns; ring the gong.
In this age, calm and lucky,
Let us, let us live and love.

In a sand dune, fine and plain,
Let us plant roasted chestnuts, five pints.
When the chestnuts shoot and sprout,
Then we'll part from the virtuous lord.

Let us carve a lotus out of jade,
And graft the lotus in the stone.
When it blossoms in the coldest day,
Then we'll part from the virtuous lord.

Let us make an iron suit of armor,
Stitch the plates with iron thread.
When it has been worn and is spoilt,
Then we'll part from the virtuous lord.

Let us make an iron ox, and put him
To graze among the iron trees.
When he has grazed all the iron grass,
Then we'll part from the virtuous lord.

Were the pearls to fall on the rock,
Would the thread be broken?
If I parted from you for a thousand years,
Would my heart be changed?

The last stanza recurs in another Middle Korean song, a love lyric, and attests to its popular origin. The use of similar popular and proverbial expressions, especially in love poems of vows and griefs, is a commonplace.

In Korean poetry of compliment the *adynaton* is an accepted stylistic device, as in the following:

> Until the short legs of the duck
> Become long as a crane's—
> Until the crow becomes white,
> White as an eastern egret—
> Enjoy enduring bliss,
> Forever.

Kim Ku (1488–1534) wrote this impromptu piece one evening when King Chungjong honored him with a surprise visit at the Office of Special Counselors. Writing to please and even inspire the king, the speaker registers his genuine affection for royal patronage. The long-legged duck and the black crane are proverbial impossibilities, as is the white raven in the West. The crow and the eastern egret are also allegorical birds in moral verse, as when the mother of Chŏng Mong-ju (1337–1392), a famous Koryŏ loyalist, warns her son never to go near the "crows tearing and cawing," jealous of the egret's white feathers. The speaker's invention lies in employing the same symbols for epideictic purposes to convey his sincere wishes for an unbroken peaceful reign.

The poem, originally intended for the king and his entourage, became popular because of its treatment of subject richly resonant in shared cultural values. In traditional East Asian society such as that of Korea, where Confucian decorum and morality were the norms, with emphasis on such social virtues as loyalty, filial piety, and faithfulness, one can see why such a poem found a place whenever there was occasion. The popular, proverbial, and *adynata*-type statements reflecting folklore motifs, together with characteristic imagery, were a commonplace in East Asian epideictic poetry. The poem was usually sung at a birthday celebration, especially a sixtieth anniversary (sixty-one in the East Asian count) when a sexagenary cycle had been completed. Such an event called for a reunion of family and clan members for celebration. When the singer presented the poem by Kim Ku (or the one following), the audience would join in, some dancing around the honored guest. The singer could be confident that his audience knew the convention, for even today such a poem is recited at an offering of a congratulatory toast to one's elders. The congratulatory *sijo* was the most popular in a society where the cult of filial devotion was extolled by the establishment for its role in daily life.

In an anonymous *sijo* poem of later date, the speaker employs the same device—not by resorting to such other commonplaces as "until (even if) Mount T'ai has become flat and the wide ocean run dry," but by a repetition of numbers in solemn, sonorous rhythms:

Enjoy a thousand years,
And then ten thousand years,
Until flowers bloom on an iron pillar,
Until fruit ripens on that iron pillar.
Enjoy one hundred million more years,
And then another myriad years.

Its confident reiteration of the carefully spaced key words is compact and effective. Such statements of perpetuity are as old as the poems and hymns of blessing and sacrifice in the *Book of Songs,* as the round number, "ten thousand" (*wan*), recurs in the formulaic phrases—*wan-shou wu-chiang* (literally, "A myriad years without limit"),[100] *chün-tzu wan-nien* ("A myriad years for our lord"),[101] or *T'ien-tzu wan-nien* (or *-shou*) ("A myriad years for the Son of Heaven"),[102] and finally *wan-yu ch'ien-sui* ("A myriad and again a thousand years").[103]

172.2 Happiness to our Lord!
May he live for ever and ever.

213.2 May our Lord for ten thousand years
Keep safe his house and home.

262.6 The Son of Heaven—may he live for ever!
Illustrious is he, the Son of Heaven, . . .

300.4 For thousands upon ten thousands of years;
Safe you shall live for evermore.

Another characteristic motif recurs in the poems of praise in the *Man'yōshū,* the eighth-century Japanese anthology:

I.36 Endlessly as this river flows,
Lofty as these mountains,
Will it [the pleasure palace] stand for aye, . . .

VI.923 Ever prosperous like those mountains
And continuously as this river flows,
Will the lords and ladies of the court
Come hither [the Yoshinu palace].

VI.933 . . . he [the emperor] rules his realm
Eternally as endure the heaven and earth
And ever long as shine the sun and moon.

XIII.3234 As long as heaven and earth shall last,
And as long as sun and moon,
May the courtiers serve him . . .[104]

But in its magnificent array of similes, in its language and style, and in its confident and jubilant tone, poem 166 especially of the *Book of Songs* stands out. It may have served as a prototype for Korean and Japanese poetry of the kind, but later imitations turned up few surprises.

166.3 May Heaven guard and keep you,
Cause there to be nothing in which you do
not rise higher,
Like the mountains, like the uplands,
Like the ridges, the great ranges,
Like a stream coming down in flood;
In nothing not increased . . .

166.6 To be like the moon advancing to its full,
Like the sun climbing the sky,
Like the everlastingness of the southern hills,
Without failing or falling,
Like the pine-tree, the cypress in their verdure—
All these blessings may you receive![105]

Such pious hope is often visible in national anthems, as in the Republic of Korea's anthem which, in addition to invoking the pine on South Mountain as an emblem of the country's stability and continuity, begins with a prayer that under the protection of God on High, the country shall last "till the Eastern Sea runs dry and Mount Paektu is worn flat."[106]

Such optimism that society and culture will last as mountains and rivers has often been challenged. In Sonnet 64 Shakespeare contemplates invincible Time, the destroyer and leveler, brandishing a crooked, cruel knife or a bending sickle:

When I have seen the hungry ocean gain
Advantage on the kingdom of the shore,
And the firm soil win of the wat'ry main,
Increasing store with loss and loss with store;
When I have seen such interchange of state,
Or state itself confounded to decay . . .

which echoes the speech of Pythagoras in the *Metamorphoses:*

I have seen oceans
That once were solid land, and I have seen
Lands made from ocean. Often sea-shells lie
Far from the beach, and men have found old anchors
On mountain-tops. Plateaus have turned to valleys,
Hills washed away, marshes become dry desert,
Desert made pools. Here Nature brings forth fountains,
There shuts them in; when the earth quakes, new rivers
Are born and old ones sink and dry and vanish.
(XV.262–270)[107]

Only poetry will outlast "fire and sword,"[108] for the powerful rime is more durable than marble, bronze, Pharaoh's pyramids, the gilded monuments of princes.[109] The poet confers immortality on great men and renders their deeds imperishable. Such forms of praise as hymns, epics, and heroic poems, especially the Renaissance epics with their theme of deliverance, are often held to be capable of conferring immortality on the subject and his nation as well as of vindicating poetry's social role. Armed with philosophy and history, precepts and exempla, Confucian encomiasts—especially the compilers of *Songs of Flying Dragons*—succeeded not only in conferring glory but in creating an image of ideal virtue, discharging their twofold duty as Confucians and encomiasts.

IV

In the poem that sings the retreat of a patron, teacher, or friend[110] the poet as a tour guide of the grounds enjoys the freedom of movement, his delineation extending to a wider range of objects: now he climbs a hill contemplating the *sic transit* or *ubi sunt* motif, now he finds himself by a lake or river musing on the currents of life and time, thought and memory, poetry and music, or describes the seasonal beauties or the emblematic seasons of life. As a poem of praise its primary concern is the dweller's moral beauties, their lasting impact on society and culture. In integrating the epideictic theme with the topographical—the description of the excellence of his estate—nature usually reflects the virtue and character of the dweller. The praise of moral and spiritual excellence calls for a context of solitude and nature. Often explored are the dialectic patterns of withdrawal and emergence, the contemplative and the active, self and world, the contemplative as a necessary stage for the active career, moral cultivation as a prerequisite for public service, the individual's moral sense as the only safeguard for institutions. In the course of describing the dweller's moral beauties, be he a Taoist immortal or a Confucian sage, through a praise of landscape, the poet reaffirms traditional cultural values and parades his knowledge of history and literature.

Written to praise the elegant life of Kim Sŏng-wŏn (1525–1598), which centered on the Sŏha Hall and Sigyŏng Arbor on Mount Star in South Chŏlla Province, Chŏng Ch'ŏl's "Little Odes of Mount Star" (c. 1585–1587) begins with a question:

"Listen, Master of the Sŏha Hall,
despite the many pleasures life held,
why did you prefer to them all
this mountain, this water?
What made you choose
the solitude of hills and streams?"

The poet then catalogues the delights of the four seasons and exclaims that Mount Star exceeds in beauty T'ao Ch'ien's Peach Blossom Spring; it is, in fact, a "world of the moon." This is a topos of outdoing, but it could also be a reflection of the patriotic theme. Virgil's panegyric of Italy (*Georgics,* II.136–176) as the ideal land once ruled by Saturn and the land of harvests and plenty (*Saturnia tellus,* 173) and his English imitators' praise of England prompted one critic to say that "A Georgic is, among many other things, always a patriotic poem."[111] The expansive landscape reflects Kim Sŏng-wŏn's own liberality, freedom, and unworldliness, and the floating clouds and water-fowl (ducks) symbolize the mind and courtesy of the host. At the end, the poet, enraptured by the music played by his host on the black lute, avers that Kim is the true immortal in harmony with the workings of the universe, metaphorically flying high on the back of the crane.[112] The crane is not only a bird of longevity but a fit symbol of unity and harmony. It soars above the world while maintaining an intimate relation with it, uniting time and space, time and timelessness.

Unlike the seventeenth-century English country-house poems, the Korean poem is characterized by the omission of the description of buildings or their pedigree. Property is not the outcome of personal virtue or economic aggrandizement. His estate is Nature itself, mirroring the state of his mind, as another sixteenth-century Korean poet (Song Sun, 1493–1582) has it:

I have spent ten years
Building a grass hut;
Now winds occupy half,
The moon fills the rest.
Alas, I cannot let you come in,
But I shall receive you outside.

His hut has no walls and doors—nothing separates him from Nature. Furthermore, as Su Shih exclaims in his rhymeprose, *The Red Cliff*, I, "each thing between heaven and earth has its owner, . . . Only the cool wind on the river, or the full moon in the mountains, caught by the ear, becomes a sound, or met by the eye, changes to colour; no one forbids me to make it mine, no limit is set to the use of it; this is the inexhaustible treasury of the creator of things."[113]

Pak Il-lo's "Hall of Solitary Bliss" was written on the occasion of his poetic pilgrimage to the Hall of Solitary Bliss on Mount Jade in Kyŏngju where the remains of Yi Ŏn-jŏk (1491–1553) are preserved and Pak paid tribute to the master's memory. Yi Ŏn-jŏk passed the civil service examination in 1514 and served as Fourth Inspector and Second Censor before he suffered the first purge and withdrew to Mount Chaok (Purple Jade) near Kyŏngju to study Neo-Confucian philosophy. In 1537 he was recalled by royal order and filled the following posts: Rector of the National Academy, Inspector-General, Minister of Personnel, Rites, and Punishments, and Magistrate of Seoul, First Counselor in the Office of Special Counselors, and Fourth State Councillor (1545). The poem, however, does not dwell on his political success and rewards but on his exemplary virtues. The poet's task is to exalt and preserve the fame of virtue. As the ideal Confucian statesman and philosopher,

> He revered the sages of the past
> and wrote his poems.
> In quiet nature he was so immersed
> that he felt at home in all situations . . .
>
> He contemplated, sought the truth,
> and carried on the ancient sages' task.

Through study and self-cultivation he preserved and continued tradition and "opened a bright new path."

> His every word is wisdom and reveals
> the long tradition and patterns of thought
> as bright as sun and moon,
> a light illuminating the dark.

As a statesman he was equal to Hou Chi or Lord Millet, ancestor of the Chou dynasty, and Chieh, a wise minister under the legendary emperor Shun. But being implicated in a political purge of 1547 he was sent into exile to the north where, like the Grand Tutor Chia I (201–168 B.C.) in Ch'ang-sha,[114] he spent seven years in cold Kanggye.

There he transformed the rigors of political winter to the bliss of virtuous spring.

Such metaphors of natural harmony as the graceful peaks, the winding stream, the straight bamboo, the caressing wind, and the dense pine grove—these were spared by Heaven and treasured by Earth so that their riches could be handed down to the true "owner." The emphasis is on the beauty, purity, and spontaneity of nature, symbolic of the subject's harmonious, enlightened state of mind. It is a center of moral cultivation, and what is praised is a way of life in the ideal setting, a mode of existence vital to the preservation of the enduring norms of the lettered class. His friends were such emblematic animals as hawks and fishes. These classical images from the 239th poem in the *Book of Songs*[115] imply, first, as in the original context, the self-contentedness of the bird and the fish as the symbols of the extent of moral transformation effected by an ideal ruler (here fish do not jump into the fishermen's nets in their eagerness to serve the owner)[116] and, second, as emblems of the workings of the Confucian Way—how it is clearly seen in Heaven and on Earth.[117] The images suggest that the classical tradition is part of the cultural heritage of the Hall of Solitary Bliss and that the master was able to maintain the ideal relationship between man and nature.

His retreat surpasses in beauty and purity the Garden of Solitary Bliss of Ssu-ma Kuang (1019–1086), Censer Peak in Mount Lu sung by Li Po, T'ien-t'ai Mountains in Chekiang, or even Peach Blossom Spring, the Chinese Arcadia. His absence is like "an empty hill without a phoenix," yet his fragrance lingers on, for the speaker sees him "in the soup and on the wall."[118] In moral and spiritual stature Yi Ŏn-jŏk is compared to Mount T'ai or the polestar, supreme emblems of Confucian moral rhetoric. The hyperbolical description (*ecphrasis*) and metonymical representation create the *locus amoenus,* an ideal microcosm that mirrors the ideal state built on the Confucian political-moral philosophy. But the disrupter of social and moral harmony is man himself, who still wrestles in the dusty world, unaware of the relative values of name and fame. Thus the poet subtly introduces a satirical bite, deriding those ignorant of the ideal pattern of emergence and withdrawal, the art of biding time, and the cultivation of the self. A victim of political machination and senseless bloodshed which upset the moral and cosmic harmony, Yi's dream of creating another golden age ("hoped/ to achieve the peace of Yao and Shun") was shattered and the country became a waste. Unlike the myth of the Golden Age and Eden, the golden age invoked here is from the Chinese political myths. Sage emperors and wise ministers are paragons of Confucian virtues, brought in to heighten and illustrate the subject's exemplary qualities as statesman. Even in exile he "achieved virtue and the forthright Way." History vindicated his name, private academies enshrined him, and he was worshiped in the Confucian Temple, the highest honor accorded a scholar-statesman. Indeed, virtue is a jewel shining in the midst of adversity, and he was able to make use of adversity as a trial of spirit, as the "wisest course" (*3 Henry VI*, III.i.25). The exiled Duke Senior muses in the forest of Arden:

> Sweet are the uses of adversity,
> Which, like the toad, ugly and venomous,
> Wears yet a precious jewel in his head;
> And this our life, exempt from public haunt,
> Finds tongues in trees, books in the running brooks,
> Sermons in stone, and good in every thing.
> *As You Like It*, II.i.12–17

Indeed, "Jade is concealed in the rock, yet the hill is refulgent with it," a passage in Lu Chi's *Essay on Literature*[119] was aptly evoked to exalt the master's rural solitude, contemplative leisure, and complete modesty.

Only virtue will serve as a bulwark against mutability. The dweller of the Hall of Solitary Bliss has conquered time by his paradigmatic acts, and his enduring virtues are bright as the sun and moon, eternal as the "clear breeze . . . That blows over the Hall" itself.

> Heaven so high and earth so rich,
> they, too, end and dissolve to dust.
> Only the cool wind is eternal that blows
> over the Hall of Solitary Bliss.

As the poet declares, "Only the presence of my teacher abides." Virtue, not fame, conquers death. Yi Ŏn-jŏk thus becomes an ideal. Cheek by jowl are the perennial contrastive values and norms of conduct, the Confucian and Taoist, world and self, man and Nature. The poet, however, affirms the values of history and culture which insisted on the correspondence of microcosm and macrocosm, society to nature. Subtly underlying the poem is the poet's conviction that the return of political-moral harmony depends upon the return of harmony between man and nature. The restoration of civil order calls for man's moral regeneration, but action might bring about a faster change, hastening the application of the Arcadian vision to the world of politics. Such a dream, combining the active and the contemplative—the heroic and the pastoral—finds expression in the country-house poems. As a man's dwelling expresses his virtue, so should a dynasty. Only a ruler's bestowal of virtue on people and country can transform chaos into order and reaffirm the values of civilization. The ideal landscape provides a setting in which to contemplate the enduring norms of history and culture.

V

Another kind of praise poetry addressed to a solitary recluse, Taoist or Buddhist, extols the subject for his rejection of worldly values in favor of a life of repose and contemplation in nature and finally his attainment of a complete harmony with nature. Such a hermit usually resides in a craggy hilltop, oblivious of custom and opinion below. Formulaic descriptions of nature are intended to merge the subject of praise with nature: he is invisible, vanishing behind clouds and mist, occasionally leaving behind a footprint on a rock or on the moss. The ascent of a mountain, emblematic trees and animals, a cool spring or torrent, or a cold moon are metaphors of the stages of spiritual quest and an entry to the realm of transcendence. They are also symbolic of the freedom and spontaneity of the hermit who rides on the flux.

Ch'iu Wei (694–789?), in "Visiting a Recluse on West Mountain and Not Finding Him In,"[120] imagines his friend riding on a firewood cart or fishing in the autumn stream. Characteristically, he does not find him:

> But the color of the grasses under new rain,
> the voice of the pines in an evening window—
> these are the promised hidden wonders,
> enough to open wide the ear and heart.

He has not achieved an encounter, but nevertheless "grasped the meaning of purity." The poet's spiritual communion with the purity and harmony of nature is enough. Hence the last line, "What need to wait around for you?"

Li Po's poem addressed to his Taoist friend Yüan Tan-ch'iu employs the same technique. Lying high in the Eastern Ridge, "far from confusion and bustle," on a pillow of blue mist, Tan-ch'iu's activities include lying in the empty woods and sleeping until the sun shines on high.

> The pine wind cleans his lapel and sleeves,
> A stony lake laves his heart and ears.[121]

Emphasis falls on the verbs, "cleans" and "laves," the red dust of the world must be laved and the heart purified before it can attain spiritual enlightenment.

Again in "While Visiting on the South Stream the Taoist Priest Ch'ang" by Liu Ch'ang-ch'ing (709–785), nature scenes are not so much to stress the priest's delights of the senses as to stand for his attributes, an inference left for the reader.

Walking along a single path,
I see a footprint on the moss.
A white cloud is low on the quiet lake,
Fragrant grasses shut the idle gate.
After a rain I see the color of the pine,
Follow the mountain to the source of the water.
Creek flowers partake of the truth of Ch'an—
Flowers and I—I've nothing to say.[122]

Images are conventional, but perhaps appropriate in their context, their values to be assessed in the light of the eremitic ideals. They are symbols for the poet's ideal of Taoist perfection, a means of elegant compliment. "A footprint on the moss," "a white cloud on the quiet lake," "fragrant grasses that shut the idle gate," the source of the water, and creek flowers. These are Truth, paradigms of natural and poetic harmony, the poet says, and in their presence he is speechless, for they embody the friend's way of life, symbolic of his happy state of mind.

In one of the poems entitled "Summoning the Recluse" or "Invitation to Hiding," the Chin poet Tso Ssu (250?–305?) expresses his longing to go into retirement with a praise of pure joys in nature:

. . . in the hills is the sound of a singing lute.
White snow still lies on the northern hill,
Red flowers dazzle the southern grove.
A stony spring laves jade-like stones,
And there small fishes float and dive.
Why do we need strings and flutes?
Hills and waters have their clear music.[123]

Tinged with a strong ethical note, this poem indirectly criticizes the times and emphasizes the need of withdrawal as the only means of preserving the integrity and freedom of the self. Poems such as this probably stand behind the examples cited, which tend to be more condensed in form (fewer details are catalogued), pointed in message, and formulaic in diction. Landscape, reduced to a few essential notations and purified into a vision, has become an embodiment of ideal resemblance between nature and man.

In "Sent to the Taoist Holy Man of Ch'üan-chiao Mountain," Wei

Ying-wu (b. 736) praises his friend in a more personal and colloquial tone.

> This morning it was cold in my office study
> and suddenly I thought of you, living in the mountains,
> in valley bottoms bundling thorns for kindling,
> coming home to cook white stones.
> I wanted to take a gourdful of wine
> to cheer you far off in evening wind and rain,
> but falling leaves have filled the empty hills;
> where could I find a trace of you?[124]

The holy man must be "in valley bottoms bundling thorns for kindling,/ coming home to cook white stones" (the food of recluses), the poet imagines. The poet wants to cheer him with wine.

> but falling leaves have filled the empty hills;
> where could I find a trace of you?

The adjective "empty" underscores first the distance between the hermit who resides in the stillness of nature and the world below; it also alludes to his mind empty of worldly knowledge and useless intellectual baggage so that it can impartially reflect the flux of existence; and finally, in Buddhist terms, it stands for the illusory nature of the phenomenal world. The question uttered by the perplexed seeker in the last line points to the convention: the hermit is everywhere and nowhere, he is Nature and can be found only by spiritual awakening. As long as we persist in the conventional effort to comprehend the virtues of the enlightened, we will fail. We can come closest to the hermit by contemplating what he stands for, and contemplation of nature—ascent to the transcendent—is a conversation with him. The distance between the poet and his friend is therefore a necessary device: the praise of a friend in Nature is the highest praise, transmuting him into a symbol, a fragrance and radiance, as Li Po has it in his poem to Meng Hao-jan (699–740):

> Ruddy-faced, you renounced carriage and cap,
> White-haired, you lie among the pines and clouds.
> Drunk with moonlight, you are often hit by "sage,"
> Bewitched by flowers, you don't serve the lord.
> High mountain, how can I gaze at you?
> Here I bow only to your pure fragrance.[125]

In Korean poetry written in the vernacular and in Chinese, most of the topoi are present in varying degrees and emphases. Send-off poems to a friend leaving for his country estate or retreat usually portray him as roaming on the cloud-capped hills and drifting on the vast moonlit seas, inaccessible to one who has not yet renounced the world, as in the following anonymous poem:

Where is your home, friend?
"Over the hills and long rivers,
In the green of a bamboo grove,
A closed wicker gate.
If a seagull hovers in the air,
Go there and ask again."

In another type of poetry addressed to an immortal (*hsien;* fairy), the poet longs for one who has fulfilled the quest for liberty and permanence. In "Little Odes to Mount Star" by Chŏng Ch'ŏl, the poet has complimented his friend as riding on a crane, the usual means of transportation for the enlightened. The following poem, "Longing for an Immortal," by Ch'oe Myŏng-gil (1586–1647), combines the search-for-an-immortal theme with old age and retirement:

A sea of clouds is dim, and in the sunset
My eyes search for P'eng-lai Isles.
Chang Ch'ien's uneven path is obstacle-ridden,
Hsü Shih's storied boat has not returned.[126]
My white hair is blown easily by autumn winds,
Hard to find magic pills to keep my face young.
Since this year, endless sad affairs—
In a narrow lane moss grows—my gate bolted.

Also known as the Blessed Isles, P'eng-lai, one of the five or three sacred mountains to the east of the Eastern Sea, is an abode of immortal sages. "The towers and terraces upon [these mountains]," according to *Lieh Tzu,* "are all gold and jade, the beasts and birds are all unsullied white; trees of pearl and garnet always grow densely, flowering and bearing fruit which is always luscious, and those who eat of it never grow old and die. The men who dwell there are all of the race of immortal sages, who fly, too many to be counted, from one mountain to another and back again in a day and a night."[127] The Chinese version of the earthly paradise recalls the well-known Western convention of idyllic enclaves, for example, in Milton's description of the Hesperidean gardens in *Comus.*[128] The great odyssey attempted by boasters and frauds to reach the mountains in search of herbs "that banish Death" was futile.[129]

On the hills, thick growing,—herbs that banish Death.
Wings grow on those who eat them and they turn into heavenly
"hsien" . . .

> Their eyes search but cannot see the shores of the Blessed Islands.
> They cannot find the Blessed Isles and yet they dare not return.
>
> Po Chü-i, "Magic"

Although the speaker has bolted the gate and severed contacts with the common herd (moss grows in the path), he still has need to untrammel and disengage himself from "sad affairs." The quest for self-renewal and permanence cannot be fulfilled by magic pills; nor will they restore the health and strength of the youth.

> The Dark and Primal Master of Sages in his five thousand words
> Never spoke of herbs,
> Never spoke of "hsien."
> Nor spoke of soaring in broad daylight up to the blue heaven.

Hence the poem's subtle compliments and satire: tribute to an immortal, be he an unnamed friend or a creature of imagination, and derision of those who attempt to quicken the numinous experience or control ever-fluctuating anarchic forces in life. Man's reconciliation with himself and discovery of a realm of bliss are open only to the power of the imagination; so the speaker devastates the illusion that the reaching of the fabled Blessed Isles might offer freedom and felicity. The poem is an affirmation of the power of active imagination and the mind's integrative capacity.

We have surveyed some major types of praise poetry in East Asia: dynastic hymns in the *Book of Songs,* panegyrics in the *Songs of Flying Dragons,* country-house poems, and finally poetic compliments to recluses and enlightened Taoists and Buddhists. The poetic praise of a ruler represents a museum of topics and utilizes to the fullest extent stylistic devices (comparison and amplification), tropes of praise with allegorical significance (the dragon, the stag, and the like), folkloristic motifs, and concepts of the macro-microcosmic correspondence. The biographical pattern explored by Confucian classics and histories served as sources for the encomiast: such major topics as the goods of nature, fortune, character, and the "places" to be used in praise (birth, childhood and youth, education, pursuits, achievements in peace and war). As in the West, the chief function of praise is witness to moral virtues; hence praise, admonition, and contemplation are mixed, often resulting in the subordination of praise to instruction. Portrayed as the paragon of Confucian virtues or a mirror for future monarchs, the ruler is often allegorized in terms of Confucian culture heroes and sage rulers. His emergence and his deeds (territorial expansion, renaissance in the arts and letters, or foundation or renovation of a dynasty) herald a return of the golden age.

More freedom is allowed in the use of topics and places in the poetic praise of the literati. The arrangement of the material depends on the social status of the subject, his profession, deeds, and the occasion for praise which often determine the importance—and omission—of certain topoi. If the subject was a public servant, such virtues as loyalty, integrity, righteousness, and fidelity are emphasized. Although addressed to specific individuals on specific occasions, most praise poems of this kind, by their stress on eminent virtues, single out only the typical, conforming to formalized patterns in the tradition. If he renounced active life in search of a happy rural retirement, he was usually pictured as having attained a complete harmony with nature, for which there is probably no counterpart in the West. In either instance, the hyperbolical praise results in the disappearance of the individual: a statesman would vanish behind Confucian cardinal virtues; and a recluse merges with nature. Whatever the stance adopted, the greatest praise transmutes the subject into a simulacrum, into an exemplar of virtue in the first, and into an integral part of nature in the second.[130] It is nature poetry written in the first-person singular that allows the expressions of the claims of the self. The discovery of the individual is therefore allied with the emergence of nature poetry that rejects the complicity of society.

2 NATURE

A SALIENT feature of East Asian poetry is the predominance of nature imagery. A discussion of the complex relation of man to nature and the multiple meanings and functions of nature imagery must take into account the cultural and intellectual traditions that formed nature poetry. Here I shall confine myself to several types of nature poetry, with special attention to the topoi important within each kind and to their place in East Asian poetry.

I

Early examples of poetic topoi may be found in the *Book of Songs*. The first 160 songs of a total of 305 are called airs (*feng* or *kuo feng*, airs of the states), folk songs from fifteen states of northern China. In the airs and in subsequent sections, the technique known as *hsing*,[1] the thematic introduction of nature scenes to state the motif of the poem, is used. The oblique relation of a nature scene implies its metaphoric function, reinforcing, at least in the earlier songs, the speaker's state of mind. There are a number of motifs; their frequent recurrence in similar contexts and themes helps us to analyze and, often, to date the poems. The number of motifs in a poem varies from one to several (e.g., poem 9.2). Often the *hsing* signals a topos, motif, and theme, in its earlier and later phases, as in the following:

9.2 Tall grows that tangle of brushwood;
Let us lop the wild-thorn.
Here comes a girl to be married;
Let us feed her horses.
Oh, the Han, it is so broad,
One cannot swim it,
And the Kiang, it is so rough,
One cannot boat it!

10.2 I go along the high banks of the Ju
Cutting boughs that have been lopped and
grown again.

At last I have seen my lord;
He has not left me for ever.

118.2 Fast bundled is the firewood;
The Three Stars have risen.
Is it tonight or which night
That I see my Good Man?
Oh, masters, my masters,
What will this Good Man be like?

68.1 The spraying of the waters
Cannot float away firewood that is bundled.
Yet those fine gentlemen
Are not here with us defending Shen.
In what month shall we get home?

There is a metaphorical connection, the speaker says, between "that tangle of brushwood" or "that mixed firewood" and a "girl to be married." Is she the one he used to meet and woo in the course of gathering firewood? Has she been married off to a distant place ("Oh, the Han, it is so broad"), unattainable and unapproachable? The poem is both a celebration of her marriage and a lament of lost love.[2] In poem 10.2, the speaker is a woman who, under the pretext of cutting firewood, goes out to meet her lover. Her momentary anxiety and disappointment in the first stanza give way to an exclamation of joy ("At last I have seen my lord;").[3] In poem 118.2, "the bundled firewood" functions as a metaphor of cohesion and solidarity.[4] Interpretations differ as to who is the speaker of the poem but, whoever he is, the poem is about marriage and family solidarity represented by the bundled firewood. Poem 68 reinforces such a reading. A frontier guard laments the absence of his wife and the hardships of his duty. He then invokes the now established metaphor of the "bundled firewood," the marriage ties that no vicissitude ("stirred waters") could destroy.[5] Here the image of the bundled firewood underwent a gradual development: the seasonal ceremony of gathering firewood, the occasion for young men and women to meet and fall in love, first was associated with courtship and marriage, then with cohesion of the family members so vital to the maintenance of order and continuity.

92.1 Even the rising waters
Will not carry off thorn-faggots that are
well bound.
Brothers while life lasts
Are you and I.
Do not believe what people say;
People are certainly deceiving you.

238.1 Thick grow the oak clumps;
We make firewood of them, we stack them.
Great is the magnificence of the lord king;
On either hand are those that speed for him.

101.4 When we cut firewood, how do we do it?
Without an axe it would not be possible.
When one takes a wife, how is it done?
Without a matchmaker he cannot get her.
But once he has got her,
No one else must he ever approach.

158.1 How does one hew an axe handle?
Without an axe it is impossible.
How does one take a wife?
Without a matchmaker she cannot be got.

Poem 92.1 illustrates how the firewood metaphor could be employed in a similar context but with a different theme, the beauty of friendship.[6] In poem 238.1, a eulogy to praise the magnificence of the king, it has acquired epideictic relevance, the well-stacked firewood representing the times of peace and plenty.[7] However, the proverbial statement in poems 101.4 and 158.1 would place them at a later stage, when a simple, yet vivid introduction of nature, once evoked to assert an analogy between nature and man, lost its dramatic, expansive force.[8] Such a formulaic statement indicates the compiler's conscious manipulation to close a gap between a public moral code and an intensely personal tone. The fourth stanza in poem 101 and the first in 158 are hortatory, the matchmaker (ax) replacing free love closely associated in ancient China with agricultural festivals, communal free time, song contests staged by groups or individuals, and with spontaneity of feeling and expression.

Poem 9 contains at least two topoi, one of which is that of firewood for courtship and marriage, and the other that of river, standing for separation.

Beyond the Han a lady walks;
One cannot seek her,
Oh, the Han, it is so broad,
One cannot swim it,
And the Kiang, it is so rough
One cannot boat it.

To the girl the song expresses the joy of marriage and the sorrow of separation; to her erstwhile lover, the disloyalty of love and the finality of separation, *odi et amo*. The rivers bespeak both the serene and tumultuous states of the mind.

61.1 Who says that the river is broad?
On a single reed you could cross it.
Who says that Sung is far away?
By standing on tiptoe I can see it.[9]

34.2 He: The ford is in full flood,
And baleful is the pheasant's cry.
She: The ford is not deep enough to wet your axles;
The pheasant cried to find her mate.[10]

37.1 If you tenderly love,
Gird your loins and wade across the Chen;
But if you do not love me—
There are plenty of other men,
Of madcaps maddest, oh![11]

129.1 Thick grow the rush leaves;
Their white dew turns to frost.
He whom I love
Must be somewhere along this stream.
I went up the river to look for him,
But the way was difficult and long.
I went down the stream to look for him,
And there in midwater
Sure enough, it's he![12]

These complaints of unfulfilled love represent various moods, all centered on the metaphor of the river. One is gently rebuking yet self-consolatory; another is a humorous dialogue, a battle of words between the sexes, with the omenistic image of the pheasant; the third is tantalizing with its stern reminder of the trial of love; the fourth portrays the dramatic moment when yearning and languishing give way to a fulfilled desire. The river both separates and unites, an adequate symbol of the encounter and parting of lovers. Its mindless, irreversible flow is as endless as her yearning, its tides as turbulent as her fears and loneliness, and its various moods as uncertain as the safety of her lover as he crosses the water. As "going into the hazelnut trees" was synonymous with love-making in medieval lyric, so "gathering firewood" and "going to the river" had emotional and symbolic associations with love in ancient China.[13]

The tenth in the *Nineteen Old Poems of the Han* represents an earlier instance of the transfer of the motif from earth to sky. The Herdboy (or Draught Ox; Aquila) and the Weaver (Vega and Lyra) constellations of Chinese astronomy, on both sides of the Milky Way (or The Han River in Heaven, River of Heaven, the Silver River), were often invoked as fit metaphors of the separation of lovers. Fated to a year-long separation, they meet once on the night of the seventh day of the seventh lunar month, when magpies form a bridge across the river of stars.[14] Some 120 poems in the *Man'yōshū* deal with the same motif, and such major poets as Yamanoe Okura (c. 660–733) and Kakinomoto Hitomaro (c. 680–700) wrote the "Seventh Night Poem."[15] The persistence and power of the motif are attested by the frequency of the river image as a symbol of separation in pre-T'ang and T'ang and Korean poetry of friendship, especially send-off poems, and of love.

We have observed the evolution of some nature imagery and the mutation of a given motif and theme, or the association of a given motif with a given theme[16] in ancient Chinese poetry. I have tried to indicate the emergence of a poetic metaphor, the poem's metaphorical structure, the way of objectifying and communicating experience. The technique of a symbolic equation, as Reckert calls it,[17] and such Japanese variants as the *kakekotoba,* a verbal counterpart of the superimposition of images, and the *honkadori,* a superimposition of themes, represent earlier modes of analogy in East Asian poetry. Symbolic equation functions as the assertion of an implicit interaction between the elements of the poem—nature introduction and human situation. Not as in earlier medieval European verse where nature scenes are presented as "a public fact," "a concept rather than a percept,"[18] the Chinese speaker's insights and associations tend to invest the imagery with a highly subjective tone. Indeed, the speaker's thought, feelings, and attitudes are embodied in a single image, appropriate for the delineation of the poem's mood and tone. It becomes the poem's principle of organization, reinforcing a correspondence between man's existence and nature's seasonal changes.

II

Poem 154, "Seventh Month," in the *Book of Songs,* is in Waley's words "a song made out of sayings about 'works and days,' about the occupations belonging to different seasons of the year."[19] The months are based on the lunar calendar which begins its year in the spring. Originating in the area of modern Shensi in the north, the poem's chief events of the agricultural year based on the local climate are:

I. Plowing.
II. Offering of lambs and garlic.

III. Spring. The orioles sing.
Girls take their deep baskets to gather the soft mulberry leaves and the white aster.
A girl's heart is sick and sad.
IV. The milkwort is in spike.
V. The cicada cries; locust moves its leg.
VI. The grasshopper shakes its wing.
We eat wild plums and cherries.
VII. The shrike cries.
We boil mallows and beans, and eat melons.
VIII. We pluck the rushes and sedges, twist thread, dry the dates, cut the gourds.
"With my red dye so bright I make a robe for my lord."
IX. We take the seeding hemp, gather bitter herbs, cut the alianto for firewood, gather harvest, and make ready the stackyards.
Shrewd frosts.
X. Boughs fall.
The cricket goes under the bed.
Make spring wine, clear the stackgrounds, hold the village feast.
XI. Sharp frost. Make fur coats.
XII. Keen winds.

The following designations from the twenty-four fortnightly periods *(ch'i)*,[20] still in use in China and Korea, indicate how the descriptions of natural phenomena served as season indicators, heralding the conventions of seasonal imagery in the literature of later periods: Awakening of Creatures, Clear and Bright, Grain Rain, Lesser Fullness of Grain, Grain in Ear, White Dews, Cold Dews, Descent of Hoar Frost, Lesser and Greater Snow. Such nature images served as important elements of poetry, its tone, mood, and symbolism. This partly accounts for the formulaic nature of seasonal images and the limited, stylized types of emotions and situations in East Asian nature poetry.

III

Description of landscape for its own sake is rare in the *Book of Songs,* for the bond between nature and man was never questioned, and nature told the poet what he was. Poetry speaks the heart's desire, and the poems were about the feelings of man, natural scenes calling up human emotions. The extended description of nature and of specifically named places and objects coincides with the emergence of the *fu,* or rhymeprose form, but the *Ch'u tz'u* or *Songs of the South* are not without a depiction of exotic landscape, where much dispersive detail is colored by local myths and allegory. This visionary landscape is a configuration of many elements, reflective, descriptive, moralizing, and political. The later Han *fu,* such as Ssu-ma Hsiang-ju's (179–117 B.C.) "Shang-lin Park" adds to these elements a catalogue—varieties of hills, rivers, birds, beasts, plants, trees, minerals, and the like—a motif that became part of the stock-in-trade of later *fu* pieces in China and *kasa* poetry in Korea. The wearisome enumeration, often drawn from a dictionary and displaying virtuosity, tends to be external in treatment, ornamental in purpose, pastiche in effect. Nevertheless, the poems in the *Ch'u tz'u* and, later, in the *fu* genre provided themes and techniques for Korean writers of *kasa* poetry from the fifteenth century onward. Some motifs, often originating in the *Ch'u tz'u,* include: a distant wandering, historical reflection with condemnation of historical misdeeds or praise of exemplary acts, moralizing on the theme of virtue unrewarded, incidental meditation on rural retirement and mutability, conclusion on a fabulous flight or a didactic note. As the *Poly Olbion, Coopers Hill,* or *The Seasons* furnished a storehouse of topics for later topographical poetry, so "Encountering Sorrow" (by Ch'ü Yüan, c. 300 B.C.), "Shang-lin Park," or "Climbing the Tower" (by Wang Ts'an, 177–217),[21] stimulated topographical depiction on more or less the same principles of selection and arrangement, especially in the journey poem, the mountain poem, and the retirement poem.

IV

How, then, did the four seasons figure in poetry, and how did the East Asian poet respond to different beauties and sensations of the seasons? Even a casual reader will be struck by the fact that the favorite seasons are spring and autumn, as if to underscore an ancient saying, "In spring the woman yearns, in autumn the gentleman sorrows,"[22] reminiscent of the passages in *Tempus est iocundum* from *Carmina Burana: Tempore brumali/ vir patiens,/ animo vernali/ lasciviens* (In the winter, a man is patient; in the spring, he's full of lust).

23.1 There was a lady longing for the spring;
A fair knight seduced her.

154 The spring days are drawing out;
They gather the white aster in crowds.
A girl's heart is sick and sad
Till with her lord she can go home.[23]

"The Nine Arguments" (*Chiu pien*) in the *Ch'u tz'u* open with a meditation on the flux:

Alas for the breath of autumn!
Wan and drear! Flower and leaf fluttering
fall and turn to decay.[24]

Winter poems are comparatively fewer than spring poems, as in classical antiquity of the West. But the use of a topos of stylized winter landscape in political, moral, and allegorical verse, especially in mirrors of mutability, is common in both cultures. Such a topos seems to have flourished in the West from the time of Renaissance, and Sackville's *Induction* to his *Complaint of Henry, Duke of Buckingham* in *A Mirror for Magistrates* may be cited as a characteristic English expression of it. But such winter landscape will be studied with the theme of mutability, of *de casibus* and *ubi sunt*.

The following examples of spring poems I chose at random; all are in the short form of verse. In the first Tzu-yeh song, the spring wind heralds the advent of the season, stirring the speaker's heart; as a result she sees strange yet lovely mountains and forest and hears the birds' limpid songs. In the second, against the flowers in the forest are set the speaker's sad thoughts, evoked by the birds. Li Po's poem is built on an opposition—green silklike grass and the speaker's homesickness—intensified by the visit of spring wind in her room. Chia Chih's begins with the usual seasonal images: yellow willow sprays, the green grass, the perfumed plum, and the eastern breeze. But the source of sorrow is the inadequacy of the breeze to expel the lengthening sorrow which is likened to a long spring day. On the other hand, Tu Fu's poem (757) exploits fully the twofold metaphorical qualities of landscape, its indifference to human sorrows and disasters and its capacity to be in sympathy with the speaker. "The flowers shed tears of grief," a pathetic fallacy employed to show a bond between man and nature and to close the gap between macrocosm and microcosm.[25]

Yakamochi's poem is, again, built on a contrast between a soaring lark singing in the tranquil sun and the speaker's burdened heart. Narihira, like Tsurayuki, blames cherry blossoms for enticing sorrow in the beholder, for their poignant transience. The departing wild geese from the spring dawn, symbolic of the season's fleeting beauty, Shunzei says, provoke tears. A spring night's dream, according to Teika, is ephemeral and unreal as the floating bridge of dreams, leaving behind only a cloud vanishing into the sky. (Perhaps the image of levitation signifies a moment of cognition, an ascent of consciousness as it attempts to free itself from the world of relations.)

Yi Cho-nyŏn depicts the spring night with the practiced eye: it is painted white; it is fragrant and beautiful—the joy of spring is so keen it resembles pain. Both poet and bird are awake, one unthinking (ignorant), the other sensitive, and only the sensitive soul notices sorrow and absence lurking behind beauty and joy. Song Sun blames the passing of spring on the wind, here perhaps standing for a political purge; Prince Pongnim, on the other hand, is aware of the fickleness of spring—blossoming flowers and trees, blue rain, and spring breezes that, like the brief career of sycophants and miscreants at court, are destined to be momentary. Kim Yu-gi, in an attempt to discover some sense of constancy in the midst of flux, singles out pine and bamboo, the traditional symbols of longevity, integrity, and constancy, and mocks the gaudy dresses of blossoms. The last three poems are about the winter of discontent, symbolic poems intended to be understood at more than one level. The last of the three examples is probably from one fully enlightened, one who has perceived the truth of the oneness of peach blossoms on the tree and of those scattered on the ground.

Built on a contrast of spring landscape (1–12) and human mortality (13–20), Horace's ode *Solvitur acris hiems* (I.4) draws lively details from reality and mythology—Zephyr, flowers, calm sea, Venus dancing with the Graces and Nymphs; but in line 13 allegorical Death abruptly intrudes, impartially knocking at the farmer's cottage and prince's palace.[26] The terror and paradox of the human condition are the theme of another poem, *Diffugere nives* (IV.7), A. E. Housman's favorite Latin lyric. The first and third stanzas read:

> The snow has fled; already the grass is returning to the fields and the foliage to the trees. Earth is going through her changes, and with lessening flood the rivers flow past their banks . . . The cold gives way before the zephyrs; spring is trampled underfoot by summer, destined likewise to pass away so soon as fruitful autumn has poured forth its harvest; and lifeless winter soon returns again.[27]

Intrusion of winter into spring and the subsequent reminder to Torquatus that no family, eloquence, or righteousness recalls a man from death—with further mythological parallels at the end—repeats the usual unresolved tension between man and nature characteristic of much of classical Western spring poems.[28] These emphasize, and so does the third spring poem by Horace (IV.12)[29] which is an invitation to Virgil recalling the threat of Death's dark fires (*nigrorum ignium*), a need to enjoy life while there is time, an attitude scorned by Shakespeare's great sonnets. And when the nymph in Raleigh's "The Nymph's Reply to the Shepherd" declares that "The flowers do fade, and wanton fields/ To wayward Winter reckoning yields," she is indeed repeating a commonplace.

Unlike Horace's spring poems, the opening lines of Chaucer's General Prologue, regarded as a good specimen of medieval descriptions of spring, presents a joyful picture as sweet showers, budding flowers, tender shoots, the mild west wind, the young sun, and singing birds all praise nature's rebirth and renewal.

> Whan that Aprill with his shoures soote
> The droghte of March hath perced to the roote,
> And bathed every veyne in swich licour
> Of which vertu engendred is the flour;
> Whan Zephirus eek with his sweete breeth
> Inspired hath in every holt and heeth
> The tendre croppes, and the yonge sonne
> Hath in the Ram his halve cours yronne,
> And smale foweles maken melodye,
> That slepen al the nyght with open ye
> (So priketh hem nature in hir corages) ;

Such rebirth is presented here as "the impregnating of a female March by a male April," "a marriage of water and earth," and a fructifying of every grove and heath by Zephyrus, "a marriage of air and earth,"[30] but such mode of depiction is rare in East Asian poetry. Making his *reverdie* "the groundsong for a pilgrimage," Chaucer celebrates not only a spring that stirs the earth but another spring, a beginning and regeneration of pilgrims as they set off to the shrine of Thomas à Becket at Canterbury.[31]

Nature's spontaneous profusion, with a catalogue of seasonal objects, is often the subject of poems centering on spring, usually in longer forms of verse such as *kasa* and *fu*. The first extant *kasa* in Korean, "Hymn to the Spring," celebrates the joys of the season by a retired gentleman:

> Winter left us yesterday; look,
> Peach and apricot blossoms in the sunset.
> Willows and plants are green in the rain.
> As if in marks of a chisel,
> As if in strokes of a brush, the hand
> Of the Creator is everywhere, gay and extravagant.
> The graceful birds in the wood,
> Drunk with spring time, flirt and sing.

The "Creator" here, also translated as the "Fashioner of Creatures (or Mutations)," occurs already in the *Chuang Tzu* and more frequently in T'ang literature. It is a "metaphysical principle," responsible for the multiplicity and particularity of the phenomenal world. At times designated as "the old man who fashions creatures," this Taoist creator is a "shaper and molder of matter," to be wondered at and admired,[32] especially for inscrutable workings of nature, but not to be appealed to. What the speaker sings in this poem is the unity of man and nature ("Nature and I are one"), not a pious worship of the supernatural responsible for the creation. Thus the speaker aptly sees at the end of his roaming the Arcadia of T'ao Ch'ien, not the shrine to the creator.

Although there are poems with descriptive details praising autumnal beauties for their own sake—especially in topographical and retirement literature—my examples are set in the evening and at night. The predominantly visual and auditory imagery seems to indicate its reputable, accepted usage in the tradition. The figural diction suggests the beauty of the season of dying as it lingers and passes and finally gives way to the season of desolation and death. Again, the general pattern is the same as in the spring poems, nature evoked for its metaphorical power to intensify a contrast or a parallel: the bright moon and autumn wind, the cold river, the sleeping fish, set against the sadness of absence and longing (Yi Chŏng); a brief worldly glory against the autumnal beauty (Tu Fu; Wŏn Ch'ŏn-sŏk); the serene, vacant landscape against the agony of the sleepless man (Li Yü); the cry of a cricket (Tzu-yeh song; Hsieh T'iao; Sone no Yoshitada; Yun Sŏn-do), a goose (Hsü Hun; Yun Sŏn-do; Yi Chŏng-bo, Cho Myŏng-ni), a quail (Shunzei), or a snipe (Saigyō) as a symbol of the speaker's state of mind; and a melancholy dusk (Shunzei; Teika; Saigyō; Wŏn Ch'ŏn-sŏk), an evening over the black pines (Jakuren), a lone traveler braving the evening wind (Teika) or spending a sleepless night in a moonlit garden (Cho Myŏng-ni) to communicate the loneliness of the spirit and, ultimately, the meaning of the human condition. Yun Sŏn-do and Yi Chŏng-bo specifically identify the season with the onslaught of old age and decay (wrinkles devour my lord; the speaker's parents get old; and frosty air turns the hair grey), the emblematic season of life.

The prevalence of autumn as the favorite poetic season—as a mood and subject of poetry—and the deliberate cultivation of the dark and mysterious, the sad and veiled, the fleeting and intangible as the highest aesthetic ideals, were responsible for a number of autumn meditations by East Asian poets. Autumn, which fuses "now" of summer's warmth and glory with the "then" of winter's coldness and desolation,[33] is a fit metaphor to capture the "evanescence of a treasured 'now,' "[34] the awful transition between being and nothingness. Thus by looking toward a vanishing actuality man seems to realize deeply the truth of split existence, "the double awareness of life as 'now' and 'then.' " That moment, Thomas McFarland says, is the lyric instant, "art's most distinctive tribute to our individual selfhood."[35] My examples, in various ways, embody "the lyric instant," reflecting the characteristic mode of existence of East Asian man and his mode of perception.

Despite conventional seasonal images, brought in to satisfy seasonal requirements and to set the background, nature depiction in these poems is not enthusiastic or detailed. The imitation of nature was not the aim, for the mimetic theory was nonexistent in East Asia. What little imagery there is, in spite of its concreteness, is evoked for its premeditated effects, attuned to the tone and mood of the poem. The brevity of the forms and the requirements of prosody all but ruled out the introduction of irrelevant detail. A choice of imagery indicates both the freedom of selection and the sanction of tradition and convention, and such a choice was dictated by the sense of the poem's total design. There is little doubt that the poets, possessed of clear vision and deep feeling, connoisseurs of natural beauty and virtuosi of word magic, were open to sense impressions. At the same time, it is difficult to determine whether the poet was speaking from firsthand knowledge or from his literary memory. As in the *Book of Songs* and in later poetry, greater compression was achieved not by overt comparison, but by symbolic juxtaposition of images, on the one hand, and of the seasonal elements and the state of mind on the other. Whether the effect intended is harmony or contrast, a harmony of man and nature, or a contrast between interior discord and exterior joy, the lyrical, dramatic use of nature imagery was less to hint at the mingling of human emotion and natural scene as to single out one intense emotion, to arrest a moment of experience, an aesthetic moment in, or beyond, time, by retracing experience in the light of tradition and convention. The paratactic syntax and the predominantly present tense seem to underscore the immediacy of the elements of experience, without the interposition of the poet. It is a rediscovery of a union between nature and consciousness, in contradistinction to the ambivalent views of nature in the West, the continual oscillation between attraction and repulsion, especially the Romantic disjunction between consciousness and nature. Reconciliation between man and nature was seldom achieved in Romantic nature poetry, which is in reality an "antinature poetry," even by Wordsworth whose real subject was the creative imagination, the workings of the mind of a poet, not nature.[36]

V

Poetry that sings the happiness of rural retirement is perhaps the most popular theme of Chinese and Korean poets. Its setting is the authoritarian state built upon Confucian political philosophy, and its season of growth is the times of political upheaval and moral chaos. Earlier examples of such poetry were produced in a period of turmoil and division between the beginning of the third and the end of the sixth century in China, between the close of the Han and the establishment of the Sui. In the middle of the third century, a group of literati, known in history as the Seven Worthies of the Bamboo Grove, renounced public life and its rewards and adopted a simple life in a bamboo grove, reminiscent of a pastoral oasis. There they indulged in a kind of pastoral friendship, with a common devotion to poetry, music, wine, and polite conversation. In an attempt to break away from Confucian rituals and morality, they found solace and meaning in Taoism, with its emphasis on individual freedom and fulfillment.[37] This is perhaps the reason why one critic views their revolt against authority and convention as the discovery of the individual and of the beauty of Nature. But the first authentic voice in this vein was T'ao Ch'ien (365–427), also known as the "Gentleman of the Five Willow Trees" from the autobiographical sketch, who at the age of forty withdrew from official life never to return, refusing to "bend his waist for five piculs of rice." In East Asia these were the beginnings of nature poetry, which flourished when dynasties changed, when standards were in flux, much as they were during pre-Augustan Rome, the Commonwealth, and post-Restoration England, when the poet painfully realized the instability of civilization and the fragility of political order. But most motifs in such poetry in East Asia were first successfully explored by T'ao Ch'ien and later accepted as the established norms.

Using a single poem by T'ao Ch'ien, "The Return," I will attempt to isolate the principal topoi in it and in other poems of his collection and to suggest some of their multiple associative significances. The poem, like other works of T'ao, is a museum of topics for the retirement poetry of later times, much in the manner Virgil's *Georgics* (II.458–540), Horace's ode (III.16), epode (II), epistle (I.10), and satire (II.6), Martial's epigram (X.47), and Claudian's *De Sene Veronensi* were to English retirement poetry in the seventeenth and eighteenth centuries. A selection of later Chinese and Korean examples in the same tradition attempts to show the persistence and power of the enduring convention.

In the Preface to "The Return," written in the eleventh month of 405, T'ao Ch'ien gives the reasons for his return to the country: "My instinct is all for freedom, and will not brook discipline or restraint. Hunger and cold may be sharp, but this going against myself really sickens me."[38] The poem therefore begins with the principal motif, that of his return as a true homecoming to himself, a discovery of the self and of the beauty of nature: "To get out of this and go back home!" The return is the result of following "the inclinations of the heart" (51) or the "promptings of his heart" ("After Drinking Wine," XVIII.9), capable only of one who knows how to "adapt to change" ("At the Year's End: A Reply to the Attendant Chang," 18), and "to follow [one's] own course" ("After Drinking Wine," XII.12), all emphasizing the topos of individual choice. Thus he declares, "To go against oneself is a real mistake." Line 35 of "The Return" amplifies his resolution: "The world and I shall have nothing more to do [with] one another." The severance of all ties with the outside world (not nature's formlessness, as in Frost) is shown by a symbolic act of closing his gate: "There is a gate there, but it is always shut." Or in less metaphorical terms, for

> Success or failure do not trouble me,
> "At the Year's End," 17
> I will not be bound by love of rank . . .
> "Written at T'u-k'ou at Night," 18
> . . . a name left to posterity
> Is no more to me than floating mist.
> "A Lament in the Ch'u Mode," 17–18

The last is an echo of the remark of Confucius, "Undeserved wealth and rank are no more to me than floating clouds" (*Analects,* VII.15).[39]

His concern is not poverty, but truth. The polemical stance underscores the speaker's moral and spiritual protest, as is true of all poetry of the kind, and the intensity of conviction and degree of firmness—firmness in adversity—provide the unifying mood and tone. It was a way to explore the reverberations, literary, social, moral, and philosophical, of the given theme and to invest it with multiple viewpoints and implications. Thus sounded the dialectical and polemical tone so characteristic of retirement poetry.

In "A Farmhouse on the Wei River," Wang Wei (699?–759?), who is a witness to a happy rural scene, exclaims at the end:

> This I admire: the simple life.
> And sad, sing: *O to be home!*[40]

Wei Ying-wu (b. 736), in "Eastern Suburb," describes his newly won freedom from a life of confinement and complexity. After a momentary savoring of bliss, his mind becomes beset with affairs again. The poem ends with a resolution:

> Finally I'll retire and build myself a hut here,
> I may then fulfill my wish to emulate T'ao.[41]

Su Shih's (1037–1101) "The Homecoming" echoes a number of familiar topics: "Oh! I will go back home," reinforced at about a midpoint, "At last, I have come home!" He praises the mindless clouds and birds which seem to live "on their own accord" and declares, a few lines later, "Let me follow but my heart." He has no ambition to acquire wealth and fame.[42]

A seventeenth-century Korean poet, Kim Kwang-uk (1579–1656), declares his independence with the familiar symbol of a "bird newly freed," already introduced by T'ao Ch'ien in "Returning to the Farm to Dwell" (I.19–20): "For long I was a prisoner in a cage/ And now I have my freedom back again."

> Bundle the piles of verbose missives,
> Burn the scrolls of empty scribbles—
> At last I ride home on a swift horse,
> Whipping the autumn winds.
> A bird newly freed cannot be happier,
> I savor freedom, sup the rustic air.

The final abandonment of the court associated with pride, deceit, and avarice was contrasted in a striking manner with the pure, constant, innocent nature and the pleasures of a secluded life by Chŏng Ch'ŏl:

> Milky rain on the green hills,
> Can you deceive me?
> A sedge cape and horsehair hat,
> Can you deceive me?
> Yesterday I flung off my silk robe—
> I have nothing that will stain me.

Pak Il-lo (1561–1643), a navy captain turned recluse, probably felt the influence of the fifth-century Chinese poet in the following:

> Sick and old you [the king] let me leave you.
> So to east of the Han River
> I return among the hills and waters.
>
> "Song of the Sedge Bank" (1611)

> So today I start out at last
> With a bamboo stick and straw sandals.
>
> "The Hall of Solitary Bliss"

> In my old age I visit hills and waters.
> I know it is a bit too late, but
> In order to meet my heart's desire . . .
> I visit the valley of the Reedy Stream.
>
> "Song of the Reedy Stream" (1636)

Most versions of seclusion poetry emphasize the renouncement of fame and fortune as necessary conditions for the enjoyment of natural beauty, a central concern of the *beatus vir* in East and in West.

The values of "The Return" are presented by a number of nature images—emblematic images of retreat—all serving as symbols for his liberated mind and individual fulfillment: the wind (called "gentle breeze" in line 9; "the liberating cleansing breeze" or "a south breeze" elsewhere) that blows his gown, the aimless clouds, the homing bird, the flowing spring, together with the pine and chrysanthemums standing on the three paths, the trees in the courtyard, and a lonely pine, all celebrating freedom, peace, and leisure; the pine, especially for firmness in adversity, a true moral symbol. At one point, the chrysanthemums and the pines are called "outstanding sentinels beneath the frost" ("A Reply to Secretary Kuo," II.10); in another poem, "As I Passed Through Ch'ien-hsi," the cypress is singled out for the same lofty character ("can endure the frost," 16). A conjunction of a group of these images, like that of grass, shade, and water in the topos of the *locus amoenus* beginning with the seventh *Idyll* of Theocritus, became the favorite device for signaling a withdrawal from the active world, either in panegyrics to innocence, simplicity, and contentment, or polemical-satiric attacks on the falsity and hypocrisy of the court. Yun Sŏn-do (1587–1671), in "Songs of Five Friends," addresses the pine and bamboo:

Flowers bloom when it is warm;
Leaves fall when days are cool.
But O *pine,* how is it
You scorn frost, ignore snow?
I know your towering self,
Straight even among the Nine Springs.

You are not a tree, no,
Nor a plant, not even that.
Who lets you shoot so straight; what
Makes you hollow within?
You are green in all seasons,
Welcome, *bamboo,* my friend.

Yun Sŏn-do's pine, like T'ao Ch'ien's, takes on a new dimension as a symbol of an isolated poet who weathers adversity, yet remains untarnished and unyielding. It signals the acceptance of solitude as the only dramatic resolution of the perennial conflict between society and individual, civic obligations and self-fulfillment, as well as a fit metaphor of the landscape of the poet's regenerated mind. The bamboo is praised especially for its hollowness—for only the empty mind can respond to natural things without prejudice—free of useless knowledge and purposive activity, shorn of such false gems as wealth and prestige.

Speak, chrysanthemum, why do you shun
The orient breezes of the third moon?
"I had rather freeze in a cruel rain
Beside the hedge of dried sticks,
Than humble myself to join the parade:
Those flowers of a fickle spring."

The author is An Min-yŏng (c. 1870–1880), and his speaker holds an imaginary dialogue with the chrysanthemum, which scorns a "fickle spring," a repudiation of a worldly career wrought with vicissitude and hypocrisy.

In lines 39–44 of "The Return" T'ao Ch'ien describes the work to be done on the farm:

The farmers tell me that now spring is here
There will be work to do in the west fields.
Sometimes I call for a covered cart
Sometimes I row a lonely boat
Following a deep gully through the still water
Or crossing the hill on a rugged path.

As in the georgic, pastoral, and *beatus ille* tradition, the poet seems to say that the land is a repository of values—harmony, order, fruitfulness set against disorder, instability, and destruction raging outside. As such, it is an emblem, as was the retired estate in the poetry from Jonson to Pope. Indeed he proclaims elsewhere that farming is his "proper occupation"[43] to which he must return. There are vivid passages about the simple, contented joys of farming:

I planted beans below the southern hill
The grasses flourished, but bean sprouts were few.
I got up at dawn to clear away the weeds
And come back now with the moon, hoe on shoulder.
Tall bushes crowd the narrow path
And evening dew soaks my clothes.
"Returning to the Farm to Dwell," III.1–6

I hold the plow and rejoice in the season's work,
With happy face I urge the farmers on.
A far wind blows across the level field
The tender shoots enfold a new life too.
"In Early Spring of the Year 403," II.5–8

But in spite of poetic tributes to georgic labor, with celebrations of the innate superiority of such paragons[44] of farming as the "wise and good" Chang-chü and Chieh-ni and such impoverished virtuous men as Ch'ien Lou, Chang Chung-wei ("was fond of poverty"), Huang Tzu-lien ("pure poverty"), Old Man Jung ("lacked respect for ill-got gains"), and even Confucius himself, the poet realizes everyday hardship:

> Through poverty I am short of hands
> And bushes make my yard a wilderness.
>
> "After Drinking Wine," XV.1–2

At one point the realistic voice of the domestic persona declares that the farmer's life is "bitter";[45] at another, the same persona insists that the work gives him "joy"[46] and it is not "worthless."[47] Indeed, in spite of his labor, he says: "Of cold and hunger I have had my fill," but he consoles himself, for lowliness and obscurity ("We who stay by lakes and streams remain obscure")[48] are better than a giddy height. The passages emphasize hard work and poverty (simplicity of life), as does Virgil in the first and third *Georgics,* and are not without somberness. Cheek by jowl are rural delights and daily hardships, the poet-farmer's spiritual excellences and utter helplessness.

The following poem by Hwang Hŭi (1363–1452) is about the rustic joys, rather than hardships, of country life:

> Spring has come to a country village;
> How much there is to be done.
> I knit a net,
> A servant tills the fields;
> But who is to pluck the sweet herbs
> That grow on the back hills?

Here the image of the retired scholar or poet-recluse who is content to live in obscurity and poverty is closer to the Horatian happy husbandman rather than to the innocent shepherd, whose emblem is a carefree grasshopper rather than a diligent ant. Spenser and Sidney seldom offer a comparison, for Elizabethan poems on the town-country or court-country motif are mostly literary tour de force; they have not yet identified the retirement with a happy country life. However, William Byrd's "The Herdman's Happy Life" may be an approximation of the Horatian tradition:

> O, happy who thus liveth!
> Not caring much for gold;

With clothing which sufficeth,
  To keep him from the cold.
Though poor and plain his diet,
  Yet merry it is and quiet.[49]

For the theme of poverty I have chosen a poem by Han-shan ("Cold Mountain"), a poor, eccentric monk-farmer of late T'ang who retired to Cold Cliff in the T'ien-t'ai Mountains, and another by Pak Il-lo, "In Praise of Poverty" (1611).

The new grain hasn't ripened yet,
But today I used up the last of the old.
I went out to borrow a measureful
And stood at their gate, hesitating.
The husband came to the door and said
  to speak to his wife;
The wife came out and said "Ask my husband!"
Too stingy to help when times are bad—
The more the wealth, the bigger the fool![50]

Through a simple episode Han-shan meditates on the right and wrong use of riches and says that the wise and good will help, but not the fool. The evils of wealth are worse when the possessor is newly rich or heartless. The humor alleviates the bitter didactic tone in the last line, which is in turn redeemed by the context.

Pak Il-lo's, on the other hand, is a conflation of motifs and techniques, some from T'ao Ch'ien, some from others. The title itself, literally "Song of the Mean Alley," was inspired by a passage in the *Analects* (VI.9), where the master praises his disciple Yen Hui, "Incomparable indeed was Hui! A handful of rice to eat, a gourdful of water to drink, living in a mean street."[51] The poem begins with an admission of the speaker's impracticality and clumsiness (cooking gruel with wet straws), but the tone is self-satiric in view of a passage in the *Lao Tzu*, 45; "The greatest skill is like clumsiness." Strategically placed at the center of the poem is a lament of the lack of a farmhand and particularly of an ox without which there is no plowing. Did Horace not say that happy the man who plows his father's acres with his own beasts (*Epode*, II.3)?[52] Then comes a wry, humorous episode, his futile efforts to borrow an ox from a rich farmer who was bribed by a peasant with wine. After a sleepless night and a disappointing morning, the speaker resolves to forgo plowing and instead contemplates the green bamboo in the winding waters of the Ch'i, an allusion to poem 55 in the *Book of Songs*. Then he invokes "the flowery reeds" and "the unsold breeze and moon," intensely polemical symbols, as we shall soon see. Then comes another quotation from the *Analects*, XIV,

11, "To be poor and not resent it is far harder than to be rich, yet not presumptuous,"[53] followed by a panegyric to a modest life. The last lines emphasize the fact that poverty cannot bend the noble mind, that his only concern is how to delight in the pursuit of the Confucian Way. Throughout his poetry Pak Il-lo emphasizes by constant references to the classics the importance of the acquisition of knowledge in the Confucian tradition. The overall pattern therefore indicates the interplay of the formal and the informal, the sophisticated and the rustic, the learned and the personal, the *utile* and *dulce,* as it seeks to adapt moderation in life and art. Thus with humor, irony, anecdote, conversations, and a bit of self satire, Pak has created a convincing picture of a poor but pure poet-farmer's life.

Although line 53 of "The Return" declares the absence of envy and greed ("I have no desire for riches"), the sine qua non of contemplative life, by implication it introduces another topos, that of sufficiency, which is hinted throughout his poems:

> More than enough is not what I desire.
> "A Reply to Secretary Kuo," 10

> Plowing and spinning supply my needs
> What do I require more than these?
> "To Match a Poem by Liu," 17–18

> All I want in truth is wheat and bean,
> With no pretensions to the sweet and fat.
> "Inspired by Events," 3–4

> Not hoping for a belly more than full
> I only wished to eat my fill of grain, . . .
> "Untitled Poems," VIII.5–6

More subtly, the same topos appears metonymically in the form of a simple dwelling, vegetarian diet, homespun clothes, uncomfortable bedding, and the like. T'ao Ch'ien's diet includes wheat, bean, garden vegetables, and fern (note the conspicuous absence of nuts and strawberries). His favorite beverage is wine. His thatched hut, also called "my wretched shack,"[54] is in a narrow lane, with a "rustic gate."[55] His roof is broken, and "a waste of weeds engulfs the courtyard."[56] He has coarse clothes for winter ("Happily content with homespun clothes"),[57] sleeping often without "covers," and "netted hemp" for the summer sun.[58] Such were the properties of the poet-farmer in retirement, and poets of later times repeated the same proud list with faithfulness, though with occasional deviation in detail.

Chinese and Korean poetry of later times evokes the same items in the inventory, all serving the purpose of underscoring rural felicity and virtuous simplicity ("to show," in Northrop Frye's words, "how little a man actually needs for the best life"[59]) and, by implication, their absence among the less-than-ideal people. The poet's abode is a grass roof with a brushwood door. Occasionally called a "snail shell,"[60] it is girt with hills and trees, replete with the music of brooks and birds. His clothes are made of coarse cotton, his hat of blue arum, sedge, or some other type of reed; and on rainy days he puts on a sedge cape and a bamboo hat. He wears a pair of sandals, carries a bamboo stick during his walk, and occasionally travels on a cow. His favorite food includes bean and barley, fresh herbs, sometimes pickled, fiddlehead fern, and turnip, and sometimes fish if he happens to be a fisherman himself.

> Boy, fetch your open basket,
> The sun is setting.
> The ferns which grew last night
> Are already withered, I fear.
> What is the poor man's daily food
> But the fiddlehead, guileless and pure?
>
> Cho Chon-sŏng (1553–1627)

> With coarse clothes, with a bamboo stick,
> I go to the mountain torrent and there
> While away my time among the pines.
> The fiddlehead fern is my breakfast;
> The fish I caught will do for a supper.
>
> Ch'a Ch'ŏl-lo (1556–1615), "The Country Life"

> Here I enjoy honest conversation with my family
> And take pleasure in books and zither to dispel
> my worries. (37–38)

Now the poet-farmer may express concern about his georgic labor, or it may be a weightier worry, a reconciliation of the two traditions and values, the Confucian and the Taoist, the social self and the natural self, much in the same manner Western pastoral poetry tried to reconcile or assimilate the Biblical and classical traditions. The poet has independence, solitude, and happiness; and the zither, like the shepherd-poet's pipe, helps him to maintain harmony of mind and of man and nature.

He needs books too, for rural retirement has provided the opportunity for study and contemplation:

I have renounced the world to have my leisure
And occupy myself with lute and books.
"A Reply to Secretary Kuo," I.5–6

When young I kept aloof from the world's affairs
And found my comfort in books and zither . . .
"Lines Written as I Passed through Ch'ü-o," 1–2

When young I had no taste for worldly things—
My whole delight was in the Classic Books.
"After Drinking Wine," XVI.1–2

The fields are plowed and the new seed planted
And now is the time again to read my books.
"On Reading the *Seas and Mountains Classic*," 5–6

Did Horace not want "books of the ancients" to quaff sweet forgetfulness of life's cares (*Satires*, II.6), taking along to his Sabine Hills Plato, Menander, Eupolis, and Archilochus? And did neoclassical English poets not insist that the contemplation of the chain of being and the book of Nature, which is the book of God, required quiet rural retreats and books?[61] Books do not mislead man. Rather, T'ao Ch'ien sought in the classics the heroic models to emulate, the ideal modes of life in adversity.

Kwŏn Ho-mun (1532–1587), in his lakeside retreat, declares, "How fresh and fervent my life/ With a long lute and piled scrolls!" Ch'a Ch'ŏl-lo, in "The Country Life," not only pays T'ao Ch'ien the compliment by quoting two lines (57–58) from "The Return,"[62] but reiterates later, "Thus with a lute and books a day passes." Chŏng Ch'ŏl, in "Little Odes of Mount Star," says:

Alone in the deep mountain
With no friend but the classics, pile on pile,
I think of the men of all times.

This is not desire for a lost perfection, but for a means of moral cultivation, how best one might refine that faculty in man in order to become a "man among men," for only through man's moral regeneration can one restore the ideal order in the city.

What T'ao Ch'ien ultimately wishes to do behind his rural enclosure is the "cultivation of the True."[63] The "True" (*chen*), a technical term figuring in the mystical philosophy of Chuang Tzu, implies self-cultivation; virtue and wisdom being the fruits of a simple contemplative life, much like the Stoics but unlike the retirement in the Horatian tradition which sought comfort or beauty or comfort alone.

The term "the True" and its modifying forms occur at least ten times in his poetry; he talks about the vision of Truth, a fundamental truth, and cultivating, holding, and preserving the truth. Although the poet often oscillates between his awareness of life's illusory quality and his attempts to find meaning here and now, he accepts both human mortality and unchanging nature.

> How endlessly vast is the universe
> And how few men will live to be a hundred!
>
> "After Drinking Wine," XV.5–6

This recalls Virgil's lines in the third *Georgic* (284–285):

> But time slides past, slides past beyond recall.
> While, spellbound, we fight off among details.[64]

Of Horace's fourth ode in the first book (I.iv.13–14): "Indeed, pale Death with foot impartial knocks at the poor man's cottage and at princes' palaces."[65] T'ao Ch'ien has discerned the ultimate design in Nature, the permanence in change, and the identity of opposites. Thus he desires to attain and preserve the vision of truth in a world of shadow: In "Substance, Shadow, and Spirit," spirit's resolution goes:

> You had better go where Fate leads—
> Drift on the Stream of infinite Flux,
> Without joy, without fear;
> When you must go—then go,
> And make as little fuss as you can.[66]

and in "The Return,"

> So I manage to accept my lot until the ultimate homecoming.
> Rejoicing in Heaven's command, what is there to doubt? (59–60)

In the Western pastoral, the poet's commitment to nature demands a commitment to the finality of death. Death may be calmly accepted or held anxiously at bay by seizing the day, as often is the case with friendship poetry in East Asia. But what characterizes T'ao Ch'ien and others like him is their joyful acceptance of the terror of discontinuity as "the ultimate homecoming," a return to the infinite flux. Such a vision has the sanction of tradition and the support of metaphysics. One who abides in the *tao,* Taoism taught, affirms both man's existence patterned after the order of nature and his ability to intuit and embody the power (*te*) of the Tao within himself. Nature scorns all distinctions of right and wrong, good and evil; it exists on its own accord, transcending human values and standards, and its freedom, freshness, innocence, and purity is its mode of existence.

I catch sight of the distant southern hills;
The mountain air is lovely as the sun sets
And flocks of flying birds return together.
In these things is a fundamental truth
I would like to tell, but lack the words.
"After Drinking Wine," V.6–10

I look at the clouds and envy the high flying birds.
Beside the stream I am shamed by the free swimming fish.
My breast has always held this vision of truth—
Let no one say I have been bound by externals.
"Lines Written as I Passed through Ch'ü-o," 15–18

The gentle rain that bathes the grove,
The clean draft that lifts the cloudbird.
I see that all these things are there
Not cut off from their natural bent.
"As I Passed through Ch'ien-hsi," 5–9

These are particular, unique instances of the truth, discovered at individual moments of time, and the total experience is deeply rooted in Nature which becomes the myth for the landscape of the mind.

He realizes painfully that "to cherish simplicity and maintain equilibrium are the excellent qualities of the gentleman. Since the time when the true morality departed the world, the Great Imposture has held sway."[67] Knowing that in his own day few preserve the truth,[68] his resolution is to cultivate the True, "proud and self-sufficient," to "embrace the plain and hold the true."[69] Hence he bids farewell to the world of power and prestige, called metaphorically "a fine net" and "a strong snare," to restore in his mind that state of harmony which, he thinks, is the "best thing" he can do in his poor hut.[70] Thus, humming to himself, he closes the door, becomes a farmer, and cherishes his garden.[71]

What the Taoist in T'ao Ch'ien desires, however, is not the immortality of body but a discovery of joy and happiness in the simple things of life. His intensely subjective tone enters into his landscape, which conveys the depths of feeling and the heights of vision. Consider how the poet communicates his joyful acceptance of life and enthusiasm for the landscape:

The hills are scoured by last night's clouds
The sky is dimmed by a film of mist.
From the south there blows a breeze
Winging over the new grain.
"Progression of the Seasons," I.5–8

> I got up at dawn to clear away the weeds
> And come back now with the moon, hoe on shoulder.
>
> "Returning to the Farm to Dwell," III.3–4

> I crush the grain to brew a first-rate wine
> And when it is ripe I pour myself a cup.
> My little son, who is playing by my side,
> He began to talk, but cannot yet pronounce.
> Here is truly something to rejoice in . . .
>
> "A Reply to Secretary Kuo," I.11–15

> I tell my wife to bring along the children—
> This is a perfect day to make an outing.
>
> "To Liu, Prefect of Ch'ai-sang," 9–10

> Seeking one good friend
> I met the one I love.
> Our own joyful hearts in harmony,
> Our houses side by side.
>
> "A Reply to Adviser P'ang," II.5–8

Nature around his garden and farm below Mount Lu in Kiangsi, the poet-farmer's blessed state, love of his family—the locus of human identity—and happiness of housekeeping[72] are an index of his spiritual freedom and contentment, "an ideal harmony of the natural and human,"[73] which can be expressed only through poetry, explorations of the landscape of the mind. Herein lies a fundamental truth which, as he says, defies words, but he has marvelously succeeded in conveying the vision. Indeed, the beauty of nature is "meaningless unless man lives in a state of joyful harmony." It is by man's state of mind that "nature becomes either a paradise or a ruin."[74]

At this point I should add that the concern of East Asian nature poetry with a happy rural life, contemplation, and finally illumination explains why love, a central topic of the pastoral of happiness in the West, received such scant attention. To the nature poet who assumes the figure of a recluse or a hermit, the central concern is not the fulfillment of the passion of love, but the attainment of spiritual peace and self-fulfillment. T'ao Ch'ien is also exemplary in bringing in family life to his retired estate ("I tell my wife to bring along the children"), that domestic happiness is not incompatible with contemplative life, a topic emulated at times by his followers.

The transcendental interpretation of nature by T'ao Ch'ien and others like him owes a great deal to the Neo-Taoism and Prajna-Buddhism, especially to their rapprochement in the fourth century. In Neo-Taoism, it is Nonbeing that is the basis of all phenomena, while in Prajna-Buddhism, it is Emptiness that is the ultimate truth behind the phenomenal world. Because there is no difference between the phenomenal world and the ultimate truth, be it Taoist Nonbeing or Buddhist Emptiness, it could be experienced in contemplation here and now. In the former it leads to the understanding of oneness of Nature, in the latter to the intuitive wisdom that all beings are participants of the ultimate Emptiness. The contemplation of the beauty of Nature is therefore a vision of the ultimate truth here and now.[75] Much nature poetry is a dramatization of the process of contemplation and the final attainment of illumination. As an instance I cite the following lyric by Sŏng Hon (1535–1598), which subtly dramatizes the theme:

The mountain is silent,
The water without form.
A clear breeze has no price,
The bright moon no owner.
Here, after their fashion,
I will grow old in peace.

The poem is so simple in its statements that one might say there is no metaphor or direct comparison. Perhaps the analysis of the interaction of images and the configuration of their relationships might yield a latent symbolic meaning. Four images in the first four lines are all from nature: mountain, water, breeze, and moon, and they are qualified by four statements that form a unity, pointing to some special relationship among them. The first set are metaphors with Taoist overtones, for nature, in the philosophy of Chuang Tzu, is not only spontaneous but is in constant flux. The second set introduces, somewhat startlingly, what might be called mercurial metaphors, metaphors of the marketplace in fact, for they implicitly denounce one way of life and uphold another. Here we are presented with the contrast between one who is attached to worldly pursuits and one who has freed himself from them. For this purpose, the poet has brought in two of the most exalted adjectives in Korean nature poetry: "priceless," here translated as having no price, and "ownerless" or "loverless" translated as having no owner. The first has two meanings: not worth putting a price on, hence unsold; and having a value beyond all price. A clear breeze is still unsold, for those who cling to worldly power and wealth cannot purchase it with all their money and power. Those who are still attached to the world dominated by chaos and absurdity are unable to infiltrate the priceless nature, which can be won only by the poet's sensibility and imagination. Similarly, the moon has no owner, nobody has yet claimed it his own. Corrupt courtiers have rank and riches, but the poet has the joy and ecstasy of nature. The love of priceless nature, the significance of which only the poet who has renounced the world knows, becomes the sine qua non of the poetic existence. Transforming and transformed, wandering in the vast realm of oneness, the poet attains great knowledge, indeed "after their fashion." In the last line, the speaker talks, somewhat ironically, as a man fully awakened, a man who has comprehended the relationship between the phenomenal world and ultimate truth and who has taken transformation as his final abode, as one who will never grow old. He is impervious to the elements of nature, for nothing can harm him or cause him to suffer. An anonymous Korean poem expresses the truth in a different manner:

> In the valley where the stream leaps,
> Having built a grass hut by the rock,
> I till the field under the moon,
> Among the vast clouds I lie.
> Heaven and earth advise me
> To age together with them.

Parallels are not lacking in those seventeenth-century English poems which condemn the world and teach the need for neo-Stoic retirement. Røstvig cites such poets as Drummond, Denham, Waller, and Habington. But, because the imagery in the Korean poetry I have considered is charged with political and metaphysical implications, involving as it does the poet's awakening and illumination, it might be appropriate to seek comparisons in the poetry about the ecstatic contemplation of the happy man, the hortulan saint, in John Evelyn's words. Such are the garden poems by More, Fane, and Marvell. I shall not pause here for the emblem of the garden (*hortus conclusus*) in the medieval tradition, where the solitary thinker withdraws from the world. There is a correspondence in the stages of contemplation between the hortulan saint and the Taoist recluse. One purifies his senses, careful to purge all desire; the other abandons all subjective values and concepts in order to free himself from their bondage. This enables the first to distinguish between the outer show and inner reality, and the second between the ways of man and the Way of Nature. This state of mind finally leads one to glimpse the shadow of God, the other to comprehend the oneness of Nature. The ecstasy attained in the first case is not of beauty, but of heavenly beauty, as Kermode reminds us,[76] and in the second, not of knowledge and virtue in the ordinary or Confucian sense, but of Great Knowledge and Profound Virtue.

That nature is unsold and has no owner recurs in Yi-dynasty retirement literature. Pak Il-lo, we recall, in "In Praise of Poverty," declares:

> Among the flowery reeds, befriending the moon
> And clear breeze, I'll grow old naturally
> Among the unsold breeze and unsold moon.

In the "Song of the Sedge Bank":

> Gulls and herons, stags and hinds
> They are my cattle that I raise here;
> And the unsold breeze and unsold moon,
> They too naturally belong to me.

And in the "Song of the Reedy Stream":

> The fields plowed by Chang-chü and Chieh-ni,
> The fishing beach haunted by Yen Kuang,
> Still unsold, natural, natural . . .

Virgil, in the fourth *Georgic* (130–133), depicts an old Corycian farmer's ideal life and praises his self-sufficiency and integrity:

> This farmer, spacing herbs among his thickets,
> And setting out white lilies, slender poppies,
> And vervain, felt sure that his riches matched
> The wealth of kings, when he came home at night
> And heaped his table high with *unbought* foods.[77]

Horace, in the *beatus ille* epode (II.47–50), praises "an unbought meal" (*dapes inemptas*) that the wife of the happy farmer provides for his evening meal.[78] Ben Jonson, in "To Sir Robert Wroth," echoes both:

> But canst, at home, in thy securer rest,
> Live, with unbought provision blest;
> Free from proud porches, or their guilded roofes,
> 'Mongst loughing heards, and solide hoofes:
> Along'st the curled woods, and painted meades,
> Through which a serpent river leades
> To some coole, courteous shade, which he calls his,
> And makes sleepe softer then it is! (13–20) [79]

And so does Pope in his portrait of Cotta in the *Epistle to Bathurst* ("soups unbought and sallads," 184). Izaak Walton (1593–1683), in the fifth chapter of *The Compleat Angler,* quotes Francis Davison's beggar's song in order to underscore the "superiority of anglers' quiet wisdom over the busyness of more practical men."[80]

> The world is ours, and ours alone,
> For we alone have world at will;
> We purchase not, all is our own,
> Both fields and streets we beggars fill . . .

Aaron Hill (1685–1750), in "The Happy Man," sings of "the unbought wealth, which nature gives."[81]

> Let me ask you who are convention-bound,
> Can you fathom those outside the dirt and noise?

T'ao Ch'ien asks this in lines 29–30 of "The Peach Blossom Spring" which became another topos in later poetry. Yi I (1536–1584), a great Neo-Confucian philosopher and poet, in the second of his "Nine Songs of Mount Ko," asks:

> Can the dusty world fathom this joy?

Yun Sŏn-do, in the sixth poem in the summer cycle of *The Angler's Calendar,* poses the same question:

> Who would know this immortal delight?

Kim Sam-hyŏn (c. 1675–1700), as he contemplates the twilight river from a pine grove, declares: "Yes, perhaps only I/ Know the beauty of these hills and streams." And Kim Su-jang (b. 1690), sitting alone in his grass hut and putting the clouds to sleep by his song, ends the poem:

> O who else knows this blessedness,
> Who says there is my equal?

The poet may go a step further and assert boldly, as does the author of the first extant *kasa* in his "Hymn to the Spring":

> I am not the only man under the skies;
> But the pleasures of the hills are mine.

Yun Sŏn-do, in one of the "New Songs in the Mountain" (1639):

> Heaven says I shall be the guardian
> To keep only the hills and waters.

And an anonymous poet concludes his "Return to the Mountain":

> Perhaps I alone, I alone
> Am guardian of these hills and streams.

And, finally, Shin Hŭm (1566–1628), more passionately:

Don't laugh, foolish people, if my
Roof beams are long or short, the pillars
Crooked. This snail shell, my grass hut,
The vines that cover it, the encircling hills
And the bright moon above,
Are mine, and mine alone.

Indeed, the criterion of true possession, says Thoreau, is not ownership but enjoyment.[82]

VI

T'ao Ch'ien, the first Chinese nature poet, is also the creator of the first Chinese literary *locus amoenus*,[83] Peach Blossom Spring. A golden era or an ideal place remote in time or space figures, for example, in the Taoist writings. The creators of these paradises fondly evoked such golden age as the days of Perfect Virtue (*Chuang Tzu,* 9), such a never-never-land (utopia indeed!) as the Village of Not-Even-Anything or the Broad-and-Borderless Field (*Chuang Tzu,* 7),[84] or such a tropic or arctic *eutopia* as the land of "Virtue Established" in Nan-yüeh (*Chuang Tzu,* 20)[85] and the country of "Utmost North" (*Lieh Tzu,* 5),[86] or a dream land of Hua-hsü which, according to the writer, can be reached only by a journey of the spirit (*Lieh Tzu,* 2).[87] They sought, in these Chinese versions of chronological and cultural primitivism, models of simplicity, freedom, spontaneity, and ease. In depicting man's first and ideal state uncorrupted by the conventional system of values and conventional standards of judgments they emphasized its "negative amenities":[88] no distinction of good and evil, no useless knowledge and writing system, free from pride and envy, sickness and decay, sorrow and anguish, lust and hate, labor and war. In the country of Hua-hsü, the inhabitants have reached such a spiritual illumination that neither water nor fire can harm their body; whereas the well-tempered people in the Country of Utmost North are great lovers of music, spending all their days singing ballads, as if they anticipated Boethius's "three harmonies." The goal of the Taoist concept of enlightened living is embodied in the Nameless Man's advice to one T'ien Ken in the *Chuang Tzu* (7): "Let your mind wander in simplicity, blend your spirit with the vastness, follow along with things the way they are, and make no room for personal views."

Belonging as he did to a civilization that sanctioned retirement on moral, philosophical, and aesthetic grounds, T'ao Ch'ien's Chinese Arcadia reverberates with multiple meanings. Unlike many Western utopias beginning with Plato's imaginary Republic, but somewhat like a society of shepherds espousing the unity of man and nature in later pastorals, his is a small agricultural community, as in *Lao Tzu* (80) and *Chuang Tzu* (10),[89] hidden behind a grove of peach trees, tucked away behind a cave in the mountain. The broad, level plain, girt with rice fields and pretty ponds, is dotted with handsome houses:

> By agreement they set about farming the land
> When the sun went down each rested from his toil.
> Bamboo and mulberry provided shade enough,
> They planted beans and millet, each in season.
> From spring silkworms came the long silk thread
> On the fall harvest no king's tax was paid.
> No sign of traffic on overgrown roads,
> Cockcrow and dogbark within each other's earshot.
> Their ritual vessels were of old design,
> And no new fashions in the clothes they wore.
> Children wandered about singing songs,
> Greybeards went paying one another calls.

Farmers work "by agreement," not from command above, and nobody imposes taxation. They follow the rhythms of seasonal cycles, hence no need for a calendar or for useless knowledge ("clever contrivances"). Nor do the self-sufficient greedless people feel a need for trafficking or commerce. The first immigrants being refugees from the disorders of the Ch'in times in the last quarter of the third century B.C., the descendants abhor strife or hostility, but still preserve civilized customs (old ritual vessels and sartorial fashions). Children sing and the aged are content with one another, happy in their simple social and economic arrangements. T'ao's other poem, "Returning to the Farm to Dwell" (I.9–17), evokes more or less the same landscape, an indication that such an ideal place could be attained in solitude—and in spirit.

The Peach Blossom Spring haunted the imagination of later poets in search of literary inspiration and the prototype, either to register a moral protest against or to lament the existing political-moral degeneration, to get away from the complexities of civilization, to pay tributes in their imitations to the creator of the *locus amoenus* (as did Wang Wei),[90] or to employ the topos metaphorically for poetic amplification. Korean poets cannot see the Korean peach blossoms without at the same time seeing the Chinese peach blossoms in Wu-ling.

> Humming a verse we reach a stream and
> Wash our cups on the sandy beach.
> Then suddenly peach blossoms float down

From the fairy land of T'ao Ch'ien.
Green hills over there must mark the place.
"Hymn to the Spring"

The scene achieves two objectives: criticism of life by invoking the values of an ordered, harmonious state of things of the past, and a criticism of the contemporary way of life from which the poet wishes to get away. The contrast of values between dream and reality, obligation and freedom, comes to a climax.

T'ao Ch'ien's Arcadia was discovered by a fisherman of Wu-ling who, attracted by rows of blossoming peach trees, rowed upstream and stumbled into a small hideout. Yi Hwang (1501–1571) wishes to keep his retreat all to himself, lest the unenlightened intrude and disturb his peace and solitude:

Only I and the seagull
Know the thirty-six peaks of Mount Ch'ŏngnyang.
Seagulls might report Arcadia is here;
Even more untrustworthy are peach blossoms.
O blossoms, do not fall, do not float down
To tell the fisherman of this sunny site.

Chŏng Ch'ŏl, in "Little Odes of Mount Star," written to praise his scholar–hermit friend through the description of the beauties of the four seasons, asks:

I follow the peach-snowed causeway
Over to Pangch'o Islet.
As I stroll by the West Brook
the stone screen accompanies me
in the water mirror, painted there, as if polished.
Why seek Peach Blossom Spring? Arcadia is here.

The rhetorical question that recurs in Korean poetry attempts to say that the Korean landscape is as good as, if not better than, the Chinese, and one need not search it in the classical model. Yun Sŏn-do, in the eighth "spring" poem from *The Angler's Calendar,* assures himself how he is far away from the dusty world, which is literally screened from view by a grove of peach trees:

Moor the boat, Arcadia is near,
Crimson petals leap on the stream.
I am far away from red dust—
And the world of men.

A discovery of another Peach Blossom Spring (here rendered as Arcadia) marks him off from the "maze of custome, error, strife," as Jonson said.

That Korean poets who had not set foot in China could view the Peach Blossom Spring through their native landscape seems to indicate that Arcadia is a "mental place"—timeless, placeless, universal. T'ao Ch'ien already declared, "A heart that is distant creates a wilderness round it."[91] An entrance into Arcadia symbolized for the poet not only the discovery of the self far away from the world of affairs and the exploration of the relative values of the active and the contemplative, but also "the clarification of his artistic, intellectual, and moral purposes."[92] It is in Arcadia that the poet learns the significance of the transformation of self by nature and the values of the creative independence of poetry. It is also here that he reaffirms "his commitment to the arts of poetry." Arcadia is indeed a "place of witness, the place where . . . the Individual Talent [is] brought into confrontation with the Tradition."[93] When poets of later times assimilated T'ao's depiction of the Peach Blossom Spring in their recreations of the interior landscape, they seem to affirm a view that "every generation is equidistant from Arcadia."[94]

VII

Speaking of the change in attitudes about mountains in English poetry, Marjorie Nicolson called it "one of the most profound revolutions in thought."[95] Before a similar change took place in Chinese poetry around the fourth century,[96] a mountain was either sacred (*Book of Songs,* 259)[97] or forbidding, inhospitable, and melancholy as in "Summons for a Gentleman who Became a Recluse":

> Wildly uneven,
> The bends of the mountain:
> The heart stands still
> With awe aghast.
> Broken and wild,
> Chilling the heart . . .
> Towering and rugged,
> The craggy rocks, frowning . . .[98]

And Sung Yü's rhymeprose, "Mount Kao-t'ang":

> Climb high and look into the distance!
> It strikes man's heart with pain.
> The twisting ranges are jagged and sharp.
> Tiered and lofty,
> The serpentine rocks are perilous.
> Cliffs collapse and tumble down.
> Soaring peaks zig-zag and criss-cross
> As if in pursuit of one another.

> Rocky edges in sidewise collision,
> Blocking the deep caves, they seem to stamp the ground.
> Stacked and massed,
> Layer upon layer, pile upon pile,
> Like the great stone pillar circled in water.[99]

But Tso Ssu (250?–305?), in "Summoning the Recluse" or "Invitation to Hiding," departed from the classical emphasis upon horror and danger associated with the mountain:

> . . . in the hills is the sound of a singing lute.
> White snow still lies on the northern hill,
> Red flowers dazzle the southern grove.
> A stony spring laves jade-like stones,
> And there small fishes float and dive.
> Why do we need strings and flutes?
> Hills and waters have their clear music.[100]

The revolutionary change in the Chinese taste is said to have taken place after the fall of the Later Han, the ensuing political confusion, the devastation of the north by the Huns in the early fourth century, and the migration of the literati to south of the Yangtze, a landscape with great natural beauty. The rapprochement of Neo-Taoism (the origin of myriad things is nonbeing) and Prajna-Buddhism (the nature of the dharma is void) provided a philosophical foundation for excursions to mystical mountain landscapes. The new metaphysics identified landscape with the *Tao* or ultimate reality. The *Chuang Tzu* already emphasized the spontaneity and naturalness of mountains, "The great forests, the hills and mountains excel man in the fact that their growth is irrepressible" (26);[101] it also stressed man's "capacity to wander," underscoring the freedom of the enlightened spirit. The Taoist *hsien* or True Man usually resides in the mountains, for example, "a Holy Man living on a faraway Kushe Mountain," who climbs up on the clouds and mist, rides a flying dragon, "and wanders beyond the four seas" (1).[102]

Hsieh Ling-yün (385–433), a Buddhist who sought a complete release from the world in the visionary landscape of mountains and waters, has often been called the father of the "mountain and water" school of poetry. His favorite imagery of crags, boulders, precipices, streams, torrents, and forests dramatizes the self in the wilderness of the mountain and of the mind, especially the isolation in quest for a transcendental vision.[103] They are also the necessary furniture for the allegorical landscape, as the poet contemplates a complex interplay of the actual and nonactual, the unity and identity of the *natura naturans* and *natura naturata* in Buddhist-Taoist terms, in hope of achieving an identification of self with the "so-of-itself." In the poetry of Hsieh and others like him, the arduous ascent stands for the stages of spiritual pilgrimage in archetypal themes of journey, quest, and initiation, as in "Wandering on Mount T'ien-t'ai" by Sun Ch'o (c. 310–397):

> I'll push through the mark of tangled forests,
> Climb the sharp acclivity of precipice and slope,
> Across Yu Creek and straight ahead,
> Moving quickly past the point where five counties join.
> Then straddling the arc of the soaring stone bridge,
> I'll peer down ten thousand feet to untold depths;
> I'll tread the slippery moss-covered stone,
> Reach for the cliff that rises like a kingfisher-colored screen,
> Snatch the strands of dodder that trail from tall trees,
> Cling to the flying stems of creeper and vine.
> But though I face a moment's danger, on the brink of a fall,
> In the end I gain forever the gift of long life.
> So long as I keep faith with the dark and hidden Way,
> I may trudge the steepest slopes and they are level plains to
>   me;
>
> . . . . .
>
> And when I've crossed Spirit Gorge and bathed myself there,
> All the nagging worries will be cleansed from my chest;
> In the swirling flow I'll wash away the last fleck of "dust,"
> Free myself from the pursuing darkness of the "five
>   becloudings" . . .[104]

The Buddhist monk Han-shan best illustrates the Ch'an Buddhist use of the mountain image, Cold Mountain being at once his name, place of retreat, and a symbol of Buddhist austerities and final illumination. Happy to sit among the cliffs or white clouds, he is out of the dusty world, far from trouble: "Thin grass does for a mattress,/ The blue sky makes a good quilt./ Happy with a stone underhead/ Let Heaven and earth go about their changes." The following tells us what he means by Cold Mountain and how to "get it":

> Men ask the way to Cold Mountain.
> Cold Mountain: there's no through trail.
> In summer, ice doesn't melt
> The rising sun blurs in swirling fog.
> How did I make it?
> My heart's not the same as yours.
> If your heart was like mine
> You'd get it and be right here.[105]

Hsieh Ling-yün, Sun Ch'o, and Han-shan may not themselves have braved craggy peaks, but they showed active appreciation of the sublime and beautiful in the mountains of Chekiang. Petrarch's famous ascent of Mount Ventoux occurred 900 years later, in 1335, but that was proved to be an allegory.[106] It required another 400 years for the Englishman to cross the Alps in the fourth decade of the eighteenth century. "Great things are done when Men & Mountains meet."[107] That was Blake.

> Thou hast a voice, great Mountain, to repeal
> Large codes of fraud and woe; not understood
> By all, but which the wise, and great, and good
> Intepret, or make felt, or deeply feel.
>
> *Mont Blanc,* 80–83[108]

That was Shelley.

> Muse of my native land! loftiest Muse!
> O first-born on the mountains! by the hues
> Of heaven on the spiritual air begot . . .
>
> *Endymion,* IV.1–3[109]

That was Keats.

In Korea there was no such transformation of the outer landscape into the realm of the enlightened mind, with labored allusions to Buddhist-Taoist doctrines, but a more simple lyrical presentation of the subject, like the poems by Li Po[110] that seem to have attracted the imagination. One favorite logograph for pennames of scholars and poets was that of *ŭn,* in the Korean reading, meaning a "hermit" or "recluse," usually portrayed as residing in the mountains, the home of the Taoist immortals and Buddhist saints as well as the *loci* of Buddhist monasteries and temples. Two famous Neo-Confucianists of the Yi dynasty wrote a poem cycle—Yi I (1536–1584), "Nine Songs of Mount Ko" and Yi Hwang, "Twelve Songs of Mount To" (1565). Chŏng Ch'ŏl's "The Wanderings" (1580) describes the eight famous views of the Diamond Mountains on the east coast of Korea, and a number of *kasa* poems deal with a return to the pleasures in the mountain.

Yi Hwang declares his love for rocks and springs, green hills and streams. In his study, perched on a terrace among natural beauty, he ponders the arcane Neo-Confucian philosophy, worries whether he has successfully eliminated all his faults or discharged his duties to a benevolent king, and finally resolves to follow the Confucian Way. In one poem, while appreciating the orchids in the valley and the clouds on the hills, the speaker says he cannot "forget the royal virtues," as if his rural leisure were a kingly gift. The king's exemplary virtues and paradigmatic deeds have insured the maintenance of order and harmony at all plains, without which there cannot be a peaceful withdrawal into nature. Awareness of the significance of the world of action as a guarantee of simplicity and naturalness recurs in the works of Yi Hwang and others, a praise of royal virtues tempered with a subtle warning of the outcome of a rule without virtue. Apocryphal stories picture an exchange of poems by king and his poet-subjects, but no nature poem was dedicated to the king and no memorial urged him to withdraw and become a recluse. In the traditional golden age the king rules effortlessly, with flowing robes and folded hands, and at such time there is no need to pitch city and court against the country, for the best aspects of the active and the contemplative coalesce.

Yi I's cycle, on the other hand, covers the four seasons and celebrates the nine scenes in the Suyang Mountain (or Mount Ko) in Haeju. His central design is to establish essential polarities that lend a polemical force to the structure—an image of the harmony and peace set against the dusty world of man ("can the dusty world fathom this joy?"). His manner, however, is less obtrusive than Yi Hwang's, who often perilously approaches poetic moralizing. In his humble study, Yi I makes "poems of moon and breeze," plays on his lute, contemplates the twilight river with the fish: "There I and fishes delight:/ Who else has a larger heart?" Or he soars to lyrical heights:

> When the sun crosses the pine cliff,
> Let us sing our fourth song.
> Rocks swim in the water's bosom,
> They weave a rainbow of another sky.
> Trees and spring are deep and good; my heart
> Dances with exalted joy.

A more discursive piece like the anonymous sixteenth-century *kasa,* "Return to the Mountain" (also known as "A Recluse"), opens with the same polemical tone: "Yesterday I believed their words:/ Today I find them false." The speaker therefore "returns" to the mountains and waters which he finds "ever the same." Under the pine and bamboo he spreads a mat and lies leisurely, "drunk from the coolness of clear breezes." He hears dogs bark and children running out to gather chestnuts. He then starts off to a stream where he feasts on his catch and wine. He "returns" home and finds himself welcomed in the same manner as T'ao Ch'ien:

Then I catch sight of my cottage—
  Filled with joy I run.
The servant boy comes to welcome me
  My little son waits at the door.

"The Return," 13–16

Befuddled with drink, tottering, tumbling,
When I finally reach the brushwood door,
My little son helps me, my slim wife greets me.

"Return to the Mountain," 37–39

IX

In "The Fisherman," a satirical dialogue in rhymeprose dating probably from the middle of the third century B.C., the enlightened fisherman admonishes Ch'ü Yüan, the inflexible idealist:

When the Ts'ang-lang's waters are clear,
  I can wash my hat-strings in them;
When the Ts'ang-lang's waters are muddy,
  I can wash my feet in them. (19–20) [111]

Thus the erstwhile upright minister of the state of Ch'u, now irreparably wronged by slander and royal folly, was gently ridiculed for his lack of wisdom and zeal for vindication.

The West has piscatory eclogues by Theocritus (*Idyll,* 21), Sannazaro, and Phineas Fletcher, a number of *Halieutica* beginning with that of Oppian, and piscatory georgics by Izaak Walton and others. Nowhere, though, does the fisherman play as important a role as in Chinese and Korean poetry, where he is the consecrated symbol of the pure wise man who lives detached from the troubled times and the confused world and devotes himself to the cultivation of the self.[112] Legendary sages and historical recluses are therefore portrayed as fishermen, paragons of the ideal mode of life. The metaphorical connotations of the water invested the symbol of the fisherman with added dimension in Confucian and Taoist traditions. It is a metaphor of the law of change (*Analects,* IX.16) [113] or of the happy, serene mind of the wise man (*Analects,* VI.21) [114] to the Confucianist and a symbol for the virtues of Tao or Way to the Taoist. To the Taoist, especially, water is yielding, tolerant, withdrawing, receptive, mystical, and creative, a supreme emblem of Nature's self-sufficiency.

The introduction of "the blue stream" in the poem by Yun Sŏn-do unobtrusively suggests the pursuit of a Taoist adept who is willing to shed worldly ties, in an attempt to comprehend the underlying unity that embraces man, nature, and all creation in the universe:

I cooked barley and fresh herbs,
A fair amount of them.
By the rock in the blue stream
I play to my heart's content.
What else do I need by the water?
I long for nothing, nothing else.

Parallels in early seventeenth-century English retirement poetry are to be found perhaps in such symbols as "gentle hills" and "stream," both standing for an obscure, happy life, Stoic virtue of contentment, and a golden mean. In Denham's *Coopers Hill* the river Thames betokens, in addition to a "political harmony of discord," the happiness of the obscure life:

O could I flow like thee, and make thy stream
My great example, as it is my theme.
Though deep, yet clear, though gentle, yet not dull,
Strong without rage, without ore-flowing full. (189–192)

The theme of solitary contemplation affected a number of poems about retirement at this period. Like the happy contemplator in East Asia, the solitude of the pensive man is happy and gay, not melancholy, as in Milton's *Il Penseroso* (1632). Thus by invoking the water symbol, Yun Sŏn-do has subtly suggested his ability to live in two apparently separate worlds, essentially one. He is on the verge of attaining that double vision, but has not yet become a fisherman himself.

A country fisherman such as Cho Chon-sŏng (1553–1627), in one of "Four Songs Calling A Boy," is out for sport:

Boy, put on a sedge cape and bamboo hat;
It rains by the eastern torrent.
With a long rod and no hook,
Let's go angling in the rain.
Quiet there, fish, don't be startled!
I came here elated, in high spirits.

But in the poems of a more polemical pattern and structure the motif fully exhibits its multiple symbolism.

Far from being merely idyllic or didactive, Yun Sŏn-do's cycle of forty poems, *The Angler's Calendar* (1651), is not a treatise on the craft with enumeration of fish, baits, the chief seasons, or each fish's favorite haunts. Built on the dialectical pattern of two modes of life and two views of world and self, the happy fisherman's discovery of self and nature is demonstrated as the result of his renouncement of the world, the obstacle to his final freedom and illumination.

Who would envy three dukes?
Who would now think of caps and gowns?

Spring, 6

Behind me the dusty world, but
Joy doubles as I sail further away.

Autumn, 2

Do not scorn the rough clouds,
They screen the mad world from us.
Do not deplore the storm and waves—
They arrest the bustle of the world.

Winter, 8

His withdrawal is not to purge pleasure or annihilate self as, for example, in some of Marvell's major poems,[115] but to reassert the ultimate harmony between self and nature. Hence the poems celebrate the newly discovered values by means of a quiet, simple, and innocent landscape, a mirror of the happy fisherman, a moral victory of self earned by seclusion.

The heart shouts its peak of joy . .

Spring, 9

Spring stirs the joy in my veins.
O how many sweet days, sheer content!

Spring, 10

Entering the boat, rod at my shoulder,
I cannot still my loud heart.
Who has painted these scenes,
Smoky rivers and suspended cliffs?

Summer, 1

Who would know this immortal delight,
The joy of a rower in sweet songs?

Summer, 10

Paddle the boat, friends, we will live,
We will live this way today and ever.

Autumn, 9

In my empty boat, wearing my reed hat,
I sit alone and my heart beats fast.

Winter, 7

Observe a post-philosopher, a singer of timeless bliss adrift on the lake in the moonlight:

Let us tread on fragrant grasses
And pick orchids and irises.
Stopping the boat small as a leaf,
I ask what I have taken aboard.
Nothing except smoke when I set sail,
When I row back, the moon is my tenant.

Spring, 7

But politics intrude when the poet speaks from his own experience of service under four kings and humiliation of fourteen years in exile. Have the sellers of ranks and riches not planted sycophantic spies?

Let's spread the net out on the shore
And lie under the thatched awning.
Moor the boat, friends, and rest—
Fan off mosquitoes, no, flies are worse.
Only one worry, even here,
Traitors might eavesdrop on our talk.

Summer, 8

The literary source of the "flies" (green flies or bluebottles) is the 219th poem in the *Book of Songs* where the flies that buzz about and settle on the fence stand for slanderers.[116] A victim of slander as he was, Yun Sŏn-do aptly recalls the classical allusion that prepares the reader for the last two lines. "Traitors" in line 6 is in the original "Minister Sang," Sang Hung-yang (152–80 B.C.) of the Former Han,[117] probably a metonymy for the poet's political foe. Although the cycle's general structure calls for a tension between opposite values and perspectives, the poet is aware of harsher realities outside, "the realistic level of ordinary human affairs," and "grim issues" are not banished from his rural contemplation. As a consequence, the poet seeks not " 'wish-fulfillment' but self-stabilization in the face of anarchic values and events."[118] The tragic story of Ch'ü Yüan, too, lingers in the poet's mind and adds weight to his concern for the relative value of loyal admonition and political action.

The sun's lanceheads are shining,
Water is calm, calm as oil.
Should we cast a net at all,
Should we drop a line on such a day?
The poem of Ch'ü Yüan stirs my fancy;
I have forgotten all about fishing.

Spring, 5

Because Ch'ü Yüan objected to the use of force and was banished from the court, he drowned himself in the Milo or Ch'u River. Hence the poet warns us not to "catch the fish of a loyal soul" (Summer 4). His political references are, however, too elusive for us to identify the objects of his scorn and repugnance. But it does not matter, for the poet attempts to create his own order with its own values, a "rallying point for his personal values and convictions,"[119] with which he can safely confront the other world.

Yun's place in Korean poetry is secure because he is a master of flawless diction and verbal harmony, and because he has the courage to insist on the place of poetry in a civilized world. He knew how to make use of his poetic genius in creating the authentic figure of the fisherman, and nowhere does the happy, contemplative poet-philosopher speak more forcibly than in the following, the fourth poem in the spring cycle:

Is it a cuckoo that cries?
Is it the willow that is blue?
Several roofs in a far fishing village
Swim in the mist, magnificent.
Boy, fetch an old net!
Fishes are climbing against the stream.

The poem opens with two questions that suggest uncertainty of the sense of sound and sight. In the next two lines we see something, though it is far away, dim, unsteady in the mist. The last two lines are brief, forceful, and speak of a practical and immediate connection with nature. What we have, then, is an ordered progression from a state of vagueness and possible illusion through a state of dim but magnificent perceptions to actual relish and delight, with the suggestion that all three stages are part of a continuous order. The poem, therefore, presents nature's mystery, beauty, and bounty in terms of illusory loveliness, real visual loveliness, and life-sustaining matter-of-factness in the form of food from the stream. The poem not only suggests the felt transcendence of the vision but reveals a consciousness of the transcience of earthly joy and beauty. The poet achieves clarity and richness of vision with the simplest vocabulary and utmost economy.

A man who is happy and gay, "a gaiety transfiguring all that dread," a gaiety that encompasses the sense of the tragic in life, is the figure of the poet in these poems. Nature poetry in Korea was inherently criticism, affirmation, doubt, and presentation of the values of life. Sanctioned by the ancient cultural and moral tradition, renunciation of public service was an expression of moral principles, the most adequate form of protest. This was especially so in a society that placed a premium on public service and its rewards. The endorsement of a simple contented life was, therefore, a symbolic protest against the absence of all that is simple, natural, and permanent in contemporary society. Unmotivated by ambition and greed, free from the vicissitudes of fortune, a simple life provided the greatest independence, freedom, and happiness. The Korean poets have given us such a sense of life, a vision that encompasses the knowledge of the whole life and the accumulated wisdom of the civilization.

There, on the mountain and the sky,
On all the tragic scene they stare.
One asks for mournful melodies;
Accomplished fingers begin to play.
Their eyes mid many wrinkles, their eyes,
Their ancient, glittering eyes, are gay.[120]

Yeats, in contemplating an azure-blue sculpted stone, adds details imaginatively to create his own image invested with added significance. By "the imaginative possession of an image,"[121] by his creative power, Yeats wished to "make one rejoice in the midst of tragedy," as he declared in a letter to Dorothy Wellesley (1935).[122] His concern with tragedy and gaiety in this and other poems of the period is to "re-make the self and so win joy in the imminent presence of death,"[123] and "Lapis Lazuli" specifies "the intimate connection between tragic joy and the poet's discovered power."[124] The final two lines create the image of the mandarins or ascetics, who comprehend and possess the true gaiety of art. The Chinese sages (or ascetics) casting glittering, gay eyes on the scene below and "accomplished fingers" strumming the lute (whose music makes us better understand and confront the tragic in life) are still in the world of cyclical nature, and their joy of liberation is achieved without self-assertion or apocalyptic vision.[125] In East Asia the unity of man and nature was achieved by obliterating subject and object, or subject merging with object. Both exist in terms of equal reality, and human response to nature was more real and valid than in the West before the advent of the Romantics. The figure of the alienated Romantic poet who seeks the triumph of his imaginative energy and expanded consciousness, whose poetry is a history of the conflict between mind and nature, is almost unknown in East Asia. A Romantic nature poet like Wordsworth wanted to exult the power of the mind over nature, not a reconciliation between the two. In "Sailing to Byzantium" Yeats wrote, "Once out of nature I shall never take/ My bodily form from any natural thing."[126] He repudiates nature and seeks gaiety and permanence in a dimension beyond or outside nature. The Yeatsian gaiety is inseparable from "terrible"—indeed, "terrible and gay," which is "the condition of tragic joy in 'Lapis Lazuli,' "[127] is usually muted or expressed differently in East Asia. The poem that at first glance seemed to offer an appropriate parallel to our context, therefore, turns out to be very different when viewed from the Yeatsian canon.

East Asian nature poetry is as protean and eclectic as the Western pastoral. It is a field in which a structural diachronist, Guillén's ideal literary historian and critic,[128] would feel at home. Without consideration of cultural assumptions and social tensions that underlie the subject, one could not proceed to discuss the author's philosophical posture toward his material and the view of life his work embodies.[129] Whether our criterion is that of distance between man and nature or that of man's willingness to adapt himself to nature, East Asian nature poetry characterizes man's closeness to nature in attempts to understand life in relation to the patterns of nature and the final acceptance of the human condition. The metaphorical images simultaneously present man and nature, self and world, time and the timeless. Man conquers time by moral beauties, solitude, or contemplation in the world of time, and each poem is the celebration of the temporality of man as well as the ultimate harmony between man and nature.

Commenting on the importance of Thoreau's *Walden* in American culture, Frye remarks:

> The theme of the sage who makes a voluntary break with society in order to discover his genuine self in a context of solitude and nature is common in the Orient and has been a major inffuence on the arts there, but it is rare in the West. Even Wordsworth, though he has much of the theory, speaks, at the opening of the *Prelude* and elsewhere, more as someone on sabbatical leave from society than as someone aloof from it.[130]

Such favorite Western concerns as man's ascendancy over nature, ambivalence toward, or revulsion from, nature, or the conflict of the natural and the spiritual are unthinkable in East Asia. Attempts at a synthesis or resolution of the perennial tension and antagonism between nature and man and nature and art include: transformation of the classical garden of *otium* by Christian meditation, reading in nature a complete revelation of the Creator, or identification of the Good and the Beautiful with insistence on "the universal order and coherence of things."[131]

But, man's unequivocal commitment to nature was never associated in East Asia with rudeness, naivete, or bestiality. Genuine appreciation of nature in East Asia, in spite of the Confucian insistence on man and society, was usually explained as a result of the complementary nature of the two views of life, the Confucian and the Taoist, the intellectual and the intuitive, the social and the natural, the active and the contemplative. Whereas the classical emphasis on man and moral cultivation in the West led to an absence or depreciation of landscape in art, in East Asia "a taste for fine arts impregnated with feeling for nature became an attribute of the intellectual." Man is never separated from nature by intellectual discrimination or by emotional response: he is one with nature and his life is patterned after natural harmony. Harmony was indeed the great norm of both Confucianism and Taoism, and Taoism as a philosophy of life and art animated much that is permanent in East Asian culture and civilization.[132] The prerequisite for a gentleman to be a social and moral exemplum was a harmony with nature. While Tzu-lu, Jan Ch'iu, and Kung-hsi Hua desired power and politics, Tseng Hsi, in perhaps the most beautiful passage in the *Analects* (XI.25), said he desired not a kingdom but a life in harmony with rituals, fellow men, and nature:

> Tseng Hsi said, At the end of spring, when the making of the Spring Clothes has been completed, to go with five times six newly-capped youths and six times seven uncapped boys, perform the lustration in the river I, take the air at the Rain Dance altars, and then go home singing.[133]

The image of man evoked in the *Analects* is one we encounter often in landscape painting, a small dot in the vast cosmos, a traveler, rider, or fisherman surrounded by soaring mountains, floating clouds, and twisted pines, hardly to be recognized. Such is the landscape of the mind, the metaphor of Nature.

3 LOVE

IT HAS BEEN suggested that the East Asian conception of love is usually presented in literature not as the "pursuit of an eternal future, but as a thing of the past, a matter for reflection, never for speculation."[1] The tone of most love lyrics is retrospective, with the result that the pathos of separation and pangs of desertion rather than the pursuit and exaltation of passion are the recurrent themes. This is certainly true after the *Book of Songs,* when Confucianism, with its stress on ethical considerations, affected in varying degrees the amatory sentiments and expressive possibilities. The link between romance and marriage—the metaphysics and phenomenology of love—was a neglected topic, resulting in a topos of the neglected wife. The position of woman and marriage customs probably had much to do with this. The social status of East Asian woman, unlike her counterpart in the age of chivalry in the West, was far above that of the horse,[2] but the love of woman was never made a virtue of and the service of woman was never likened to a ritual worship. In traditional East Asian society, man was sovereign and he did not accept the social, intellectual, and emotional equality of the sexes. Misogynic scorn or excessive adulation is rare in poetry, but the power of a woman was acknowledged in history and literature. The *Book of Songs* declared (264.3):

> A clever man builds a city wall,
> A clever woman overthrows it.[3]

Such imperial favorites as Lady Li of the Warrior Emperor of the Han and Precious Consort Yang (whose beauty "shook an empire" in "A Song of Unending Sorrow") of the T'ang emperor Hsüan-tsung were worth a kingdom. But such a disharmony between beauty and inward virtue, often held to be responsible for a fall from weal to woe, was the stuff for the mirror literature. A comparative absence of poems of wooing (the come-live-with-me motif) and of *carpe diem* and *carpe florem* in later times indicates that in China and Korea courtship was seldom codified as in the Western Middle Ages. The exception, however, is the *Book of Songs,* which contains a large number of songs of courtship of folk origin.

I

Courtship was carried out in the open, usually at the time of spring festivals: a young man meets a girl near the town gate (138), at the corner of the wall (42), by the willows of the Eastern Gate (140), or by the river (108). In the third month festival, a girl gives her lover a peony, symbol of youth and delight, joy and love (95); in another poem (64), she throws a quince, then a peach, and finally a plum to her lover, receiving in return a girdle-gem, green stone, and jetstone. More secret courtship occurs in poem 76, where the girl, mindful of family and village people, urgently pleads:

> I beg of you, Chung Tzu,
> Do not climb into our homestead,
> Do not break the willows we have planted.
> Not that I mind about the willows;
> But I am afraid of my father and mother.
> Chung Tzu I dearly love;
> But of what my father and mother say
> Indeed I am afraid.[4]

Unlike the *pastourelle,* this does not seem to be a chance encounter, but a prearranged meeting.

Contrarily, "The Mulberry Trees on the Field Path," a 54-line pentasyllabic ballad dating from the Later Han, describes the meeting of a prefect and the beautiful Lo-fu and her successful resistance of his advance. The prefect does not flatter or promise a gift but bluntly asks her to ride with him. The girl does not escape by feigning or making impossible demands—a motif seldom found in East Asia—but repulses him by humiliating him, a kind of baffling ruse, narrating a career of her husband (imagined or real) in appearance or rank. It is regrettable that the ballad ends with Lo-fu's reply, although the reader will have guessed the outcome.[5] Stories of shepherdess and rustic maidens baffling and ridiculing knights and lords by a battle of words or clever tricks, such as in "L'autrier jost'una sebissa" (The other day along a hedgerow) by Marcabrun (fl. 1130–1150),[6] the ballad cycle of "The Baffled Knight," or in the fabliaux in the West and in folk tales in East Asia, are well known, and this Chinese ballad may represent a folk pastourelle of the day.[7]

The next poem (23) opens with the magnificent juxtaposition of two images: a dead roe (not an emblem of passion, as in the West) under the rushes and a yearning lady covered by a fine knight:

In the wilderness there is a dead roe,
Wrapped with white rushes.
There is a girl longing for spring,
A handsome man seduces her.

In the forest there are elms,
In the wilderness there is a dead deer,
Bound with white rushes.
There is a girl like jade.

Slow, easy, easy!
Don't touch my sash,
Don't make the dog bark.[8]

The whole meaning of the poem, Archibald MacLeish says, lies in that equation of the two images, the dead roe and the giggling girl. MacLeish continues: "The emotion of the poem is in the place between—the place where they are together—where they meet . . . death and passion, the human comedy and indifferent death . . . The emotion it holds is held between these two statements in the place where love and time cross each other."[9] Thus in the guise of a *pastourelle* the poem subtly conveys "the knowledge of the defeat of love by time."

In the following anonymous Korean *sijo* of folk origin, wit and frankness find expression:

O dearest, when I hold your wrist,
You beam with delight.
When I scratch your back over your shoulder,
You come closer and embrace.
"Darling, easy now, stop,
My heart pounds and whelms me."[10]

Is she so much in control of the situation that she can say composedly how far the lover may go? Whatever the answer, it is a pity that such aspects of courtship and the cultivation of frankness were allowed only in anonymous folk songs.

II

The praise of the beloved's beauty first articulated in the *Book of Songs* recurs in stylized motifs from the sixth century in China and occasionally in Korea. The lady's face is like the "mallow flower" (83), her thick hair "billows like clouds" (47), her brow is "white and well-rounded" (47), culminating in the description of a noble lady, a synthesis of admirable attributes befitting her station. Here the description starts with the hands and moves upward (57.2):

> Hands white as rush-down,
> Skin like lard,
> Neck long and white as the tree-grub,
> Teeth like melon seeds.
> Lovely heads, beautiful brows.
> O the sweet smile dimpling,
> The lovely eyes so black and white.[11]

In later lyrics (*tz'u*), such stylized figures of comparison recur: cloudy or dark green hair, also called "fragrant cloud"; willow waist; eyebrows like distant mountains; fragrant dimpled cheeks; eyes like autumn waves; limbs jade trees and jasper branches; and skin smooth as jade. Later, enumeration of the qualities of the lady or parts of her body occurs also in drama and romance, at times in the manner of burlesque, recalling the *Blason anatomique du corps féminin*. We are familiar with such improbable comparisons in the idealization of the beauty of the sonnet lady: tender breasts are flowers; her lips cherry, roses, or ruby; hands ivory; teeth like pearls; eyes twin stars, suns, or sapphires set in snow; eyebrow an arch of ebony; hair twisted golden wires or a golden snare. Spenser, in *Amoretti* 15, and Shakespeare, in sonnet 130 ("My mistress' eyes are nothing like the sun"), gently repudiate the Petrarchan convention prevalent among the poets of the sonnet sequences: the first with a Neoplatonic moral in the last two lines, while the second with a series of refreshing departures, culminating in the last lines:

> And yet, by heaven, I think my love as rare
> As any she belied by false compare.

The following anonymous Korean poem singles out three items for praise, an indication of the popularity of the convention:

> Eyebrows like a moth's antennae,
> Teeth like a row of melon seeds,
> Your smile a tricolored peach blossom
> Half opening after a night rain.
> When your mother bore you, dear,
> You were made to love me only.

The last two lines demonstrate the poet's originality in handling an otherwise familiar topic. In the colloquial style and startling turn we hear the personal, convincing voice of the persona, whose concern is not only to praise the lady's unadorned beauty—all objects of comparison are drawn from nature—but to possess the woman he loves. The emphasis is upon "only," and not without a warning. Poem 143 likens the lady to a "moon rising white," bright in splendor: another poem (47) makes a most startling comparison:

> How comes it that she is like a heavenly one,
> How comes it that she is like a god?[12]

The lover identifies his beloved as more than human, an incarnation of some divine being, radiating her grace and charm like a goddess. Happily or unhappily, the motif is seldom taken up in later times, and the celebration of the beloved in a language recalling that of *amour courtois* is rare.

A series of rhymeprose on the theme of "Stilling the Passions" extols a beautiful woman as both wise and good:

Curbing Excess

Ah, this lovely woman of alluring charms!
Her face is radiant and filled with color.
Within all Heaven's bounds she has no equal,
Throughout a thousand years she is unique.

Ts'ai Yung (132–192)

Rectifying the Passions

Ah, the unusual beauty of this lovely woman!
Complaisant she is, and wisely understanding.
In response to supernatural harmony her substance was formed:
She embodies the lush beauty of the orchid and the purity of jasper.
Among [beauties of] past time rarely equaled,
In present time none can compare with her.
Like far-reaching rays emitted by the morning sun
The clear glance pours out from her eyes.
In her blooming beauty she crowns our time
And is just as virtuous as that woman of Shen.

Ying Yang (?–217)

Stilling the Passions

Ah, the precious rare and lovely form
She stands out unique in all the age.
Though hers is a beauty that would overthrow a city
She intends to be known for her virtue.

In purity she rivals her sounding pendant jades
In fragrance she vies with the hidden orchid.

She disowns tender feelings among the vulgar
And carries her principles among the high clouds.

T'ao Ch'ien[13]

Affected compliments expressed in standard clichés and prefabricated formulas indicate that they are exercises on a conventional topic. Hyperbolic praise of the lady as the living embodiment of the ideal—she is a harmony of beauty and virtue, an emblem of a particular class—renders her emotionless and unattainable. Her indifference and disdain, a consequence of the perfection attributed to her, should not discomfort the speaker; but the emotional distance is a device to vindicate the speaker's renunciation, which prevents despair. Far from dramatizing the fluctuation of emotions (such as at once extolling the lady as noble and debasing her as insensate), the root of tensions in the courtly love lyric, the poems are occasions for complaints, a search for retreat, stability, and a point of rest; and through this convention (whose value must be judged by the standards of the time) early Chinese poets may have learned to express their versions of frustrated love. The chief concern of the series is not so much the praise of the lady as the frustration caused by her beauty and goodness. But he seldom declares, "She is my joy and solace, a source of knowledge, an incitement to virtue and perfection of my nature. Therefore in spite of her imperviousness I will continue to pursue her and love her." Nowhere does the speaker say that his love for a paragon is ennobling or that suffering caused by unfulfilled love purifies and enriches his life, as, for example, in two sonnets of *Astrophil and Stella* (62 and 108):

I joyed, but straight thus watred was my wine,
That love she did, but loved a Love not blind,
Which would not let me, whom she loved, decline
From nobler course, fit for my birth and mind:
   And therefore by her Love's authority,
   Willd me these tempests of vaine love to flie,
And anchor fast my selfe on *Vertue's* shore.
   Alas, if this the only mettall be
   Of Love, new-coind to helpe my beggery,
Deare, love me not, that you may love me more.

So strangely (alas) thy works in me prevaile,
   That in my woes for thee thou art my joy,
And in my joyes for thee my only annoy.

Likewise, despite such similarities as the convention of hiding the identity of the beloved, the threat of gossip and slander, an exchange of poems describing the parting of love at break of day, and the cult of beauty and refinement, nothing in love of Heian Japan (or elsewhere in East Asia) corresponds to the courtly love tradition in the West. We will look in vain for such dominant virtues of Western courtly love as courtliness, *jovens, mesura,* in Japan. The Heian gentleman, heavily powdered and perfumed, described as beautiful as a woman, constantly wetting his long sleeves, can hardly be compared to a troubadour.[14] Although Peter Dronke has convincingly shown that *amour courtois* (*cortez' amors* of Peire d'Alvernhe) is "no new feeling," but one of the eternal aspects of man, that "poetry of the courtly experience has always existed, and is not confined to a 'courtly' class,"[15] there is no counterpart in East Asia to a "litany of the virtues of the loved lady" from the Halberstadt miscellany, which presents a "fusion of the lady's own qualities with the graces she can bestow through love."[16]

Est tocius mundi gaudium,
viri solacium,

augmentatrix leticie,
fuga tristicie,

honestatis conservacio,
amoris mitigacio,

angelicus
intuitus,

splendor siderum,
honoris exemplum,

cordis elevacio,
omnis amaritatis consolacio.

(She is the joy of all the world, the solace of her man, the increaser of joy, the flight of sadness, the preserver of honour, the gentleness of love, the angel's glance, the brightness of the stars, the example of honour, the exaltation of the heart, the consolation for all bitterness.)

Indeed the celebration of the beloved's beauty as the manifestation of an inner perfection of the soul, of the ultimate beauty ("But that which fairest is, but few behold,/ her mind adorned with vertues manifold," *Amoretti,* 15), is a subject singularly neglected. No East Asian way of thought—be it Confucianism, Taoism (in spite of its rich feminine symbolism), or Buddhism—supplied the mystical or noetic language of love.

III

The definition of love may take the forms of simple declarations: love is a deceit, love is a torment, love is dream and death; or it may be worked out metaphorically throughout a poem; all attempt to probe love's contrary moods, diverse responses, joy and tyranny, continuity and mystery. Love is a flame that no water can quench:

> A mountain in spring catches fire.
> Unopened flowers burn.
> Yet there is water there
> To put out the flames.
> Where is the stream that can kill
> The fire that burns deep within me?
>
> Kim Tŏng-nyŏng (1568–1596)

We are not told who has kindled a fire in the victim's breast, but the speaker acknowledges the irresistible power of love which wounds his heart. The familiar trope is very ancient, as in "Invocation to Aphrodite" by Sappho:

> . . . my lips are stricken to silence, under-
> neath my skin the tenuous flame suffuses;
> nothing shows in front of my eyes, my ears are muted in
> thunder.[17]

Fire (durable, consuming, or quenchless) in which the lover chokes, smolders, and burns is a common metaphor of courtly love. Fire converts into itself that with which it comes into contact, but also destroys the "brief, bright human moment,"[18] linking it to the imagery of melting and dissolution (hence such conceits as a fly, a moth, a self-consuming candle, a dewdrop). Petrarch compared himself to a "salamander living in the flames of love," which is contrasted to the icy heart of the lady.[19] The fire-ice contrast was fondly repeated by such English courtier poets as Wyatt ("I feare, and hope: I burne and frese like yse") and Spenser ("My loue is lyke to yse, and I to fyre"; *Amoretti,* 30). Romeo declares, "Love is a smoke made with the fume of sighs;/ Being purg'd, a fire sparkling in lovers' eyes;/ Being vex'd, a sea nourish'd with [lovers'] tears" (I.ii. 196–198). Ōtomo Yakamochi (718–785), after a dream vision of a young woman, declares (*MYS,* IV.718):

Omowanui	Having seen your smile
Imo ga emai wo	In a dream by chance,
Ime ni mite	I keep now burning in my heart
Kokoro no uchi ni	Love's inextinguishable flame.[20]
Moetsutzuzo oru.	

Ki no Tsurayuki (884–946) says smoke rises from his bosom, burning forever like Mount Fuji (*SKKS*, VI.1008). But seldom does the East Asian lover build an altar to the lady with his burning heart as a sacrifice (*Amoretti*, 22) or hope to melt the lady's icy heart: he is content to fry in love's fire.[21]

Love is a sickness for which there is no remedy, and no famous physician can cure it: it can be cured only by a return of the lover's affection.

They say in this world, we have
Many remedies and brilliant swords.
But no swords to cut off this love,
No remedies that make me forget him.
I'll not forget until I am dead,
Cut off this tie, forever bury him.

Only death, the anonymous Korean woman poet declares, will liberate her from her agony, but she heroically clings to her hope. There is no room for Reason to intervene as a doctor and guide, as in Shakespeare's sonnet 147 ("My reason, the physician to my love"). Love's illness also inflicts mortal wounds, as Meng Chiao (751–814) points out in his "Impromptu" in which love's stabbing is compared to the wound inflicted by sharp swords: "Woman's beauty too close will wound your life . . . The peril of love is not in loving too often,/ A single evening can leave its wound in the soul."[22] Meng Chiao is undoubtedly referring to genuine love, where quality and intensity count, where one night is enough to fathom the ardor and despair of love. Or it can carve out a piece of heart from a languishing patient:

I reviewed my heart one day, and
Found a piece of it missing.
I have not fasted or wept,
But—was it taken off of itself?
Think, love, you produced this sickness;
You can cure me, you alone can.

The following remarkable Korean *sijo* vividly captures the torments of love. She is, the nameless speaker says, willing to suffer the most unimaginable torture inflicted upon her, but that is nothing compared with a life without love. The poem appeals wholly and directly to the senses, and succeeds because the speaker has found the objective correlative to express the inexpressible in a most original way. The result is a stunning definition of the power of love.

If you bore a hole in my heart,
Twist a slack rope of straw,
Thrust it in that round hole,

Have two lackeys hold both ends
And pull this way and that—
I'll have it your way and suffer,
No matter how great the pain:
But if you ask me to live without you,
That, I tell you, I cannot bear.

Often the physical symptoms of love vividly describe the incurable disease and offer an indirect definition of love. Sappho likens the assault of love to a sudden, violent gust that shakes the mountain oaks: "Love shook my heart, like a wind falling on oaks on the mountain."[23] Or the turmoil of her mental and physical state, underscoring the inevitability of her suffering: "Again love, the looser of limbs, shakes me, a creature bittersweet, inescapable."[24] Archilochus, inspired by Homer, expresses his helpless state:

Miserable I lie in longing, lifeless, pierced through the bones with bitter pains by the will of the gods.[25]

For such was the desire for love that twisted itself under my heart and shed a thick mist over my eyes, stealing the tender spirit from my heart.[26]

The mist falling on the eyes and the stealing of the spirit, as Maurice Bowra points out, come from the language of death in the *Iliad,* obliquely equating love with death. Also, "Love, like a smith, smote me again with a great axe and soused me in a wintry torrent."[27]

"This mad and beastly passion," Robert Burton says, "is usually called by physicians Heroical Love, or Noble love, because noble men and women make a common practice of it, and are so ordinarily affected with it" (*The Anatomy of Melancholy,* III.ii.1/2). In East Asia such disease often afflicted male and female folk poets who shared a number of distressing symptoms—paleness, leanness, loss of appetite, sighing, weeping, sleeplessness, madness, and ultimately death. Indeed, love is "a plague, a torture, hell, bitter-sweet passion, sweet-bitterness, a delicious pain, a gay torment" (III.ii.3). There is no end to the psychological and emotional conflicts and paradoxical symptoms of passion:

Of hopes begot by fear, of wot not what desires:
Of force of heav'nly beams, infusing hellish paine:
Of living deaths, dear wounds, faire stormes and freesing fires . . .
Astrophil and Stella, 6.2–4

Love is, Burton concludes, "a bottomless pit." Or when Romeo "runs through the repertory in oxymora"[28] betraying his knowledge of Petrarchan conventions:

O loving hate!
O anything, of nothing first [create]!
O heavy lightness! serious vanity!
Mis-shapen chaos of [well-seeming] forms!
Feather of lead, bright smoke, cold fire, sick health!
Still-waking sleep, that is not what it is!

Romeo and Juliet, I.i.182–187

Lady Kasa of eighth-century Japan equates love and death:

Omounishi	If it were death to love,
Shinisuru mono ni	I should have died—
Aramaseba	And died again
Chitabi zo ware wa	One thousand times over.[29]
Shinikaeramashi.	

The figure of love as a mystery (a labyrinth or a maze) is a commonplace:

What was love in fact, what was it?
Was it round, was it square?
Was it long, was it short?
More than an inch, more than a yard?
It seems of no great length,
But somehow I don't know where it ends.

"It seems of no great length," avers the anonymous Korean poet; it is so near and so far at the same time; it is endless and boundless especially in the sorrow it brings—heart entangled in a net of yearning, underscoring love's painful enlacement and the sorrow of separation ("Cut and cut, it will not sever; loosen, it's entwined as ever").[30] Another anonymous Korean poem advances a view that, as the footprints in the riverbed are no sooner made than washed away, so the speaker cannot fathom the depth of love.

No matter how often you walk
The fine sand in the riverbed,
No footprints will remain.
However strong her love for me,
A wind-tossed boatman
Cannot fathom its depth.

The anonymous *Man'yō* poet echoes the same sentiment and the same proverbial folk wisdom and diction (XI.2442):

Ōtsuchi mo	The great earth itself
Toraba tsukimedo	Might be exhausted by digging,
Yononaka ni	But of love alone in this world
Tsukisenu mono wa	Could we never reach the end.[31]
Koi nishi arikeri.	

Ōshikōchi no Mitsune (859–907) seems to concur:

Waga koi wa	My love
Yukue mo shirazu	Knows no destination
Hate mo nashi	And has no goal;
Au wo kagiri to	I think only
Omou bakari zo.	Of meeting as its limit.[32]

Love involves the whole of existence; it is at once fine, vast, inconstant, and frail. Only by cataloguing its manifestations can one approximate such sorrows in life:

Yearning is the heart, and the eyes seek love.
Fine as a floating thread, vast as the sea.
But the moon's not always full and the flowers are soon faded.
I have such sorrows in my life, and most for her.

Wu Jung[33]

True love entails not only sympathetic relationship and dedication but surrender and annihilation of self. It unites contrary qualities, yin and yang, and transforms the lover into a new being, bound by inseparable destiny. I have become you, and you have become I. No less than a total give and take will achieve this identification. The lovers' separation will then result in death, for each possesses the other's heart and soul. The following poem by Kuan Tao-sheng recalls some Mozarabic *kharjas* in its subtlety:

You and I
Love each other so
As from the same lump of clay
Is moulded an image of you
And one of me.
In a moment of ecstasy
We dash the images to pieces,
Put them in water,
And with stirring and kneading
Mould again an image of you
And another of me.
There and then,
You will find yourself in me.
I myself in you.[34]

The medieval conceits of the fusion of identities and of the migration of man's heart to the lady's might be cited as Western parallels.[35]

Finally I cite a Korean example of folk origin from *The Song of a Faithful Wife, Spring Fragrance,*[36] the anonymous romance originating sometime before the nineteenth century. A satirical imitation of the genre, its humorous attack on the ruling social and literary conventions, especially the traditional educational system and pendantry, has entertained the reader. When the hero, Dream Dragon, tries his hand at defining love to impress and persuade his girl, Spring Fragrance, his wit and humor run to excess. But the young man's exuberance and overindulgence—he was sixteen—emphasize the power of love which he attempts to recreate by the stock-in-trade of love rhetoric. In order to hide artifice and create the illusion of spontaneity, he seizes on the efficacy of the key word "love" and mixes learned and folkloristic similes:

> Love, love, my love,
> Love high as Witches Mountain or the moon shining upon the 700-li Tung-t'ing Lake,
> Love deep as the green sea and boundless as the sky above,
> Love like the moon on a thousand autumnal peaks as it shines upon the Five Mountains,
> Love of Duke Mu's daughter for the fluteplayer as she learned to dance,
> Love like the evening sun and the moon upon the peach and plum blossoms seen through the screen,
> Love that abounds in the winsome smiles and graces of a moth-eyebrowed girl,
> Love that brings us together through three lives, bound by the Old Man of the Moonlight,
> Love without reproach between husband and wife,
> Love lovely as a well-rounded peony on the eastern hill in the rain,
> Love joined on end like a brocade woven by the Weaver in the Milky Way,
> Love concealed like the seams in the quilt of a singing girl,
> Love long drooping like the fronds of the weeping willow by the river,
> Love piled up like the grains in the southern and northern granaries,
> Love deeply etched in every corner like silver and jade inlays in the chest,
> Love of the golden bees or the white butterflies as they hold the flowers and dance over the pink-green hills in the spring breeze,
> Love like a pair of mandarin ducks bobbing on the clear green stream,
> Love of the Herdboy and Weaver on the night of the Double Seven,
> Love of Master Liu-kuan's disciple Hsing-chen frolicking with the Eight Immortals,

Love of Hsiang Yü—whose strength can pluck up the hills—
meeting the beautiful Lady Yü,
Love of the Brilliant Emperor for Precious Consort Yang,
Love swaying gracefully like the searoses on a stretch of Bright
Sand Beach,
Everything about you is love,
My love,
My lovely one, my love![37]

IV

Poems celebrating the fulfillment and ecstasy of love are comparatively few, and even behind the few that concern the present lurk a fear of separation, the insubstantiality of joy, and a plea for indulgence.

The south side of the painted hall their tryst;
She leans one instant quivering on his breast:
"So seldom can I come to you, my love,
That all the love you ask of me, I give!"[38]

Li Yü (937–978)

The anonymous Middle Korean song whose simplicity and charm of the language is seldom surpassed, contains the elements of the *propemptikon:* the beloved departing, the dejected lover, pleas and conflicts, and a final renunciation:

Will You Go?

And will you go away?
Will you thus forsake me,
Leave me, and go away?

How can you leave me so
That loved you every day,
How can you leave me so?

I could cling to you, stop you,
But fear you would never return,
Scared by my salt tears.

Go, then, I'll let you go.
But return soon, soon return,
As easily as you leave me now.

In the second stanza, the propemptic speaker attempts to reason, plead, and reproach the departing beloved. The third stanza is an instance of *renuntiatio amoris:* she tries every appeal she knows to win him back, but realizes the inevitability of his journey. She then overcomes her grief and decides to let him go, but with the propemptic "remember me" topos.[39]

In the following two poems, the speaker tries to hold back the departing lover.

> Do not draw back your sleeves and go,
> My own,
> With tears I beg you.
> Over the long dike green with grass,
> Look, the sun goes down.
> You will regret it, lighting the lamp
> By the tavern window,
> Sleepless, alone.
>
> Yi Myŏng-han (1595–1645)

> A horse neighs, wants to gallop:
> My love clings to me, begs me to stay.
> The moving sun has crossed the hill.
> I have a thousand miles to go.
> My love, do not stop me:
> Stop the sun from setting!

In both, night, the usual time for love, becomes instead a time for separation. The speaker in the first offers a gentle repudiation to the heedless lover, but not a catalogue of impending dangers that await the traveler, as in the following *tz'u* by Chou Pang-yen (1056–1121) where the lady pleads:

> "Where are you going to spend the night?
> They've called the third watch from the city wall.
> Your horse will slip, the frost's so thick;
> You'd do much better not to go;
> There's hardly anyone about at all."[40]

The speaker in the second asks, not without self-mocking irony, his lady to stay the course of the sun: only if she could tie the sun down, their love would continue. But nature is not responsive: day will not last forever. He is aware of the irreversible movement that brings grief. The first also resembles the famous poem by the woman poet Hwang Chin-i, where she likens her lover to a flying stream never to return and pleads that it pause and enjoy the beautiful stillness of the moonlit night.

> Do not boast of your speed,
> O bluegreen stream running by the hills:
> Once you have reached the wide ocean,
> You can return no more.

Why not stay here and rest,
When moonlight fills the empty hills?

Couched in the metaphorical (or metaphysical) language characteristic of her poetry, the speaker has successfully transformed the passion of love and reconciled the tension between the tranquility of nature and the turmoil that besets her. In East Asian love poetry, the moon is often a sympathetic companion, a confidant, or a mediator. The moon's changing phases are also compared to the stages of human love, especially love's inconstancy. But here Hwang Chin-i has gone a step farther —she says she is the moon that overflows nature with beauty and stillness. Is she the full moon, the Buddhist symbol of enlightenment? Or the new moon that inspires hope in her beloved? Could she but have power to reverse the course of the stream. The hills are, however, empty, emphasizing her desolate state of mind as well as the illusory nature of the phenomenal world, the insubstantiality of love. Joy coexists with sorrow; its momentary enchantment is the more poignant because it is fleeting. So why not prolong that joy even for a moment?[41] Another of Hwang Chin-i's poems elaborates on the same motif:

Blue mountains speak of my desire,
Green waters reflect my Lover's love:
The mountains unchanging,
The waters flowing by.
Sometimes it seems the waters cannot forget me,
They part in tears, regretting, running away.

She likes to hope that she will never change like the mountains, but the waters that stand for her beloved are not so. They tumble along, but not without sadness: do they also lament the transience of earthly love?

What if the willow has ten thousand strings;
Can they tie down the spring breeze?
What if the butterflies search out nectar;
Can they stop the falling blossoms?
What if we feel secure in the time of our love;
What will become of it if she leaves me alone?
Yi Wŏn-ik (1547–1634)

Love depends upon the lady's loyalty, her whims and graces, says Yi Wŏn-ik. As the willow's strings cannot tie down the spring breeze and keep it from scattering the blossoms, so he will be made miserable by the beloved's disloyalty. If only she could surpass spring and stay its beauty. But the speaker was no Meleager of Gadara (c. 140–70 B.C.) or Cavalcanti; he was unable to create her as flower of flowers, spring of springs, or confer on her the transcendent power and supernatural grace as in Cavalcanti's "Fresca rosa novella."[42]

The poignancy of the bitter moment of parting is evoked magnificently in one of the Tzu-yeh songs:

> I heard my love was going to Yang-chou
> And went with him as far as Ch'u-shan.
> For a moment when you held me fast in your outstretched arms
> I thought the river stood still and did not flow.[43]

The lovers can make the river stand still, stop the flow of time and eternalize the moment, thus conferring immortality on the union. Man and nature are at peace: or is love stronger than nature? I have discussed in Chapter Two the function of the river metaphor in East Asian love lyrics starting from the *Book of Songs*. Its mindless, irreversible flow is as endless as yearning, its tides as turbulent as tears and agonies. The motif was later transferred from earth to sky when poets employed the myth of the ill-fated Herdboy (Aquila) and the Weaver (Vega and Lyre) constellations of Chinese astronomy, on both sides of the Milky Way, as fit metaphors of lovers' separation. This and other examples skillfully refine through the use of the same metaphor the dramatic potentialities inherent in the tradition.

> The white-footed girl of Tung-yang,
> The skipper of a white boat from K'uai-chi,
> They look at each other—the moon hasn't set,
> For no reason their hearts break.[44]
>
> Li Po (701?–762)

> Holding hands, we look at each other's tearful eyes,
> Without a word, choked by frozen sobs.
> Think of the thousand miles of misty waves stretching ahead,
> And the deep layers of evening clouds in the vast Southern sky![45]
>
> Liu Yung (fl. 1034), Tune: "Bells in the Rains"

Here are examples where parting took place in the past:

> Cut a running stream with a prized sword—
> It will never be severed.
> My thoughts that follow your course
> Are as endless as the stream.[46]
>
> Li Po, "Written in Behalf of My Wife"

The last line echoes the last two lines of a poem by Hsü Kan (171–218): "Thoughts of you are like the flowing river—/ when will they ever end?"[47] And Li Chih-yi (c. 1073), in a lyric to the tune, "Song of Divination":

> I live at the upper end of the River,
> And at the lower end live you;
> Every day I long to see you but cannot,
> Though from the same River we drink.
>
> When will the River go dry?
> When can my sorrow come to an end?
> Only may your heart be like mine,
> My love for you will not be in vain.[48]

Like Sappho before her, the speaker in the anonymous Middle Korean "Song of P'yongyang" says she cannot mind her wheel. The lover across the Taedong River flowing past the city of P'yongyang has possessed her heart.

> Although P'yongyang is my home and capital
> And the walls have all been repaired,
> If I must part from you, be left behind,
> I'll stop spinning, and stop weaving,
> Follow my own love with salt tears.
>
> Were the pearls to fall on the rock,
> Would the thread be broken?
> If I parted from you for a thousand years,
> Would my heart be changed?
>
> Not knowing the Taedong that flows on,
> You pushed the boat off, O boatman.
> Not knowing the sorrow that kills me,
> You had him board the ferry, boatman.
> Once he has crossed that awesome water,
> He will pluck some other flower.

The middle stanza, a love vow couched in *adynata,* was popular during the period and recurs elsewhere. Time will, she avers, never untie the thread. And the anonymous English song says that "The moon shall be a darkness,/ The stars shall give no light,/ If ever I prove false/ To my heart's delight." The final stanza, addressed to the boatman, ends with the graphic portrayal of the fated betrayal: a new love will drive away the old. Her heroic determination to follow him and her pledge of unswerving loyalty notwithstanding, the inexorable water flows on. The persistence and power of the imagery are attested elsewhere, in the Toscan folk songs and *kharja,* as well as in the following love song by women in the Cambridge manuscript (*Carmina Cantabrigiensia,* 14).[49]

Nam languens	Languishing
amore tuo	for love of you
consurrexi	I arose
diluculo,	at dawn
perrexi-	and made my way
que pedes nuda	bare-footed
per nives et	across the snows
[per] frigora,	and cold,
atque maria	and searched
rimabar mesta,	the desolate seas
si forte ventivola	to see if I could find
vela cernerem,	sails flying in the wind,
aut frontem navis	or catch sight of the prow
conspicerem.	of a ship.

But who is this stricken woman, abandoned to languish in an anonymous Korean song? The reasons for the flowering of women's love songs in thirteenth- and fourteenth-century Korea are obscure; but these unknown song writers, like their sisters of later times, left some of the most moving lyrics in the language. Women poets of the Yi dynasty (1392–1910) were mostly *kisaeng,* known by such memorable professional names as Bright Jade, Thousand Brocade, Laughing Spring Breeze, Bright Moon (Hwang Chin-i), Small Cypress Boat, Cold Rain, Cassia Maiden (the traditional name of courtesans in the West was Flora).[50] As professional entertainers, they wrote and sang poetry, danced, played musical instruments, and were known chiefly for their literary and artistic achievements. Such a *kisaeng* as Hwang Chin-i, for example, was eagerly sought out by contemporary men of letters. Gallus' Lycoris (Cytheris), Tibullus' Delia (Plania) and Nemesis, Propertius' Cynthia (Hostia), Catullus' Lesbia (Clodia), Ovid's Corinna—how much do we know about these women? They (and later the sonnet lady, for example, Petrarch's Laura, Constable's Diana, Daniel's Delia) were immortalized by their poet-lovers.

> She is the whole of my inspiration.
>
> Propertius, II.1.4[51]

> my verse your virtues rare shall eternize,
> and in the heuens wryte your glorious name.
>
> *Amoretti,* 75.11–12

In Korea it was women who conferred lasting fame on themselves.

In the limited examples of poems on the parting of lovers at dawn, most elements in the Western *alba* are present: secret or prearranged meeting, the consummation of love, the cock motif, the renewed desire for prolongation of night, consolation of the loved one, separation at dawn, and the like. An earlier example of the dawn-dialogue occurs in the *Book of Songs* (96), and the *Man'yōshū* preserves similar poems.

The Lady: The cock has crowed;
It is full daylight.

The Lover: It was not the cock that crowed,
It was the buzzing of those green flies.

The Lady: The eastern sky glows;
It is broad daylight.

The Lover: That is not the glow of dawn,
But the rising moon's light.
The gnats fly drowsily;
It would be sweet to share a dream with you.

The Lady: Quick! Go home!
Lest I have cause to hate you![52]

Here the identity of the lover and the lady is not given, although some translators make him to be a courtier. One of the pair tries to persuade the other that it is not the cock but the buzzing of green flies, not the glow of dawn but the rising moon's light. Their fear of rumor and slander, the element of danger, finds expression in the last lines.

Towards the east it is still dark,
But he bustles into jacket and skirt.
He bustles into them and hustles into them;
From the palace they have sent for him.

The dew of the night is not yet dry,
But he bustles into skirt and coat,
Hustles into them and bustles into them;
To the palace they have summoned him.

'He is breaking the willows of the fenced
garden.
The mad fellow in his flurry—
Never can he judge the time of night;
If he's not too early, then he's too late.'[53]

In poem 100, the man is a high official summoned by the court, and the poem is a satiric, humorous portrayal of the man who has lost all sense of time.

A remarkable feature of Japanese examples—and later in some *tz'u* and Korean poems—is the threat to kill the cock, as in the following from the *Tales of Ise:*

Yo mo akeba	When daylight comes
Kitsu ni hamenade	I shall toss him in the cistern—
Kutakake no	That miserable rooster
Madaki ni nakite	Who crows too soon
Sena o yaritsuru.	And drives my lover away.[54]

Po Chü-i's famous *tz'u,* "Hua fei hua," may be cited as a later specimen:

A flower, not a flower;
A mist, not a mist.
At midnight coming,
At daybreak gone.
Came like a spring dream, for a short stay,
Gone like a dawn cloud, without a trace.[55]

The poem magnificently underscores the finality of separation—that each meeting is by itself, and that it was the last and cannot be repeated again. The following three anonymous Korean poems sufficiently demonstrate their kinship with the genre of *alba:*

When the candle was growing dim,
My love stole through the window.
Now the dawn moon goes down;
Once again I am in his arms.
How can I forget my love
Even my white bones turn to dust?

This night I have met my love—
O cock, do not crow.
Day will soon break, I know,
Without your telling me so.
Not this night, not just this night,
Your cry will break my heart.

Of all the birds and beasts
The cock and the dog should be disposed of.
When my beloved sleeps in my arms
Inside the white walls and gauze window,
The cock crows and wakes him up.
When he steals into my inner gate,

The dog barks and drives him away.
When the chicken- and dog-pedlar comes along,
I'll bind and pass them on.[56]

In one of the *Man'yō* poems by Prince Yūhara, the speaker asks the moon god to "make this night as long . . . / As five hundred nights in one" (VI.985).[57] In a variant form of the *sijo,* the anonymous poet or poetess invests the same motif with a new dimension and subtle humor and wit:

One, two, three, four, five, six, seven,
Seven stars in the Northern Dipper,
I respectfully submit a petition:
  Last night I met my beloved,
  But before I poured out my heart,
  Day broke, and I was heartbroken.
  Please send out three sentry stars
  To check night-fleeing
    dawn-hustling
      little stars!

Addressed somewhat pedantically to seven stars of the Dipper, the petition begins by enumerating every star of the Great Bear. The first line consisting only of numerals engenders not only dramatic immediacy but suspense. The second part is the prayer proper, offered in the form of a confession to the celestial confidants. Three sentry stars, supposed to guard the northern sky, are requested to restrain the little sleepy stars which disappear as soon as day breaks.

All the poems cited deal with passionate, often adulterous, love, the lovers opposed to conventional morality and society. As in the Western *alba,* love-making is associated with night, and dawn is a separator and destroyer of a momentary bliss, underscoring an impermanence of passion and an inevitability of separation. But seldom do the lovers declare that only in death will they enjoy eternal union. Structurally, the dualistic opposition between inside-outside, night-day, desire-reality exists, together with psychological conflict, portrayed in dialogue poems. However, dawn and light are not invested with religious values, such as God's light, spiritual awakening, or eternal bliss. If "the conflict of two worlds, the problem of choice, and the necessity for action" are basic ideas to the structure of the Western medieval *alba,* "expressed in the thought forms of Christianity,"[58] East Asia offers no counterpart.

A curious ninth-century Korean poem—also the most famous of all Old Korean poems—is "Song of Ch'ŏyong" (879). The author of the poem is, according to our source, one of the seven sons of the Dragon King of the Eastern Sea. He called himself Ch'ŏyong and married a beautiful woman. Seeing that she was extremely beautiful, an evil spirit transformed himself into a man and attacked her in her room while Ch'ŏyong was away. But Ch'ŏyong returned and witnessed the scene, and calmly he sang the following song, which so moved the evil spirit that it went away:

> Having caroused far into the night
> In the moonlit capital,
> I return home and in my bed,
> Behold, four legs.
>
> Two have been mine;
> Whose are the other two?
> Two had been mine;
> No, no, they are taken.

The Ch'ŏyong mask was later used to exorcise the evil spirits, usually on New Year's Eve. Traditionally, Ch'ŏyong was considered to be a shaman—he expelled the demon not by confrontation but by means of song and dance, thus shaming the demon into submission. His identity became a popular topic of speculation, and one critic traces him to an Arab or Central Asian merchant who came to Korea in the ninth century. Whatever his identity, he may have been a variant of the figure of the *exclusus amator,* the shut-out lover who grieves at his lady's doorway. In Greek and Latin examples,[59] the lover usually sings a lament or a plea before the locked door of his mistress, after he had been refused admission. Sometimes, in Roman examples, the wounded lover attacks the door with axes, crowbars, and torches. Contrarily, Ch'ŏyong's calm handling of the situation has been described as magnanimous, fatalistic, magical, and the like. Nobody has yet ventured a reason why the motif was not taken up by later poets.

V

Poems of disappointment and sorrow from desertion or separation take various forms. The *Book of Songs* has already explored some major motifs and themes, beginning with the physical effects on the lover caused by betrayal. In the first, the disappointed lady says,

> 86.1 . . . all because of you
> I leave my rice untouched.[60]

In the second, another victim exclaims:

145.1 Day and night I can do nothing:
As a flood my tears flow . . .[61]

The last two lines are refrains with minor variations: "For my heart is full of woe" (st. 2) and "For on pillow I toss and turn" (st. 3), the last one of the clichés in later poetry. In poem 72, a single day's absence is likened first to three months, then three autumns, and finally three years (also in 91).[62]

The torments of hopeless love, like passion in Sidney's *Arcadia,* are portrayed as darkness and violent weather:

30.3 A great wind and darkness;
Day after day it is dark.
I lie awake, cannot sleep,
And gasp with longing.[63]

The intensity of the lover's heartache even causes the death of Nature. The fructifying force of love gone, Nature too conspires against her ("Western wind, when will thou blow,/ The small rain down can rain?"):

201.3 Zip, zip the valley wind
Across the rocky hills.
No grass but is dying,
No tree but is wilting . . .[64]

Another favorite metaphor is the storm-tossed bark, and instability (also floating duckweed, mud in turbid water, rudderless boat, to name only a few) is the familiar symbol of the tribulations of the unrequited love in Western poetry:

26.1 Tossed is that cypress boat
Wave-tossed it floats.
My heart is in turmoil, I cannot sleep . . .[65]

45.1 Unsteady is that cypress boat
In the middle of the river . . .
Oh, mother, ah, Heaven,
That a man could be so false![66]

The first is a lament by a woman who was about to be married off against her wishes; the second concerns a broken vow. The third and fifth stanzas of the first contain genuinely moving passages:

26.3 My heart is not a stone;
It cannot be rolled.[67]

This is not the familiar Petrarchan conceit for the hardness of the lady's heart; saturated with sorrow and tears, the speaker declares that her heart is heavier than a stone. Or in another simile,

26.5 Sorrow clings to me
Like an unwashed dress.[68]

The fifth stanza of poem 35, which begins with the familiar wind and darkness motif ("Zip, zip the valley wind/ Bring darkness, bringing rain"), presents in vivid, homely language the truth of the affair:

35.5 Why do you not cherish me,
But rather treat me as an enemy?
You have spoilt my value;
What is used, no merchant will buy.
Once in times of peril, of extremity
With you I shared all troubles.
But now that you are well-nurtured, well-fed,
You treat me as though I were a poison.[69]

The speaker is the rejected first wife who reminds the guileful husband that, unlike the concubine he has just acquired, she is not merchandise. You have only taken advantage of my loyalty and diligence and have forgotten what hardships I have borne to maintain the poor household. Now that things are better, you turn me down. Your betrayal has made a mockery of the bond of marriage. Far from considering me a "sweet enemy," you attack me as your true enemy of happiness, a poison that kills your worthless dalliance.

The speakers in some Korean "lost love" poems refuse to abandon hope and await a recanting of the loved one.

My mind is foolish,
And all that I do seems vain.
Who would come to the deep mountain
With its thick clouds, fold upon fold?
I look to see whether you come by chance,
Whenever the fallen leaves rustle in the wind.

Sŏ Kyŏng-dŏk (1489–1546)

A flickering shadow haunts the window.
I start up, open, go out.
Only clouds passing the misty moon—
No, it was not the one for whom I've been waiting.
I'm lucky, night doesn't look in to laugh;
But what if it happened in broad daylight?

Anonymous

The faint moon in a heavy frost;
A solitary wild goose flies cackling.
Love, I fancied it brought me news.
Was it a letter from my love, indeed?
No, I hear only the bird
Among the clouds, incredibly far.

Anonymous

Night draws near in a dead village,
A dog barks far away.
I open the cottage door:
The chilly sky and the moon
Be still, stop barking at the moon
Asleep over the bare mountain.

Ch'ŏn Kŭm

Startled by the rustle of fallen leaves, a flickering shadow on the paper screens, the cackling of a solitary goose, or a barking dog at the moon, the "foolish" lover looks out the window. "I'm lucky, night does not look in to laugh," says the anonymous speaker in the second. People would have laughed at his (or her) anxious behavior during the daytime, but darkness is a confidant, and at night the poignancy of desire for reunion is most uninhibited.

That night is deceiving and the solitary lover is responsive to the slightest sight and sound ("A lover's eyes will gaze an eagle blind,/ A lover's ear will hear the lowest sound"; *Love's Labour's Lost,* IV.iii. 334–335), is also a commonplace in Chinese and Japanese poetry:

All night I could not sleep
Because of the moonlight on my bed.
I kept on hearing a voice calling:
Out of Nowhere, Nothing answered "yes."[70]

Tzu-yeh Song

I await the moon in the western chamber
Where the breeze comes through the half-opened door.
Sweeping the wall the flower shadows move:
I imagine it is my lover who comes.[71]

Yüan Chen, "The Story of Ying-ying"

Kome ya to	Although I am sure
Omou mono kara	That he will not be coming,
Higurashino	When the locusts shrilly call
Naku yūgure wa	I go to the door and wait.[72]
Tachimataretsutsu.	Anonymous

Hito ni awamu	The night of no moon
Tzuki no naki yo wa	There is no way to meet him.
Omoiokite	I rise in longing—
Mune hashiri hi ni	My breast pounds, a leaping flame,
Kokoro yakeori.	My heart is consumed in fire.[73]
	Ono no Komachi (9th century)

The objects that evoke memory and desire are many: such gifts as a fan or the loved one's belongings; the fragrance of such seasonal indicators as the plum, orange, peach, paulownia or the cries of the cuckoo, *hototogisu* (woodthrush), firefly, cicada, locust, cricket, and goose; the moon, wind, and rain, the Milky Way, or occasions of seasonal festivals. In fact, the anonymous "Ode on the Seasons," a Middle Korean calendrical folk song, compares the stages of a woman's love to the four seasons. So does another folk poem, "Song of the Lantern Feast" (c. 1725)—the first five stanzas of which survive—built on the monthly observances of folk origin. The endless longing of the victim of inconstant love is magnificently conveyed by Sappho in a deceptively simple, subdued tone:

Midnight,
        and the small hours
creep on,
        the Pleiads
& the Moon
          have set,
I lie alone.[74]

These poems drive home the painful awareness of the gulf that separates reality and show, truth and semblance. Love is mutable and illusory, and no gaiety and continuity of nature can assuage the sufferings in the heart.

Such are the themes of the anonymous Middle Korean song, "Spring Overflows the Pavilion," sung by a female entertainer (sts. 1–3):

Were I to build a bamboo hut on the ice,
Were I to die of cold with him on the ice,
O night, run slow, till our love is spent.

When I lie alone, restless, vigilant,
Only peach blossoms wave over the west window.
You have no grief, welcome the spring breeze.

I have believed those who vowed to each other:
"My soul will follow yours forever."
Who, who persuaded me this was true?

A spring in her heart is dead, killed by the loved one. But can there be another spring outside? The poem is more than an expression of a discord between the lover's internal condition and the weather outside. After an imaginary coaxing dialogue in the fourth stanza, the fifth transforms the tone of the poem by having the treacherous man express his wish for fulfillment: he will be able to transform the icy bamboo hut into a love grotto.

> A bed on Mount South, a jade pillow, gold brocade,
> And beside me a girl sweeter than musk,
> Let us press our hearts together, our magic hearts.

The love grotto (which resembles a Gothic cathedral) where Tristan and Isolde fed upon the light from each other's eyes was in the wilderness, but adorned by three lime trees with singing birds, the shade, and the sun. The ideal landscape was the right place for ideal love (actually adulterous love sanctioned by God himself), separated from the outside world by a bronze door that can be opened only by true lovers.[75] But here the speaker's desire for preservation of love in absence is so strong he (actually she in disguise) says he can transform a bamboo hut into an ideal place. A similar sentiment is found in a dialogue poem in the *Man'yōshū* (XI.2824–5):

Omou hito	Had I foreknown my sweet lord's coming,
Konto shiriseba	
Yaemugura	My garden, now so rank with wild weeds,
Ooeru niwa ni	
Tama shikamashiwo.	I had strewn it with pearls!
Tama shikeru	What use to me a house strewn with pearls?
Ie mo nani sen	
Yaemugura	The cottage hidden in wild weeds
Ooeru oya mo	Is enough, if I am with you.[76]
Imo to oriteba.	

The next poem by Chŏng Ch'ŏl is also on the cruelest season:

> Flowers are in splendid show,
> Butterflies fly in pairs.
> Willows are green, luxuriant,
> Orioles sing in pairs.
> Birds and beasts are loving, always two together—
> But why do I dwell here alone?

In Nature every creature rejoices in spring and finds fulfillment: "in pairs" repeated twice, followed by "always two together," and culminating in the climactic word "alone" in the last line, underscoring the ironic relationships between man and nature. What the speaker underscores is the chasm between external harmony and internal turmoil—that happiness in nature should make him sigh—the burden of one of the *Cambridge Songs, Levis exsurgit Zephirus* (sts. 4–6):

Quod oculis dum video et auribus dum audio, heu, pro tantis gaudiis tantis inflor suspiriis.	I see it with my eyes, I hear it with my ears, But in my heart are sighs, And I am full of tears.
Cum mihi sola sedeo et hec revolvens palleo, si forte caput sublevo, nec audio nec video.	Alone with thought I sit, And blench, remembering it; Sometimes I lift my head, I neither hear nor see.
Tu saltim, Veris gratia, exaudi et considera frondes, flores et gramina; nam mea languet anima.	Do thou, O Spring most fair, Squander thy care On flower and leaf and grain. —Leave me alone with pain![77]

Another poem by Chŏng Ch'ŏl is a variation on the same theme in which the poet gently chides the false lover who, unlike the returning spring, does not send a word:

I bade you farewell, my love,
When fallen leaves danced in the wind.
Now snow and ice have melted,
Blossoms will soon adorn the day.
But you send me no word—
Alas, my love, no word.

The disjunction between the peacefulness of nature and the anguish in the heart—like the joyous *Natureingang* followed by the torments of a frustrated lover—is a common device in all love poetry.

A number of poems in the *Book of Songs* use beast imagery to reproach the heartless male lover. In poem 63 a fox walking along the dam on the Ch'i is a sly, unprincipled man, the cause of the speaker's pain, as the third line in each stanza declares: "Oh, my heart is sad."[78] He has no robe—he is morally naked; he has no belt and coat—he does not guard against moral degradation. In poem 151, the image of the pelican (or cormorant) which does not wet its wings and beaks provides the central metaphor:

The pelican stays on the bridge;
It has not wetted its beak.
The fine gentleman
Has not followed up his love-meeting.[79]

As the pelican who behaves contrary to its nature, so the fine gentleman "Has no right to his dress" (st. 2) either because he has seduced a young girl and then abandoned her, as in Waley, or because he has neglected his duties because of his unslakable desire for the young lady, as in Karlgren's version.

Poems 35 and 199 introduce another imagery, that of the dam:

"It is the Wei that makes the Ching look dirty;
Very clear are its shoals."
You feast your new relations,
And think me no fit company.
"Do not break my dam,
Do not open my fish-traps.
Though for my person you have no regard,
At least pity my brood."[80]

Here the abandoned lady or first wife reproaches her treacherous man and says that, although the evil influence of the second lady has blinded him, she still hopes he will show consideration for their children.

What kind of man is that!
His heart is very intriguing;
Why does he come to my dam,
And does not enter my gate?
Who are following him?
I call them cruel ones.[81]

The speaker says, in the last stanza, that she has composed the poem as a therapy in order to sustain the wrongs done her by her unfaithful husband who does not come to see her or enter her home. "What kind of man is that?" is repeated three times (sts. 1, 3, 4), to register her indignation, self-debate, and jealousy. He is not "a spectre or a demon," hence his behavior is the more inexcusable (st. 8). "He does not fear Heaven" (st. 3)—he has no sense of shame and decency. Humiliated and troubled, hers is a cry of the heart: "If you would come but once!" (sts. 5–6). The poem is a process of catharsis, and her attempt to face the great difficulties and impose some sense of order on her turbulent emotions is convincing.

The traditional reading of these poems was allegorical, and the animal imagery seldom reappears in love complaints, except for the fourth stanza of "Spring Overflows the Pavilion," a Middle Korean love song:

"O duck, beautiful duck, why do you come
To the swamp, instead of the shoal?"
"If the swamp freezes, the shoal will do."

In the coaxing dialogue, the first is uttered by the woman, who addresses the man as "duck." The adjective "beautiful" also means "inexperienced" and "foolish" in the original. The duck is a symbol for a carefree young man who frequents the gay quarters, trafficking between the swamp and the shoal.

Catullus' two lines in song 85 best summarizes the topos of dilemma:

> Odi et amo, quare id faciam, fortasse requiris?
>   nescio, sed fieri sentio et excrucior.
>
> (I hate and I love
> well, why do I, you probably ask
> I don't know, but I know it's happening
> and it hurts.) [82]

Or Shakespeare in his sonnets to the dark lady (e.g., 129, 137, 147). But already Anacreon said, "Again I am in love and not in love, am mad and not mad."[83] "Half of him watches the other half," comments Bowra, "and is amused by the spectacle."

The topos of dilemma sometimes leads to that of role-reversal. The reversal of role is often implied, when the lost lover dramatizes his disbelief and surprise at his changed state and indulges in a nostalgic recollection of past delights.

> Together—I wish I could hate her,
> Parted—I wish I could forget her.
> I wish she had never been born,
> Or I had never known her.
> I'd rather die before her:
> Then she could ache for me.

In the above poem by Ko Kyŏng-myŏng (1533–1592), unrewarded love and unpropitious trials compel the speaker to harbor malice—he wants to see her pine, albeit for a moment. The emotional damage done him is immeasurable; it is her turn to taste the pangs. The following anonymous poem denounces the loved one—the grammatical subject unspecified in the original—and wishes the disloyal love the same agony and torments the speaker has suffered. Love's pains cannot be syllogized, no matter how mighty a pen: they are best learned by experience. No amount of witchcraft, surgery, or a long voyage will do any good (compare Propertius, I.1). As grief and tears have made me an expert, so, the speaker argues—first in a lyric by the tenth century Chinese poet Ku Hsiung, followed by the anonymous Korean *sijo*—will you find out what unswerving love entails:

Tune: "Declaring My Inner Feelings"

All night long you have deserted me; whither gone?
No news has come;
My scented chamber is closed.
Brows knitted, moon just setting,
How can I bear not to grope for you,
Weeping under my lonely coverlet?
Change your heart into my heart,
And learn the depth of my pining.[84]

Were you to become I, and I you,
Born in each other's world,
You would have a hard time of it
And suffer a heartbreak as I have.
You would know then, taught in turn,
How I have grieved all my life.

One senses a need for revenge, but the serene tone is praiseworthy, in contrast especially to Propertius' denunciation of Cynthia and his heaping of invectives and curses upon her so that in her turn "she be shut out from bliss and endure another's haughty scorn" (III.25).[85]

The occasion for the next dramatic monologue by Shin Hŭm (1566–1628) is unknown. Time is whenever, and place is the human heart. The dramatic tone, which has immediacy and intensity, indicates that what it presents is the metaphysics of love:

I would draw her face with blood
That lies stagnant in my heart.
And on the plain wall of my room,
I would hang it up and gaze.
Who has made the word, "Farewell"?
Who causes me to love and wither to death?

The first four lines deal with the transformation of the tyranny of passion which is the tyranny of time. Passion knows no relief or end within temporal existence. The mode of existence of love is also paradoxical, compounded of hope and despair, joy and sorrow, confidence and fear. The knowledge that even his beloved will be subjected to decay and corruption brings the speaker to oppose time. The ideal image of love, which can never be satisfactorily expressed, can perhaps be realized through painting. Through art he hopes to stay the march of time. Through the portrait he wants to approximate the ideal image of the beloved in his heart, which he cannot wholly attain in life. It is an emblem of impossible love and the mind's freedom from it, the knowledge of which man can discover in the world of time. Another voice demands, "Who has made the word, 'Farewell'?" Exclamation is at once the occasion for the contemplation of time-bound love, the freedom from which may be won through the metamorphosis of the sufferings lodged in his heart. Such Renaissance conceits as engraving the image of the lady or friend on the lover's heart or the eyes as windows through which such a portrait could be seen are well-known.[86]

Poems on the theme of the neglected or forsaken wife are as old as the *Book of Songs*. Later examples, notably those by Ts'ao Chih (192–232), are commonly read as political allegories, his hope for mending the strained relations that existed between him and his elder brother Ts'ao P'ei (Emperor Wen of Wei) and protestations of his loyalty to him.[87] Korean imitations and adaptations owe as much to Ts'ao Chih as to the poems in the *Ch'u tz'u,* as the unemployed or exiled courtier's longing for the center of power is expressed through terms drawn from the experience of love. Such are Chŏng Ch'ŏl's two hymns to constancy (literally the Fair One), which derive their artistic detachment from parallels established between his frustrations and the rejected woman's disappointment in love. But such allegories are not our concern here.

"A Woman's Sorrow" by Hŏ Nansŏrhŏn (1563–1589) is a dramatic narrative in the *kasa* form and a museum of topics. The introduction of the theme of sorrowful reminiscence is followed by a recollection of her happier childhood and girlhood. She was brought up to be "a bride fit for a gentleman," as in the first poem in the *Book of Songs:* "Lovely is this noble lady/ Fit bride for our lord." But one brought her by a matchmaker was a careless knight who seeks diversion in a tavern, and the remainder of the poem is a moving account of the hazards of such a union. The beauties of spring and autumn (the plum trees, the autumn moon, crickets) and the terrors of summer and winter (dreary rain and snowy nights)—all intensify her agony. Her despair reaches a point that she even thinks of ending her own life. "A desire to die possesses me, and to see the lotus-covered dewy shores of Acheron."[88] But the speaker regains her poise and says, "No, I must unravel my sorrow calmly." The music in which she seeks consolation only echoes in the empty room. She hopes to see him in a dream, but fallen leaves rustling in the wind deny a dream vision. Hers is a separation worse than that suffered by the Weaver and the Herdboy in the sky, and the water that separates her from her beloved is vaster and more terrifying than the Milky Way. She seems to share Donna Julia's feelings expressed in her farewell letter to Don Juan: "Man's love is of man's life a thing apart,/ 'Tis woman's whole existence"

(I.194.1–2). "Parting is all we know of heaven,/ And all we need of hell," Emily Dickinson says. Indeed no mortal can match her in her sorrow. When Sidney suggests, "Fool . . . look in thy heart and write," he implies that inspiration precedes study of tradition but does not rule it out; much of Hŏ Nansŏrhŏn's success derives from her mastery of rhetorical devices, as much as from the controlled pathos of the situation, the candor of feeling, and the inner debate.

> . . . my face that once was beautiful,
> Where did it go? Who disgraced it so?
> Turn away from the mirror, look no more.
> Who, who will look at me now?[89]
>
> I will hear nothing from him, not a word,
> Yet I dare to hope he will remember me . . .
>
> When the autumn moon enters my room
> And crickets chirp on the couch,
> A long sigh and salty tears
> Endlessly make me recall details of the past.[90]
>
> Oh, to sleep, and see him in a dream;
> But for what reason and by what enmity
> Do the fallen leaves rustling in the wind
> And the insects piping among the grasses
> Wake me from my wretched sleep?[91]
>
> Numberless are the sorrowful;
> But none can be as wretched as I.
> Think, love, you caused me this grief;
> I know not whether I shall live or die.

These are some of the more familiar motifs we encounter in many similar poems. Although ours here is full of art, written in a polished and graceful style, its distinctive qualities are best measured in terms of the demands of the convention.

Of course, the poem resembles a forensic speech, in which the plaintiff offers ample evidence to accuse the defendant's course of action in the past.[92] In an attempt to influence her audience (husband, judge, and the public), she narrates the wretched life she has experienced throughout the seasons, with a recapitulation at the end that "None can be as wretched as I," and intimates that the reader, versed in the affairs of heart, will approve the sincerity and truth of her argument. Her strategies are sound: the defense of her plight and condemnation of the disloyal husband. Although the poem is addressed to her husband ("Think, love, you caused me this grief"), it is also spoken to the audience, who finds the unjustly suffering woman's plea justified and concurs with her that his unjust treatment of her is the cause of her misery ("I know not whether I shall live or die"). A number of "lost love" poems (as in *Book of Songs,* 35, 45, 201) adopt such a stance to complain—if not accuse—the past action of the loved one and ask the reader to judge what should be fit punishment for the treacherous one. On the basis of the evidence presented, the reader may side with the plaintiff that his or her case is justified and that society will find the defendant—real or feigned—guilty. The brevity of some East Asian verse forms does not allow a full citation of facts or proofs and a restatement of the same at the end, but such a short poem as *sijo* could adopt the forensic stance in a reduced form as, for example, in "I reviewed my heart one day." The argument of the poem is: you (the loved one) sliced a piece of my heart away; the pain caused by the wound kills me; you can put the slice back, but you don't want to see me restored. The unwritten conclusion is: your treatment of me is inhuman. The implied plea to the reader is: deliberate on the case and pass judgment on the accused.

Upon the death of his mistress Lady Li, the Warrior Emperor of the Han (reigned 140–87) wrote:

> The sound of her silk skirt has stopped.
> On the marble pavement dust grows.
> Her empty room is cold and still
> Fallen leaves are piled against the doors.
> Longing for that lovely lady
> How can I bring my aching heart to rest?[93]

Note the contrast between the magnificent atmosphere of cold silence and the throbbing heart of the deserted lover, one of the earliest devices to underscore the ironic indifference of nature to human suffering. In Theocritus' second idyll, Simaetha is languishing for her lover, Delphis:

> Now quiet is the wind, and quiet the sea,
> but in my heart no quiet comes to me.
> I'm burned to death, I'm wretched and betrayed . . .[94]

So is Dido's agony of passion contrasted with the peace and stillness of night in the fourth *Aeneid:*

> It was night, and over the earth weary creatures were tasting peaceful slumber; the woods and wild seas had sunk to rest—the hour when stars roll midway in their gliding course, when all the land is still, and beasts and gay

> birds, both they that far and near haunt the limpid lakes, and they that dwell in fields of tangled brakes, are couched in sleep beneath the silent night. But not so the soul-racked Phoenician queen; she never sinks to sleep, nor draws the night into eyes or heart. Her pangs redouble, and her love, swelling up, surges afresh, as she heaves with a mighty tide of passion.[95]

In Ovid's *Metamorphoses,* nocturnal silence enframes the tales of erotic violence and passion (Lucaon, Medea, Scylla, Myrrha). Other symbolic landscapes recur throughout: midday heat introducing the tales of lust (Io, Arethusa, Circe); peaceful sylvan scenes with shady woods and clear pools as the setting for rape and death or for the ironic reversal of the hunter and the hunted (Actaeon and Callisto, Narcissus and Echo). In addition to providing a unifying motif and tone to the work, such Ovidian scenes, at once mysterious and alluring, establish a correspondence between the reality of nature and an inner world of free desires and intensify the sense of victim's helplessness, "the arbitrariness and incomprehensibility of a world in which man has little or no power to protect his person."[96]

Also, the harmony of nature and the disharmony of the lover's anguish in the pastoral should perhaps be mentioned. Often the unhappy lovers escape to the ideal tranquility of nature, seeking a release from the chaos of human emotion, only to realize that nature cannot offer a refuge. Writing on *The Shepheardes Calender* where Colin accepts the incongruity of man and nature, Isabel G. MacCaffrey succinctly comments on the essential function of love to the design of the pastoral:

> The life of Colin Clout, then, traces for us the line of human life as it diverges psychologically from the life of nature, while remaining physically bound to it. The event which allows this divergence to manifest itself is a familiar one in pastoral poetry from Theocritus to Marvell. It is love, the disturber of pastoral harmony, a metaphor for the troubling of human life which we call sin—that is, the dominance of passion. It is, as Colin says, the result of pride . . . In consequence the orderly cycle of human life is turned awry, its promise blasted.[97]

Theocritus often depicts "the tension between commitment to the real world with all its passion, frustration, and tyranny of Aphrodite and the desire for an escape into an idyllic refuge of pastoral repose."[98] On the other hand, Spenser's chief concern is to realize the "need for us to accept a nonliteral, invisible reality as the one most relevant to us as human beings."[99] Indeed, "man must suffer inevitable outrage from the forces released in nature at the Fall, and against these forces there is no remedy within nature itself, or within the power of mere 'natural man.' Poetry cannot provide a talisman against death, nor heal the wounds of love, nor recreate the state of innocence. Yet the power of imagination in man is a real power, if rightly understood as 'an unnatural rage'; it gives us access to a transnatural realm of being where our ultimate destiny lies."[100] The congruence between macrocosmic disorder and ravages of love is also a device in East Asian love lyric. But there is no exact parallel to the Western pastoral in its handling of the theme of love. True, human passion is often depicted as disruptive and destructive, nature serving as a refuge for the tormented lover; but that emotion is seldom measured against the ideal landscape or explored in its relation to the demands of reality. Passion is morally suspect, it is implacable and to be suppressed—Confucian ethics taught long ago that private disorder breeds social chaos. But its meditation as a dramatic situation, or the resolution of the lover's pains and the joy of imagination, or the reconciliation of passion and reason is usually ignored or forgotten.

Contrarily, the setting of the anonymous Middle Korean song, "Winter Night," is a tempestuous night that scatters sleet and snow, the fit metaphor of the speaker's state of mind. Sleepless with longing, tossing and turning, the speaker asks:

> The sleet falls thick and fast;
> Do you come, false love, who made me
> Lie awake for half the night?
> Are you crossing the pass
> Where the wind cries in the bushes?
>
> *Fires of hell or thunderbolts*
> *Will soon consume my body.*
> *Fires of hell or thunderbolts*
> *Will soon consume my body.*
>
> On what wild mountain shall I seek you?
> I will do anything, anything you say,
> The this and the that, whatever you ask of me.
> I will follow you anywhere, I swear.

The enigmatic second stanza may have been a refrain: the flames of her passion scorch her like fires of hell or thunderbolts, her carnal desire provokes the infernal or celestial punishment, or she negates self through an excess of sense delight.[101] The cries of her heart, or rather the dramatization of the hypothetical situation, are nevertheless energetic and convincing.

In the poem sent to her distant lover in the capital, Hongnang, a famous *kisaeng* and dancer of the sixteenth century, employs the traditional symbol of parting, the willow spray, but gives it a personal touch:

I send you branches of the willow—
Plant them, my Lord, to be admired,
Outside your bedroom window.
Perhaps the night rain will make them bud:
Think, then, that it is your girl,
That has come to you!

Night's fecund rain will revive the broken branch, which is endowed with the magical power of her enduring devotion. The third stanza of "Ab la dolchor del temps novel" ["In the sweetness of the budding spring"] by Duke William IX of Aquitaine (1071–1126/7), seventh Count of Poitou, offers a striking parallel:

La nostr'amor vai enaissi
Com la branca de l'albespi
Qu'esta sobre l'arbre tremblan,
La nuoit, a la ploja ez al gel,
Tro l'endeman, que.l sols s'espan
Per las fueillas verz e.l ramel.

(Our love affair will be reborn
Like a branch upon a hawthorn
Which, trembling over the trunk, will sway
At nighttime in the hail and rain,
But come the dawn, the sun's bright rays
Make leaf and branch all green again.) [102]

"A hawthorn branch," part of a long simile (*com* . . .), required the sun's bright rays to revive. The sun may, as has been pointed out, have a weightier symbolism here, in line with the poem's design of contrasting the idealized and sensual elements. The Korean willow sent by Hongnang, on the other hand, will need only the night rain to bud; and the total identification of the heartbroken lady with the willow spray engenders a more poignant tone.

In the next poem Hwang Chin-i wishes to prolong the night. The speaker desires not the protection of darkness but the claim of subjective time. Befitting the most subjective of all human experiences, the course of time depends upon the speaker's attitude toward and comprehension of the nature of love, and it is the degree and quality of intensity that can conquer the sun or the moon. Night is time, as was the sea (or river) elsewhere:

I cut in two
A long November night, and
Place half under the coverlet,
Sweet-scented as a spring breeze.
And when he comes, I shall take it out,
Unroll it inch by inch, to stretch the night.

This recalls *Pervigilium Veneris* (*Vigil of Venus,* 56), the anonymous spring poem written sometime between the second and fourth centuries: "destinenda tota nox est, perviglanda canticis" (we must hold the whole night back, keeping vigil with our songs).[103]

Frustrated by the cruel mistress, the poetic persona in the following poem, after a tormented night, has waited for the coming of the cheerless dawn hoping that light will disperse his "deep troubled self":

A rain came overnight;
Pomegranates are in full bloom.
Having rolled up a crystal screen
By the square lotus pond,
Can I unravel this deep troubled self—
Ruled by whom? Who knows?

Shin Hŭm (1566–1628)

He cannot trace the source of his frustrations; he does not know who rules his heart.

VI

Love poems on the dream motif take various forms: some are written from the recollection of an emotion; some are stereotypes, tending to be formulaic; others are wish-fulfillments in which the speaker indulges in false delights. One such classical prototype, according to Sung Yü, is the amorous dream encounter of King Huai of Ch'u with the goddess of Mount Wu, who appeared to him in the forms of clouds and rain. In Korean poetry, however, such amatory nymphs or specters seldom make an appearance.[104] In Chinese and Korean stories bearing in their titles the word "dream," however, the dream motif is used as a device to launch a story on its way or to cloak the true intention of the work. In the *Dream of the Red Chamber* and the *Nine Cloud Dream,* a Korean romance by Kim Man-jung (1637–1692), dream stands for the wonders and sorrows of the red dust.

The comparison of the experience of love with dream is often a fit metaphor of the conflict in the mind of the lover, where pains of love coexist with joy, and of the ephemeral quality of carnal love. In "Hua fei hua," we recall, Po Chü-i compared a brief moment of enchantment to "a spring dream," a painful yet precious memory of the past. In another *tz'u,* to the tune of "Memories of Fairy Grace," by Li Ts'un-hsü (885–926), the speaker portrays the poignant moment of parting with the characteristic simile:[105]

Feasted once
        in deep peach glades
one song
    phoenix to phoenix
    danced and sang
I recall
    —how long!
            saying goodbye to her
Tears mingled together
            hand on arm to the door
        like a dream
        like a dream
faded moon
fallen blossoms
        thick mist
            over all

Tarquin, in *The Rape of Lucrece,* reflects on the evanescence of amorous delight:

What win I, if I gain the thing I seek?
A dream, a breath, a froth of fleeting joy.
Who buys a minute's mirth to wail a week?
Or sells eternity to get a toy?

Joys of passion are fleeting as the twinkling of an eye. The act of love, as Shakespeare says in sonnet 129, can be a bliss, but once over, it is regretted; before, it is a joy proposed, afterwards only a dream, at once hateful and irresistible.

A bliss in proof, and [prov'd, a] very woe;
Before, a joy propos'd, behind a dream.

Dream is therefore a fit metaphor for the lover who strives to seize what is impalpable and to express the haunting perturbations and paradoxes.

Myŏngok, a famous *kisaeng* from Suwŏn, knows that dream visits are "only a dream." Nevertheless she entreats her beloved to appear in dreams. Kakinomoto Hitomaro echoes the same feeling (XI.2418):

Ikanaran	How named is the god
Na wo ou kami ni	Whom I would entreat with offerings,
Tamuke seba	That I may meet my love,
Waga mou imo wo	If but in dream?[106]
Ime nidani min.	

Did Petrarch not visit Laura in sleep where she announced her death, and did Laura, after her death, not continue to visit him in his dreams? And did Sidney not declare that as soon as sleep closed his eyes, "The first that straight my fancie's error brings/ Unto my mind, is *Stella*'s image, wrought/ By *Love*'s owne selfe"? (*Astrophil and Stella,* 38.5–7) If there is no other way to fulfill my desire, Myŏngok seems to say, give me an eternal dream:

They say dream visits
are "only a dream."
My longing to see him
is destroying me.
Where else
do I see him but in dreams?
Darling, come to me
even if it be in dreams:
let me see you, let me
see you time and again.

Such nocturnal life resulting from the pangs of absence was also a troubadour commonplace, as in the following verse epistle by Folquet de Romans.[107]

Que la nueit, quan soi endurmiz,
s'en vai a vos mos esperiz;
donna, ar ai eu tan de ben
que quan resvelh e m'en soven,
per pauc no.m volh los olhz crebar
quar s'entremetton del velhar;
e vauc vos per lo leich cerchan,
e quan no.us trob, reman ploran;
qu'eu volria toz temps dormir,
qu'en sonjan vos pogues tenir.

(For at night, when I am asleep, my spirit goes forth to you;
lady, then such happiness is mine that when I wake and memory returns,
I scarce believe my eyes, for they struggle to wake; and I search
through the bed for you, and when I find you not, I abide weeping;
for I would like to sleep ever so that I might hold you in my dream.)

To Wei Chuang (858?–910), waking from a happy dream brings "grief too much to bear":

Tune: "The Taoist Priestess"

Last night at midnight,
By the pillow I saw her clearly in my dream—
We talked a lot—
Her face, unchanged, like a peach blossom,
Her eyebrows lowered like a willow frond.

Half shy, half joyful,
She wanted to leave but lingered, lingered.
Now awake, I know it was a dream,
My grief is too much to bear.[108]

A similar sentiment is found in Ono no Komachi, who regrets waking up and losing the image of her lover. She would prefer perpetual night, if it brings about a reunion:

Omoitsutsu	Thinking about him
Nureba ya hito no	I slept, only to have him
Mietsuramu	Appear before me—
Yume to shiriseba	Had I known it was a dream,
Samezaramashi wo.	I should never have wakened.[109]

The speaker in the next poem by Saigyō (1118–1190) knows that his wish for perpetual dream meetings can lead him to the "darkness of everlasting night," the opposite of salvation. Still, he prefers the bond of earthly love to sacred love.

Au to mishi	We met in love,
Sono yo no yume no	And would that I should never wake
Sameda are na	From such a night of dreams,
Nagaki neburi wa	In spite of the ignorant darkness
Ukaru bekeredo.	With its everlasting sleep of vain desire.[110]

To the anonymous Japanese poet in the following, waking is so sad she would rather not dream of the beloved.

Yume yo yume	Dreams, listen, my dreams!
Koishiki hito ni	Do not bring me together
Aimisu na	With the man I love—
Samete no nochi wa	When once I have awakened
Wabishikarikeri.	It makes me feel so lonely.[111]

Kim Sang-yong (1561–1637) also realizes that love is as deceitful as dream. His lady's promise to visit him in a dream vision cannot be materialized, for torments of love deny him a visionary experience:

Love is a deceit—
She does not love me.
She says

She comes to me in dream:
It is a lie.
All night awake and restless,
Where shall I see her, in what dream?[112]

The next anonymous Korean poem censures dream for failing to wake her when the deceitful lover returns. The boundary between dream and reality has been abolished, and past and present, knowledge and ignorance, love and pain coexist in a continuous flow:

O dream, foolish dream, think now,
You sent him away when he came.
Better to waken than dream he leaves me.
But ah, to wake and find him gone—
Henceforth, wake me, shake me awake,
Having seized him if he came.

Yi Myŏng-han (1595–1645) develops the conceit of the path of dreams (one of the major topics in Japanese love poetry) that his frequent dream visits to his lady have worn the stone path flat. Was it because society declared that physical union was impossible in reality? Or was it a visit to the dead mistress? The track upon which the speaker advances and withdraws, retracing his own footsteps, is a fit symbol for the denial of fulfillment and the persistence of pain. The last two lines are realistic and they drive home the insubstantiality both of dream and love:

If my dreams
Left their footprints on the road
The path under my love's window
Would be worn down, though it is stone.
In the country of dream
No roads endure, no traces remain.

One of the interesting features in Japanese examples on this topic stems from the Japanese fear of vulgar tittle-tattle. One must therefore exercise utmost caution even in the world of dreams, as in the following poems by Fujiwara no Toshiyuki and Ono no Komachi, where the lover looks, hesitates, and shrinks from men's eyes:

Suminoe no	To Suminoe shore
Kishi ni yoru nami	Waves advance across the sea:
Yoru sae ya	Must I see him
Yume no kayoiji	Even in the night look round
Hitome yokuramu.	And hesitate upon the path of dreams?[113]

Utsutsu ni wa	In the waking world
Sa mo koso arame	Such caution may be well advised:
Yume ni sae	But even in dreams
Hitome o moru to	To see him shrinking from men's eyes—
Miru ga wabishisa.	This is wretchedness itself.

To the conceit of the path of dreams Ki no Tsurayuki adds the dew-tear analogy. The lover on the path of dreams gets his sleeves wet from the dewdrops, tears of longing:

Yumeji ni mo	On the path of dreams,
Tsuyu ya okuramu	Perhaps there too the dewdrops form,
Yomosugara	For these sleeves that hastened
Kayoeru sode no	All night long upon that road
Hijite kawakanu.	Are soaked, and will not dry.

Here are more Japanese examples:

Kado tatete	Since I had shut the gate
To mo sashitaruwo	And locked the door,
Izuku yuka	Whence did you, dear one, enter
Imo ga irikite	To appear in my dream?
Ime ni mietsuru.	

Kado tatete	Though you had shut the gate
To wa sashitaredo	And locked the door,
Nusubito no	I must have come to you in your dream
Horeru ana yori	Through the hole cut by a thief.[114]
Irite mieken.	

Hito no mite	Tonight I am coming
Kototogame senu	To visit you in your dream,
Ime ni ware	And none will see and question me—
Koyoi itaran	Be sure to leave your door unlocked![115]
Yado sasuna yume.	

The next poems, exchanged after a night of love between an Imperial Huntsman (Ariwara no Narihira, 825–880) and the Ise shrine Virgin, offer typical examples of classical Japanese love poetry on the dream motif. These occur in the sixty-ninth episode from the *Tales of Ise.* The first is by the Virgin.

Kimi ya koshi	Did you come to me,
Ware ya yukikemu	Or was it I who went to you,
Omōezu	I cannot even think:
Yume ka utsutsu ka	Was it a dream, or was it real?
Nete ka samete ka.	Were we sleeping, or awake?

Kakikurasu	In deepening
Kokoro no yami ni	Darkness of the heart I wander,
Madoiniki	Lost in bafflement:
Yume utsutsu to wa	Let one wise in worldly love decide
Yohito sadame yo.	What is dream and what reality.[116]

Finally, instead of evoking the assistance of dream vision which might endure forever, another miracle is sought by the forsaken lover: metamorphosis—in dream or after death. Earlier examples in Egypt and elsewhere are either associated with love-worship or erotic wish-fulfillment: in Egyptian love songs, the speaker wishes to be his lady's negro girl—so that he can view the whole of his love's body—a washer-woman, a ring, or simply her old dress. In the Greek *Anacreontea* (XXII):

I wish I were your mirror, that you might always gaze on me, I wish I were your dress, that you might always wear me. I'd like to be water to wash your body, perfume to anoint you, lady, the breastband on your bosom and the pearl on your throat, and even your sandal, if you tread me underfoot.[117]

Earlier we have discussed the praise of a beauty that begins the Chinese rhymeprose on the theme of "Stilling the Passions." The poems are noteworthy for the speaker's wishes for a metamorphosis to achieve a union. The general formula is, "I wish I were . . . but it wouldn't last," as in the following earlier examples:[118]

I imagine I might be the powder on your face
But soiled by dust its radiance is gone.
Chang Heng (78–139)

I imagine being the vibrant reed in your mouth,
But the notes are solitary and not worth listening to.
Ts'ai Yung (132–192)

In a version by T'ao Ch'ien (365–427), which shows a considerable advance over the earlier models, such conceits receive fuller treatment. The speaker wishes to be the collar of his lady's dress, the girdle of her skirt, the gloss on her hair, her penciled eyebrow, the reed for her mat, the silk for her slipper, her daytime shadow, nighttime candle, bamboo for her fan, and finally wood of the wu-t'ung tree for her lute. The poem ends with the same conventional formula: "I level all cares and cling to integrity,/ Lodge my aspirations at the world's end." Such elements as the superiority and inaccessibility of a woman, the vertical, not horizontal and mutual, relationship, with little action, and the emphasis on the state of emotional suspension and frustration may recall the medieval chanson, but the chanson lovers, unlike the Chinese ones, at least look toward the future with desire and hope.[119]

In the *Man'yō* poems, the poet wishes that his love were a bracelet (IX:1766); the second wishes to be the cloud (XIV.3510); and the third to be a tree or a stone (IV.722):

Wagimoko wa Kushiro ni aranan Hidarite no Waga oku no te ni Makite inamashiwo.	Would that my love were a bracelet! Trying her to my left arm, I would start my journey. Furu Tamuke
Misora yuku Kumo nimogamona Kyō yukite Imo ni kotodoi Asu kaerikon.	O that I were the cloud That sails the sky! Today I'd go and talk to my wife; Tomorrow I'd come back again. Anonymous
Kakubakari Koitsutsu arazuwa Iwaki nimo Naramashimonowo Mono mowazushite.	Rather than that I should thus pine for you, Would I had been transmuted Into a tree or a stone, Nevermore to feel the pangs of love. Ōtomo Yakamochi[120]

In the following Korean examples, one wishes to be a cricket so that he can wake the lady from her sleep of oblivion, and another wants to be metamorphosed into a cuckoo in order to tell her all his woes:

If my lovesick dream became a cricket
In the long, long autumn night,
It would enter my love's room
And wake her from her sleep,
The sound sleep that has forgotten me.

Pak Hyo-gwan (c. 1850–1880)

I have lived anxious and hurt.
Enough, enough, I would rather die,
Become the spirit of the cuckoo,
When the moon is on the bare hills,
And sing with bitter tears,
Sing to him my forbidden hopes.

Anonymous

In Pak Hyo-gwan's poem, as in the anonymous *Man'yō* poem above (XIV.3510), the lyric persona wishes to bridge the spatial distance, suggesting a movement from one world to another where he will be with his beloved, as in Bernart de Ventadorn's *Tant ai mo cor ple de joya* ["My heart's so full of joy," 49–52], in which the speaker wishes to be a swallow so that he can fly into the lover's chamber:

Ai Deus! car no sui ironda,	O God! why am I not a swallow
que voles per l'aire	so I could fly through the air
e vengues de noih prionda	and go in the depths of night
lai dins so repaire?	into her chamber?[121]

The third Korean example is by Kim Sam-hyŏn (c. 1675–1700), where the speaker wishes to enter, mingled in wine, his beloved's body, not only to marvel at her interior but to "set her heart aright."

Let my soul dissolve in her wine
And flow down within her.
I'll make nine turns,
Visiting every nook and cranny.
I'll then set her heart aright
That has preferred another to me.

Sonnet 63 by Barnabe Barnes (1569?–1609), who repeats "poore Petrarch's long deceased woes," comes to mind:

Or that sweet wine, which down her throat doth trickle,
To kiss her lips, and lie next at her heart,
Run through her veins, and pass by Pleasure's part![122]

Contrary to Barnes's artful and flippant display of conceit, Kim Samhyŏn's poem has a clear motive and gives the illusion of telling a convincing story about a deceitful woman.

In the story of the metamorphosis of Alcyone and Ceyx into halcyons, Alcyone, who is called *fidissima* (loyalest of wives, XI. 415), through her conjugal devotion attains a triumphant metamorphosis.[123] But such happy transformation and rewarded love are reserved for folk tales and romances. The thwarted lover's desire to pass from the realm of man into the realm of nature as a cricket or a cuckoo is hardly a happy ending. But to them love was all of life, and their desire for metamorphosis is poetic inevitability. All these poems on dream and metamorphosis drive home the tragic dilemma of man, torn between a longing for and an attempt to seek liberation from love.

VII

The disintegration in the eighteenth century of the Confucian cosmic and moral order which had dominated the world of letters prompted a flourishing of popular songs in Korea. The growth of new poetry, together with the rise of the novel, drama, genre painting, and popular entertainment, were related to the rise of the middle class and changes in approach to life. A new frame of reference for this popular poetry of folk origin was man himself, his spontaneous approaches to reality and his search for the possibilities of fulfillment. Most of this new poetry is frank and humorous, often satirical and burlesque. I will cite one example:

> "Heat for sale, ladies, heat,
> Early heat, late heat,
> Several year old heat . . .
> On dog days under the bright moon,
> Eight limbs entwined on a wooden bed,
> Five viscera burn with fever,
> Heavy breaths, beads of sweat . . .
> I sell that sweltering heat.
> Or on a long November night,
> Under the thick quilt on a warm floor,
> Two bodies turned into one,
> Hands and feet cramped and aflame,
> Throat parched with thirst,
> Calling for a bowl of cold water . . .
> That heat is also on sale,
> But it's up to you, ladies, to choose."
> "O vendor with many wares,
> Who'll refuse the two kinds of heat?
> So if that's what you have,
> That's the kind I need."

Is it a satire on newly rising merchants and moneylenders and the materialist view of life that dominated certain classes of people? Longer poems of folk origin, like this one, often indulge in cataloguing. A poem about opening of windows in the heart in order to dispel the fire and smoke of love enumerates four kinds of windows, two kinds of hinges, and a type of metal lockbar. Other satirical poems have as their objects an old woman who seduces a handsome youth, an apostate nun, or a mother-in-law with a questionable past.

I have surveyed some types of East Asian love poetry, focusing on certain thematic patterns and principal images. The combinations and permutations of topics are many, as they are in the West, but certain Western types such as the *scala d'amore* or the religious *alba* received scant attention in East Asia. Equally striking is the conspicuous absence—or relative neglect—of such topics as *carpe diem, carpe florem,* praise of the lady's body as landscape or garden (Campion's "There is a garden in her face" would be a monstrosity in East Asia), the eternizing conceit, and antipraise.[124] Love was seldom conceived as a mode of knowledge or of education—there was no East Asian Plato, Capellanus, or Castiglione. Nor was there a tradition and convention to purge love of sensuality, to endow it with spirituality, or to regard it as the ideal mode of behavior. Conflicts between love and honor or love and duty were reserved for the romance—comedy of love—and drama, owing perhaps to the brevity of East Asian lyric forms which did not allow an exploration of such complexities. Furthermore, some major poets in China and Korea, such as Tu Fu and Yun Sŏn-do, seldom wrote about love.

Love between the sexes that did not involve procreation was incompatible with Confucian society, and conflicts between desires for self-fulfillment and social convention were a recurrent theme in the romances and novels. "In mutual pleasure and in common will/ Resides the love of two fine lovers."[125] Passionate love outside the marriage bond was usually looked upon as subversive of public morality, if it did not involve a courtesan, entertainer, servant, or slave girl. Therein lies the reason why authors of love poems in Korea were female entertainers or anonymous poets. Refusing to recognize the differences of rank, they sought to proclaim the triumph of true love. At times, their wish for transformation of a secret love into something more open and official cost them dearly, as it did Dido in the fourth *Aeneid.*[126] Their love was bound to be tragic, because it had to be unfulfilled.

One possible reason for the minor place love lyrics occupy in the poetical hierarchy of China and Korea may have been Confucian decorum and morality. Viewed as a private affair, love was deemed unworthy of serious concern by men of letters. Love lyrics of the literati are usually finger exercises or imitations of anonymous folk poetry, deemphasizing passion and fulfillment. We tend to remember them not because they loved, but because they left lukewarm verse. Moving love lyrics in China and Korea occur outside the main stream of literature, in China in the anonymous *yüeh-fu* songs of the Southern dynasties and in *tz'u,* in Korea in folk poems in the vernacular. Some of these, especially Middle Korean love lyrics, like Liang palace poetry on the neglected lady, often became the objects of Confucian inquisition in the fifteenth century.[127] Confucian strictures on passionate desire and fulfillment also resulted in the poverty of erotic imagery. Except for the image of "clouds and rain" in China and "spring breeze" in Korea, metaphors for love-making are rare. Physical aspects of love were equally restricted in Japan, except for woman's hair.

These factors must have contributed to the persistent tendency in Korean love poetry—an indirect, retrospective stance, with emphasis on parting, desertion, separation, and neglect, and the resulting physical and mental anguish. Even in Heian Japan where women occupied a higher position than their sisters in East Asia, poems of separation and desertion are staples. Indeed, the sadness of separation was thought to be more poetical than fulfillment. Inspired by Buddhism, Japanese poets viewed passion ("entanglement in desire") as "darkness of the heart"—an error, confusion, or fleeting dream.[128] The fusion of dream and reality, so prevalent in East Asian love poetry, seems to indicate that dream is a device of authentication to "establish the presumed reality and truth" of experience. It may also have been a device to avoid public censure or, more important, to "create a new unreality of the real so that the real could be brought into art in a manner proper to the illusion of art."[129] Love is so real and intangible, so irresistible and unreliable that it is viewed by the East Asian poet as part of the essential human inconstancy, insecurity, and suffering.[130] In spite of a relatively limited repertory of themes, however, Korean women and folk poets successfully explored the latent possibilities in every type and motif known to them, often revitalizing the language of love.

4 FRIENDSHIP

IN EAST ASIA friendship is treated with far more reverence, passion, and idealism than is romantic love. The harmonious, virtuous relationship between man and man—its constancy and equality, affection and devotion—found more expression in literature than love between man and woman. "To the European poet the relation between man and woman is a thing of supreme importance and mystery. To the Chinese, it is something commonplace, obvious—a need of the body, not a satisfaction of the *emotions*. These he reserves entirely for friendship."[1] I cannot agree that East Asian poetry excludes love, but there is probably more poetry on friendship than on love in China and Korea. Romantic love is fickle, inconstant, irrational, and disruptive; it seizes, as Montaigne remarks, "only by one corner."[2] Friendship, on the other hand, embraces the whole man and engages the whole person. Thus the matter-of-factness often evident in the love lyrics by Chinese and Korean literati disappears in the poetry of friendship, which is often couched in the language of love, making it difficult at times to distinguish the boundary between the two.

The Confucian classics are replete with famous friendships in legend and history, and standard encyclopaedias and story collections assign a whole section to the subject.[3] Collected works of men of letters in China and Korea are mostly put together by the subject's friends, who also wrote, among other things, prefaces and postfaces, accounts of conduct (*hsing-chuang*), tomb inscriptions (*chih*), epitaphs (*pei*), invocations used at the spring and autumn sacrifices (*chi-wen*), appreciations (*tsan*), and elegies (*wan*).[4] The tributes to the dead belong properly to the literature of praise, but the examples attest to the role of friends in society and culture. The pervasive influence of Confucian thought, which glorified faithful friendship as one of the five universal ways of man,[5] coupled with social conditions in China and Korea, where women were not equals of men and marriage was a legal institution for procreation, had much to do with this phenomenon. Seldom, if ever, are women invited (unlike in Epicurus) to join a circle of friends. Here the view of the Chinese and Korean literati was that of Montaigne, who believed that the "ordinary capacity of women is inadequate for that communion and fellowship which is the nurse of this sacred bond; nor does their soul seem firm enough to endure the strain of so tight and durable a knot."[6] It is on the essential value of friendship, as distinct from other forms of love, that Western and East Asian philosophers and writers seem to agree.

I

Poem 165 in the *Book of Songs* celebrates the duty and value of friendship. From the Son of Heaven to the plain multitude, everyone needs friends for his perfection:

Seeing then that even a bird
Searches for its mate's voice,
How much more must man
Needs search out friends and kin . . .[7]

The first stanza establishes, following the *hsing* technique, a parallel between the birds leaving the dark valley to mount the high tree in search of their mates and man searching out friends ("Ying, ying cry the birds,/ Leave the dark valley,/ Mount to the high tree./ 'Ying' they cry,/ Each searching its mate's voice.") .[8] The fifth stanza contains a moral: a loss of man's innate virtue will bring disorder and division. The following *sijo,* one of the moral verses by the sixteenth-century Korean poet Chŏng Ch'ŏl, voices a similar concern:

No one is more trustworthy than a friend
Among those unrelated by blood.
He points out my mistakes
And urges me to virtuous deeds.
How can I make myself a man
Without a tried, devoted friend?

A fuller formulation on the subject is found in the *Analects.* Friendship can exist only among the good, for the master declared that a gentleman "must refuse the friendship of all who are not like him" (I.8; IX.24) .[9] Only those who have taken goodness *(jen)* as their abode and standard and whose aim is the cultivation of goodness can establish a reciprocity of equals (XV.9) .[10] Disciples of Tzu-hsia, when asked by Tzu-chang, answer: "Go with those with whom it is proper to go;/ Keep at a distance those whom it is proper to keep at a distance." Tzu-chang offers a rebuttal: "A gentleman reverences those that excel, but 'find room' for all" (XIX.3) .[11] Elsewhere (XVI, 4), Confucius endorses three sorts of friends who are profitable: the upright, the truthful, and the well-informed. Three harmful friends include the flatterer, those who are meek and compromise with principles, and those who talk cleverly.[12] The upright and faithful are of good faith with their friends, true to their word (V.25; VII.24),[13] and as companions on the path to virtue, they embody faithfulness, the single virtue emphasized throughout the *Analects*. Indeed, "the foundation of that steadfastness and loyalty for which we are looking in friendship is trust, for nothing endures that cannot be trusted."[14] The well-informed are men of education and culture, as Master Tseng says in the *Analects* (XII.24): "The gentleman by his culture collects friends about him, and through these friends promotes Goodness."[15] "A friend is an aid to virtue."[16] Likeness of character and excellence attract one another, not fame and name, utility or advantage, for the friendship of pleasure and utility is inferior to that of virtue and character. The Confucian view that virtue is the basis of friendship and the sine qua non of its preservation resembles the Greek and Roman outlook.[17] Forming a faction based on selfish interest is therefore rightly scorned in the *Book of Changes* (Hexagram 13, "Fellowship with Men"), factionalism that plagued the political order in China and Korea.

Contrarily, the three harmful friends—the flatterer, the opportunist, and the clever talker—are foes of friendship in moral lives, both in East Asia and in the West. Flattery and clever talk are characteristic of small men, according to the *Li chi* or *Collected Ritual,* which likens the friendship of a gentleman to water and that of a small man to sweet wine. The former leads to perfection, the latter to ruin.[18] Indeed, no danger is more deadly to friendship than servility, sycophancy, and flattery.[19]

In addition to the discretion required in the choice of friends, the master enjoined his disciples to inform their friends loyally, guide them discreetly (XII.23),[20] and be "critical and exacting with regard to their conduct" (XIII.28).[21] Frank admonitions and corrections are "one of the chief duties of friendship"[22] but should be offered in a "spirit of charity."[23] Erring friends should be guided gently and discreetly, for excessive scolding "leads to estrangement" (IV.26).[24] Even among old friends, one should "maintain the same scrupulous courtesy," a virtue amply embodied in Yen P'ing-chung, Confucius' example of a good friend (V.16).[25] Faithful and trustworthy, "if one has not seen one's friend but hears rumors to his prejudice, one does not believe them."

> Rumour is a pipe
> Blown by surmises, jealousies, conjectures,
> And of so easy and so plain a stop
> That the blunt monster with uncounted heads,
> The still-discordant war'ring multitude,
> Can play upon it.
>
> (2 *Henry IV,* intro. 15–20)

Suspicion and calumny are unthinkable in a true friend, who "keeps his friend straight when he is near, praises him when he is far, participates in his happiness, and is ready to die for him in his distress."[26]

Letters and poems to distant friends, which occupy a great part of the collected works of Chinese and Korean literati, testify that friendship transcends distance and vicissitudes. Friends need not live together—although some thought otherwise—but the pain of separation and the longing for reunion are so intense we are led to believe that they preferred the presence of friends to solitude, whether self-imposed or enforced. In some of the moving poems and epistles (which valued "epistolary presence" of friends), poets also poured out their view of life and their moral, philosophical, and aesthetic stance. Some are protestations of innocence or vindications of moral persuasion. Some are celebrations of the joys of the contemplative life. Some are invitations to cultivated leisure, to discover new values, and to share the beauties of nature and delights of country vegetables and wine. But others are consolation for the victims of fickle fortune or a pledge of loyalty in times of need. True friends remain steadfast in adversity, which is the test of friendship, and one who abandons his wife and children to help out his friend or follow him to death is a recurrent subject in folk tales and stories.[27] Therefore,

> . . . when two people are at one in their inmost hearts,
> They shatter even the strength of iron or of bronze.
> And when two people understand each other in their inmost
> hearts,
> Their words are sweet and strong, like the fragrance of orchids.[28]

Such friendship is "inconceivable to anyone who has not tasted it,"[29] and its essence could probably be best expressed through the *adynata,* as in the following "Oaths of Friendship":

> Shang Ya!
> I want to be your friend
> For ever and ever without break or decay.
> When the hills are all flat

And the rivers are all dry,
When it lightens and thunders in winter,
When it rains and snows in summer,
When Heaven and Earth mingle—
Not till then will I part from you.[30]

Such were the views of friendship in East Asia, fully sanctioned by the Confucian classics and emphasized by history and literature as a cultural force. The reverberations of the human, moral, and literary dimensions of friendship are constantly rediscovered and sung in poetry, often as compensation for the whips and scorns of Time. Passion for friends, man's search for individuality and freedom, selectivity, and dialogue in themselves were seldom disparaged by the Establishment, which for all its authoritarian nature never viewed them as secretive or subversive as long as they were not a threat. Some unfortunate ones were felled mercilessly, because they were labeled "seditious," scapegoats of political maneuver. Glorification of true friendship, I believe, was a built-in safety valve in authoritarian society, permitting man to grow in warmth and wisdom, to discover the mysteries of mutuality, and to challenge the tyranny of Time.

II

Waley once remarked that it would not be an exaggeration to say that half the poems in the Chinese language are poems of parting or separation.[31] All learned men in China and Korea aspired to official careers and were subjected to changes of fortune and policy. Promotion and demotion as well as the disgrace of exile necessitated separation. Also, the vagaries of court life sent officials home as a gesture of moral protest, a renunciation of worldly career, or a return to nature. The vastness of Chinese territory, the hazards of travel, the difficulties of communication, and the importance of the family in traditional society are cited as contributory to the outburst of grief. Will I see him again? What if a war should break out or a pestilence should sweep the country? A place requiring a day's journey is described as "the edge of the world," and the same topos persists in Korea, a country many times smaller than China. The number of send-off poems in both countries attests to the importance not so much of the rituals of parting as of the social and psychological dimensions of friendship itself.

The times depicted for parting are often conventionally given as autumn and winter, the seasons of decay and death, but the chilly sky and water do not deter the traveler. The anguish of the speaker is mirrored by nature, which mirrors his state of mind:

The river darkens, rain about to fall;
Waves turn white as the wind comes up.
Ho Sun (d. 518)[32]

The birds' anguished cry in the north wind—
Lang Shih-yüan[33]

The following poem by Yi Chŏng-bo (1693–1766) succinctly offers the reason for the tearful parting in autumn:

Man's greatest sorrow is the sorrow of parting
That wrenches our soul.
Among tall sweet grasses and green willows,
Parting on a lone bridge
Darkens your heart.
When a goose cries and fallen leaves sough,
Who won't shed tears at my song?

The solitary boat "becomes one with the blue sky," says Li Po in "Seeing Meng Hao-jan Off to Kuang-ling": "Now, only the Long River flowing to the sky's end."[34] Chŏng Chi-sang (d. 1135) says his tears are sources of the Taedong River:

After a rain on the long dike grasses are thick.
With a sad song I send you off to Namp'o.
When will the Taedong River cease to flow?
Year after year my tears will swell the waves.

As in love lyrics, the sea or river is separation, and "the endless white clouds"—dark or drifting clouds or steep mountains elsewhere—are another symbol to underscore the vastness of distance and the enormity of sorrow. The ship might on occasion suggest the ship of life that braves, for example, "Rockes, or Remoraes" (Donne's "To Sir Henry Wotton"), but seldom, as far as I know, is it employed in Korea as a metaphor of the ship of poetry, with poetic efforts likened to sailing.

"Parting is a time for thoughts,"[35] declares Yin Shih (c. 600), although "Human parting is not new" ("Seeing a Friend Off on a Long Journey" by Tu Fu).[36] The sorrow of separation is known only to a friend:

But if you have never endured far separation,
How can you know the yearning for an absent friend?
Chang Hua (232–300)[37]

We are like "wind-driven reeds" (Yin Shih), buffeted by winds and waves. Some like Lu Lun (b. 748) groan and grieve:

We weep, facing each other with no word,
What can we expect from this world of wind and dust?[38]

Meng Hao-jan (689–740) accepts the life of solitude:

All I can do is keep to my lonely solitude,
And just close the gate of my old garden.
"Farewell to Wang Wei"[39]

Tu Fu (712–770), in "Bidding Li Hsien Godspeed at T'an-chou," puts it in a manner which by his time was almost a commonplace: "Now the cold clouds and cold chrysanthemums will double my loneliness without your company."[40] Most, like Meng Hao-jan, accept the inevitability of parting and offer as expressions of affection "a single twig of spring"[41] (a plum branch; Lu K'ai, fl. 400–450) or a twig of willow —the traditional parting gift—or nature itself, the best compliment to a friend, for he comprehends the value of such a gift:

A poor friend has no other parting present
Than the blue hills—your companion in your journey.[42]

Wang Wei's "To Meng the Sixth on His Return to Hsiang-yang" exemplifies a send-off poem with admonition, the first of Menander's three kinds of propemptikon. Menander's view that this category illustrates the teacher-pupil relation will not hold, for advice is offered also from equal to equal. Meng, who has led a life of withdrawal, is probably on his way to accept a position, but Wang Wei is averse to Meng's move. Having tasted the repose in nature, how could he think of fortune making? A poet-friend silenced is as good as dead. Hence the last line, "Why then aspire to glory with your literary talents?"[43]

Advice to prefer contemplation to action, nature to society, is a perennial subject in Chinese and Korean poetry, an indication of why the themes of friendship are closely allied with those of the seasons and nature and of withdrawal. Retirement poetry is very old in East Asia and the West, and though it is not the direct concern here, we may recall two epistles by Horace, one addressed to Aristius Fuscus (I.10; written in 21 B.C.) and another to Scaeva (I.17), whose contents would have been perfectly acceptable to Chinese and Korean poets. What Horace asks for is not wafers or honeyed cakes, but plain bread, unhurried pleasure, and sleeping until sunshine. Wishing to "live in accordance with nature" (I.10.12) and be happy with what he has, Horace declares that "he has not lived amiss who from birth to death has passed unknown" ("nec vixit male, qui natus moriensque fefellit"; I.17.10).[44] Donne's verse epistle, "To Sir Henry Wotton," concerns the relative values of life at court, in the city, or in the country, part of a contemporary literary debate in the circle of the Earl of Essex. Like the snail, Wotton is told, the wise man takes refuge in himself, preserves his own little world intact, and lives a life free of all evils:

> Be then thine owne home, and in thy selfe dwell;
> Inne any where, continuance maketh hell.
> And seeing the snaile, which every where doth rome,
> Carrying his owne house still, still is at home,
> Follow (for he is easie pac'd) this snaile,
> Bee thine owne Palace, or the world's thy Gaole.[45]

In all these examples, such Menanderian topoi as expressions of indignation with the traveler for his heartlessness or attempts to talk him out of going (except for bidding him to drink one more cup[46]) with a list of anticipated dangers (you are going to a tundra, a journey on untrodden terrain is no fun, the bandits will waylay you, the country folk will not stand your eccentricities) are rare.[47] Also, seldom does one find a friend saying, I will follow you to the end of the world, as here:

> feremus, et te vel per Alpium iuga
> inhospitalem et Caucasum
> vel Occidentis usque ad ultimum sinum
> forti sequemur pectore.

(Bear them we will, and whether o'er the ridges of the Alps and savage Caucasus, or to the very farthest corners of the West, thee will we follow with stout heart.)

Horace, *Epodes,* I.11–14[48]

> cum quo Rhipaeos possim conscendere montes
> ulteriusque domos vadere Memnonias;

(With you I would be ready to climb the Scythian mountains, or explore the distant lands of Africa.)

Propertius, I.6.3–4[49]

III

Longing for the absent friend is intensified by the characteristic sights and sounds of the seasons—whether serene or tumultuous—or the sight of such mementos as the black gauze hat, rumors about him, or the memories of happy days together. On a moonlit spring night, Wang Ch'ang-ling (698–755?) imagines his friend sitting by a river and humming a plaintive eastern song. No matter that myriad leagues separate us, the wind will carry the fragrance of orchids and azaleas, and in it we are one in the appreciation of spring. Wei Ying-wu (b. 736) recalls the flowers of the year before and declares that "Spring only brings me grief and fatigue" ("Sent to Li Tan and Yüan Hsi").[50] In "The Retired Official Yüan's High Pavilion," Tu Mu (803–852), on his visit to his friend's high pavilion, asks:

> Who shall teach me to blow the long flute
> Leaning together on the spring wind and playing with the moonlight?[51]

What concerns the poets is lack of participation in the refined enjoyments and unhurried pleasures of the quiet life and the time of day sets a parallel between a serene nature and their serene relationship as well as a contrast between the present and the past.

Tu Fu knows that literature seldom leads to a life of worldly success ("Thoughts of Li Po from the World's End"),[52] but in "Remembering Li Po on a Spring Day" (written in 746) he asks:

> When can we meet over a pot of wine,
> Again to study and discuss literature?[53]

Tu Fu and Li Po planned a hermitage together, but the latter was away in some remote hills in search of the elixir of life ("Thinking of Li Po on a Winter Day") or "the precious herbs" ("Presented to Li Po"; 744), or simply "remained a vagabond just for a cup of wine" ("No Recent News of Li Po").[54] In "From the Mountains: A Letter to P'ei Ti," Wang Wei (699?–759?), who styled himself a "dweller in the mountains," writes:

> We must wait for mid-spring. Plants and trees will sprout, spring hills will be lovely to look at. Minnows will leap from the water, white gulls spread their wings. Dew will wet the grass in the green slope, morning pheasants will sing in the barley fields.
>
> It is not long to wait. Will you wander about with me? If you were not endowed with the pure and spontaneous mind, would I invite you to join me in the idle activity? In this lies a profound meaning. Please don't take it lightly. The yellow-dye-tree gatherer, my messenger, is leaving, so I must close.[55]

Both were dwellers in the mountains. Li Po, known as a banished immortal, delighted in mountain landscapes for their expressions of freedom and independence; Wang Wei, on the other hand, was something of a mystic, a Buddhist quietist, who left jewels of nature poetry which reveal his attainment of harmony with nature. They understood the workings of the way (*tao*), nature as the manifestations of *tao,* and took transformation as their final abode. Such transcendental appreciation of nature owes a great deal to Neo-Taoism and Prajna-Buddhism, and one who has comprehended the secrets of action and inaction is often portrayed as one who has achieved identification of self and nature.

Pyŏn Wŏn-gyu (fl. 1881), who has retreated to nature with a herd of deer as his companions, wishes to send his friend (Yi So-sŏk) a painting of the sound of autumn.

> Day after day I live, deer for companion,
> Bright moon on the waters and clouds on the hills.
> Nothing except these in the crevice of my heart—
> Shall I send you a painting of autumn sound?

He can transform, he says, autumn sounds into a painting, silent poetry (or a soundless poem), a metaphor for painting.[56] His life of integrity in nature and the fact that his friend understands his kind of life are a compliment.

Chapter six, "The Great and Venerable Teacher," of the *Chuang Tzu* presents a friendship among such enlightened ones.

> Master Ssu, Master Yü, Master Li, and Master Lai were all four talking together. "Who can look upon nonbeing as his head, on life as his back, and on death as his rump?" they said. "Who knows that life and death, existence and annihilation, are all a single body? I will be his friend!"
>
> The four men looked at each other and smiled. There was no disagreement in their hearts and so the four of them became friends.

> Master Sang-hu, Meng-tzu Fan, and Master Ch'in-chang, three friends, said to each other, "Who can join with others without joining with others? Who can do with others without doing with others? Who can climb up to heaven and wander in the mists, roam the infinite, and forget life forever and forever?" The three men looked at each other and smiled. There was no disagreement in their hearts and so they became friends.[57]

Chinese and Korean literature attests to such ideal friendships, beginning with the Seven Worthies of the Bamboo Grove in the middle of the third century. Renouncing public life, they withdrew into a bamboo grove where they indulged in a kind of pastoral friendship with a common devotion to poetry, music, wine, and polite conversation. Korean emulators of these Chinese paragons are legion, one of the earlier groups being the Seven Worthies of the Left Bank at the end of the twelfth century. Poetry written by such a group is best studied through their poems on wine; the function of wine in friendship I will discuss later.

Contrarily, if friends did not share one's moral convictions, failed to discern the motives behind withdrawal, or seemed to be taking a wrong course of action, they did not hesitate to sever the bonds. Hsi K'ang's (223–262) "Letter to Shan T'ao," a defense of his philosophy of life, may be cited as an example:

What is esteemed in human relationships is the just estimate of another's inborn nature, and helping him to realize it. When you see a straight piece of wood, you do not want to make it into a wheel, nor do you try to make a rafter of a crooked piece, and this is because you would not want to pervert its heaven-given quality, but rather see that it finds its proper place. Now all the four classes of people have each their own occupation, in which each takes pleasure in fulfilling his own ambition. It is only the man of understanding who can comprehend all of them. In this you have only to seek within yourself to know that one may not, out of one's own preference for formal clothes, force the people of Yüeh to wear figured caps, or, because one has a taste for putrid meat, try to feed a phoenix a dead rat . . . If you insist on my joining you in the king's service, excepting that we will rise together and will be a joy and help to one another, one fine day you will find that the pleasure has driven me quite mad. Only my bitterest enemy would go so far. The rustic who took such pleasure in the warm sun on his back, or the one who so esteemed the flavor of celery that they wanted to bring these things to the attention of the Most High: this showed them to be well-meaning, but it also showed their complete ignorance. I hope you will not do as they did. This being the way I feel about it, I have written to explain it to you and at the same time to say farewell.[58]

The following quatrain addressed to Chŏng In-hong (1535–1623) by the Korean poet-politician Kim U-ong (1540–1603) is probably the shortest declaration of rupture of friendship.

Do not seek out a mountain dweller,
The hilly paths are dark as pitch.
I've nothing to offer you—
A slice of moon on a cliff top.

Both were involved in political upheavals and suffered exile. Chŏng's faction for a brief period was victorious, and he was drawn into a group of cunning ministers. As a hermit in a mountain hideaway (or it may have been a place of exile), Kim U-ong views the outside world as enfolded in darkness. He is a slice of moon hanging on a rocky eminence scorning the mad world below. If you still think of me, the poet says, look at my emblem in the sky—it is better to maintain a distance until you come to your senses.

An exile's longing for a friend is as endless as the moon's rays, which he sends to his friend as a token of undying affection. The author of the following poem is Kim Chŏng (1486–1521), who had held such positions as Inspector-General, Deputy Director of the Office of Special Counselors, and Minister of Punishments. Implicated in the 1519 literati purge, Kim was banished to remote Cheju Island off Korea's southernmost coast, where he was ordered to drink poison.

> In a trackless land no one visits me,
> My lonely self surrounded by thorns.
> My dream takes me to frontier passes,
> I regard my servants as brothers.
> Grief and illness craftily invade my sidelocks;
> I've no clothes for wind and frost.
> My longing is like the bright moon,
> I send its distant rays to the world's end.

Extension of the identification of self or friend with the bright moon results in a version of the "nature reversed" topos, a staple in the poetry of praise. Sŏ Ki (1523–1591) compliments Chŏng Kae-ch'ŏng (1529–1590) as a phoenix, an auspice of a golden age and a symbol of the sage, and goes on to declare that his absence causes the disharmony of heaven and earth.

> Good customs of Yao and Shun are all gone,
> A phoenix departed, nothing goes right.
> Heaven and earth forget a season's return.
> In the cold, hungry world where can I see spring's light?

The world has turned into a cold and hungry place, and nothing but a return of spring will bring about a miracle. His friend is "spring's light," a principle of growth and the miracle of nature.

Po Chü-i (772–846), known for his affectionate friendship with Li Chien (764–821) and Yüan Chen (779–831), recalls, in "To Li Chien" (818), his active days at court:

> Yet even now I fancy my ears are full
> Of the sound of jade tinkling on your bridle straps.[59]

On his way to a new appointment as governor of Hangchow in 822, Po Chü-i thinks of his deceased friend Li Chien, his gift of a black gauze hat:

> The gauze hat still sits on my head;
> But you already are gone to the Nether Springs.[60]

We may recall that true friendship is immune to outside forces, never spoiled by suspicion and prejudice. A friend's reputation is a matter of utmost concern, and no matter how grave the charges brought against him, they will not disrupt the bonds. This factor is especially important in the Confucian bureaucracy, often threatened by political factions and the ruler's whims. Upon hearing the news of Po Chü-i's banishment, Yüan Chen wrote:

> The lamp had almost spent its light: shadows filled the room,
> The night I heard that Lo-t'ien was banished to Kiu-kiang.
> And I that had lain sick to death sat suddenly in bed;
> A dark wind blowing rain entered at the cold window.[61]

Written long after Yüan Chen's death, "On Hearing Someone Sing a Poem by Yüan Chen" illustrates the full poignancy of the poet's inner tumult when a single line of Yüan's poem suddenly stirs his memory and causes him to experience Yüan's presence:

> Once lately, when someone was singing,
>   Suddenly I heard a verse—
> Before I had time to catch the words
>   A pain had stabbed my heart.[62]

This leads to the topic of the dream vision of an absent or dead friend. The identification of love and dream so characteristic of the love lyric reappears with varying intensity. Desire for a dream encounter and a friend's visit in midnight dreams are commonplace. Here I will cite two pairs of friends, Tu Fu and Li Po, Po Chü-i and Yüan Chen. Tu Fu's two poems on "Dreaming of Li Po" were written probably when Li Po was banished to Yeh-lang in the south but before he was pardoned in the early summer of 759. The enormous distance notwithstanding, Li Po's soul appears in dream, a sign of how constantly Li Po is in his thoughts. But his is not the soul of the living man, fears Tu Fu; did he die in exile? In the second poem, however, the fact that he has dreamt of Li Po for three nights, says the poet, is a result of the friend's affectionate concern for him. Korean poets thought likewise. Water imagery in both poems underscores the poet's fear of Li Po's possible drowning: "The water is deep, the waves are wide: don't let the water-dragons get you" and "The waters are so rough. I am afraid the boat will capsize."[63]

Po Chü-i has a number of such poems, but none are more moving than those on Yüan Chen. In a poem of 805 the poet declared:

> The bond that joined us lay deeper than outward things:
> The rivers of our souls spring from the same well![64]

In "Dreaming that I went with Lu and Yu to visit Yüan Chen," written in exile, the poet calls at Yüan Chen's home:

When he saw me coming, a smile came to his face.
He pointed back at the flowers in the western court;
Then opened wine in the northern summer-house.
He seemed to be saying that neither of us had changed;
He seemed to be regretting that joy will not stay;
That our souls had met only for a little while,
To part again with hardly time for greeting.
I woke up and thought him still at my side;
I put out my hand; there was nothing there at all.[65]

The preface to another poem, entitled "The Letter" in Waley's translation, says: "After I parted with Yüan Chen, I suddenly dreamt one night that I saw him. When I awoke, I found that a letter from him had just arrived and, enclosed in it, a poem on the paulovnia flower." Like Tu Fu before him, Po Chü-i says that a dream visit was a proof that he was in his friend's mind constantly:

When dawn came, I dreamt that I saw your face;
It must have been that you were thinking of me.

The gist of the poetic letter evolves around "A single tree of purple paulovnia flowers," "a symbol to express 'thinking of an absent friend'." Is the flower an emblem of love and union that transcends space and time? Is it, as Guillén remarks, an "exercise in continuity and a demonstration of permanence"?[66] Or does it underscore the permanence of poetry, more enduring than a flower bound to follow the course of nature?

Night was late when you finished writing,
The mountain moon was slanting towards the west.
What is it [that] lies aslant across the moon?
A single tree of purple paulovnia flowers,
Paulovnia flowers just on the point of falling
Are a symbol to express "thinking of an absent friend".
Lovingly–you wrote on the back side,
To send in the letter, your "Poem of the Paulovnia Flower".
The "Poem of the Paulovnia Flower" has eight rhymes;
Yet these eight couplets have cast a spell on my heart.
They have taken hold of this morning's thoughts
And carried them to yours, the night you wrote your letter.
The whole poem I read three times;
Each verse ten times I recite.
So precious to me are the fourscore words
That each letter changes into a bar of gold![67]

A gift befitting the station of king, or perhaps more durable than marble, bronze, and gilded monuments of princes. There is irony here, "a bar of gold" meaning more precious than a bar of gold. As Horace said,

> gaudes carminibus; carmina possumus
> donare et pretium dicere muneri.
>
> (Poems you love, and these I *can* give, knowing
> The proper value of what I'm bestowing.)
>
> *Odes,* IV.8.11–12[68]

Indeed, by cherishing Yüan Chen's gift—a poem—and by addressing to him a verse epistle, the poet is affirming the dignity and worth of poetry. Poetry confers immortality, defying separation imposed by time and space, the human condition.

Po Chü-i's poems to Yüan Chen move the modern Chinese reader as much as the following by Wordsworth and Coleridge do the English reader. Dedicated to Coleridge, *The Prelude* concludes with a moving tribute to that poet's productive days:

> Thou in delicious words, with happy heart,
> Didst speak the Vision of that Ancient Man,
> The bright-eyed Mariner, and rueful woes
> Didst utter of the Lady Christabel;

Wordsworth continues:

> When thou dost to that summer turn thy thoughts,
> And hast before thee all which then we were,
> To thee, in memory of that happiness,
> It will be known, by thee at least, my Friend,
> Felt, that the history of a Poet's mind
> Is labour not unworthy of regard:
> To thee the work shall justify itself.[69]

When on several evenings in January 1807 the poem was read to him, Coleridge's reply was, "To William Wordsworth: Composed on the Night After His Recitation of a Poem on the Growth of an Individual Mind."

> Friend of the wise! and Teacher of the Good!

So begins the poem, which shows how Wordsworth's and his own life are interwoven. *The Prelude* is a testimony to the affectionate and poetic friendship that bound the two. Indeed,

> Nor less a sacred Roll, than those of old,
> And to be placed, as they, with gradual fame
> Among the archives of mankind, thy work
> Makes audible a linked lay of Truth,

> Of Truth profound a sweet continuous lay,
> Not learnt, but native, her own natural notes!

The poem concludes with Coleridge's moving appreciation of his friend's encouragement and loyalty and with a humble resolve to rise above his dejection:

> And when—O Friend! my comforter and guide!
> Strong in thyself, and powerful to give strength!—
> Thy long sustained Song finally closed,
> And thy deep voice had ceased—yet thou thyself
> Wert still before my eyes, and round us both
> That happy vision of beloved faces—
> Scarce conscious, and yet conscious of its close
> I sate, my being blended in one thought
> (Thought was it? or aspiration? or resolve?)
> Absorbed, yet hanging still upon the sound—
> And when I rose, I found myself in prayer.[70]

IV

The Angler's Calendar (1651), a cycle of forty poems by Yun Sŏn-do (1587–1671), sings of the joys of a fisherman, an emblem of a contemplative man riding happily on the waves of flux. The verbs in the envoi in ten poems on each of the seasons are consistently in the form of a command: set sail; heave away; spread sail; scull the boat; lower sail; stop the boat; moor the boat; drop anchor; and put the boat ashore. In addition to the frequency of such verbal endings as *-ra* (attentive), *-cha* (propositive), *-ka?* (rhetorical interrogative) and *-ya* (exclamation), the cycle is in the interrogative style, with abundance of such verbal endings as *-rya* (exhortive interrogative), *-sonya* (exclamative doubt), *-ko* (present and future interrogative), *-ŏ* and *-ni* (present interrogative), and *-ri* (future interrogative). The frequency with which such questions appear is a striking feature of Yun's and, indeed, other *sijo* poets' art. To whom is the speaker addressing his questions or giving his command? To whom is he postulating a dialogue? His other self, an absent friend, a listener or reader, to give voice "to what does not exist, to articulate emptiness, deprivation, and nonbeing"?[71] "All poetry is interrogative in its process of probing and in the radiation of wonder."[72] The pursuit of wisdom begins in wonder, a desire to question and explore. As poetic description is not assertion, so the poet's interrogative temper does not have to be in the form of question. Probably all good poetry exemplifies the process of query. "The poem as poem arouses further query—through its articulation in the form of criticism, through its articulation (exhibitive and active) by other poems of the same tradition or movement, or through its cultivation of the desire for poetry. It arouses query through its contagion of seeking, in any mode, any medium, any degree."[73] In fact, the whole cycle is an invitation to contemplation of self and world, being and nonbeing. This ability to ask his other self and friend to contemplate absence and time indicates Yun's mastery of his art.

> Is it a cuckoo that cries?
> Is it the willow that is blue?
>
> Spring, 4
>
> Did you hear the oriole's calling
> Here and there in the green verdure?
>
> Summer, 7
>
> What will the mood of the sky be?
>
> Summer, 9
>
> What is more transcendental
> Than the life of a complete angler?
>
> Autumn, 1
>
> You say the joys of all seasons are equal?
>
> Autumn, 1
>
> Where is it, friends, where am I?
> Is there any separation of heaven and earth?
>
> Autumn, 8
>
> Stop the boat, what does it matter
> If I catch any fish or not?
>
> Winter, 7

The last verb of the cycle is aptly in the propositive:

> Let us lean from the pine window and gaze
> As the moon crosses the winter sky.
>
> Winter, 10

A constant reference to friends, an essentially dramatic stance, an alternation of speech and silence, and a persistence of the interrogative mode help to establish an intimate and dynamic relationship with the audience.

V

In send-off poems, we recall, the traveler is sometimes asked to dismount and drain another cup, as in the following by P'ei I-chih (c. 815):

The red candles are snuffed and brighten again;
The green flasks are refilled to the brim.
I care not that the road ahead is long;
Only I fear that this night may be too short.[74]

Poems of welcome sparkle with wine, when friends celebrate a reunion and pour out their stories and drown the woes suffered during separation. In traditional Chinese and Korean poetry, wine is, first of all, a symbol of release from anxieties, fears, changes, and ultimately death. To T'ao Ch'ien (365–427), as to Horace ("memory-drowning Massic," II. 7. 21), wine is a "Care Dispelling Thing,"[75] serving to "exorcise all our concerns,"[76] liberating man from life, "brief as the startling lightning bolt"[77]—further qualified elsewhere as "dusty net" and "dream illusion." Wine works the same with Tu Fu, who declares "One cup will dissolve a thousand worries"[78] and "relieve the mind."[79] It is also the best of medicines to dispel cares and troubles in Korean poetry. Details of ceremony are dispensed with, and poets indulge in relaxation and conviviality:

Having drunk till tipsy,
We take our places, sit around.
My mob of worries announce:
They must bid me farewell.
Boy, pour wine to my cup,
I'll send them off with a toast.

Chŏng T'ae-hwa (1602–1693)

Ten thousand acres of green waves
Cannot wash away my thousand cares.
But with one bottle of wine
I've cleansed them all—
That's why Li Po was forever drunk
Never waking from his sleep.

Anonymous

How many kinds of wine are there?
Clear and turbid . . .
If you can drink your fill,
What matters which is which?
When you've bright moon and clear breeze,
Why worry if you cannot wake up.

Shin Hŭm (1566–1628)

In a dialogue with wine, a type of wine poetry, the poet often debates the pros and cons of its attributes. In one such poem, Chŏng Ch'ŏl extols the virtues of wine and concludes that he cannot sever the ties:

Listen once again to my word,
I feel I cannot live without you.
I can forget because of you
The hard, rugged things in life.
It is too late now to abandon you
In order to love strange faces.

Beautiful scenes of nature or feelings of zest also call for wine, as when T'ao Ch'ien calls in the neighbors to share wine[80] or Li Po enjoys the splendid moonlit night with wine.

Equally, chilly winds or signs of snow in the dusk—or simply bad weather (a theme as old as Alcaeus) [81]—call for friend and wine:

I have just finished brewing some Lu-i wine,
And my little red-clay stove will warm us.
There are signs of snow in the gathering dusk;
Is it not the moment for a drink together?

"A Query to Liu the Nineteenth"[82]

Snow reminds Po Chü-i that he, too, is aging, his future in the hands of the unknown. Hence frost is usually blamed for turning one's hair grey, a commonplace in East Asian poetry. Warmth, relaxation, friend, and wine will challenge the winter landscape, but the poet has stopped short of saying, "Let's enjoy life's pleasures," the Epicurean standard. Exploration of the antithesis of nature and human existence is a favorite subject of Horace:

Horrida tempestas caelum contraxit, et imbres
  nivesque deducunt Iovem; nunc mare, nunc siluae
Threicio Aquilone sonant. rapiamus, amici,
  occasionem de die, dumque virent genua
et decet, obducta solvatur fronte senectus.
  te vina Torquato move consule pressa meo.

(A dreadful storm has narrowed heaven's expanse, and rain and snow are bringing Jove to earth. The sea, the woods, now roar with the Thracian north wind. Let us snatch our opportunity from the day, my friends, and while our limbs are strong and the time is fitting, let seriousness be banished from the clouded brow! Bring thou forth a vintage trodden in my Torquatus' year.)

Epodes, XIII.1–6[83]

Vides ut alta stet nive candidum
Soracte, nec iam sustineant onus
  silvae laborantes, geluque
    flumina constiterint acuto.

dissolve frigus ligna super foco
large reponens atque benignius
  deprome quadrimum Sabina,
    o Thaliarche, merum diota:

(Look how the snow lies deeply on glittering
Soracte. White woods groan and protestingly
  Let fall their branch-loads. Bitter frost has
    Paralyzed rivers: the ice is solid.

Unfreeze the cold! Pile plenty of logs in the
Fireplace! And you, dear friend Thaliarchus, come,
  Bring out the Sabine wine-jar four years
    Old and be generous.)

Odes, I.9.1–8[84]

To accept the onslaught of frost and snow, the inevitability of death and eternal sleep—indeed to "surrender one's body to change" as T'ao Ch'ien says—is often the keynote of such poetry.

The evening of life will be fast coming upon me . . .
Let me forget it all by being utterly drunk.

Tu Fu, "New Years Eve in the House of Tu Wei"[85]

Sky and earth are my curtains,
Sun and moon my lamp and candle.
I'll channel the North Sea waters,
Sluice them to my wine jar.
I'll then watch Canopus in the South
And forget treacherous old age.

Yi An-nul (1571–1637)

The mere forgetfulness sought by Tu Fu and Yi An-nul, however, may not be enough, if it does not help to obliterate self and world, consciousness and nature: T'ao Ch'ien says he is no longer aware that "I" exists ("Twenty Poems After Drinking Wine," XIV.8) and "forgets Heaven." Li Po concurs in the following excerpts from "Drinking Alone by Moonlight":

Once I am drunk
  losing Heaven and Earth . . .
Not to know
  that my self exists—
Of all my joys
  This is the highest.

With three cups
  I understand the Great Way
With one jar
  I am at one with Nature.[86]

In wine, T'ao Ch'ien avers, there is "a taste of profundity."[87] It is a leveler that "makes a sage," an immortal, as when Cho Chon-sŏng (1553–1627) exclaims that he is a Fu Hsi, the legendary Chinese culture hero and sage ruler:

Boy, lead a cow to the northern village,
Let's taste the new-made wine.
Having drained it to the lees, I'll return home
On cow-back under the moon.
Hurrah, I am a Fu Hsi tonight,
The ancient glories are at my fingertips.

Indeed, he who follows the "promptings of his heart" ("Twenty Poems After Drinking Wine," XVIII.8) is able to seize the present, transcending past and future. As Horace advises Leuconoe,

. . . sapias, vina liques, et spatio brevi
spem longam reseces. dum loquimur, fugerit invida
aetas: carpe diem, quam minimum credula postero.

  (Be wise, strain clear the wine
  And prune the rambling vine
Of expectation. Life's short. Even while
  We talk Time, hateful, runs a mile.
    Don't trust tomorrow's bough
    For fruit. Pluck this, here, now.)

Odes, I.11.5–8[88]

Tu Fu, in the second of two poems on "Meandering River" concurs:

O wind and light and time, roll on;
Let us not quarrel; let us enjoy life.[89]

Or:

So long as we are alive and can meet, let us drink the cup.
"New Year's Eve in the House of Tu Wei"

It is not surprising, therefore, when Wang Chien (c. 830) goes out to meet his friend who is coming back from the war, with a flask of wine:

Yet I never weary of watching for you on the road.
Each day I go out at the City Gate

With a flask of wine, lest you should come thirsty.
"Hearing That His Friend Was Coming Back from the War"[90]

Although tranquil talk alone is "better than any medicine"[91] to Po Chü-i when visited by a friend during his illness, or silence is enough to open their minds when friends meet, as in Kuei Tzu-mou ("Face to Face"),[92] wine is a staple in a banquet.

How great a thing is a single cup of wine!
For it makes us tell the story of our whole lives.
"Rejoicing at the Arrival of Ch'en Hsiung"[93]

When Po praises his friend, Hsiao Chü-shih, it is because Hsiao can drink and makes the host feel at ease:

And with *him* at least I find myself at ease.
For *he* can drink a full flagon of wine.[94]

"Wine is a spy-hole into a man," said Alcaeus, revealing the true man.[95] Po could not drink alone without tried friends:

Wine was before me, but suddenly I could not drink;
I was thinking of those who have been my life's delight.[96]

Therefore, when Ts'ui, governor of Chiang-chou, invites him at his mountain retreat to a banquet at Yü Liang's Tower, Po Chü-i accepts the invitation wholeheartedly: "The consideration you show is beyond all bounds."[97]

In the spring of 759, Tu Fu and Wei the Eighth met again after a long interval under the light of the same lamp:

. . . you send the boys to set out wine and a meal,
spring scallions cut in night rain,
new cooked rice mixed with yellow millet.
Meetings are rare enough, you say;
pour the wine till we've downed ten cups!
But ten cups do not make me drunk;
your steadfast love is what moves me now.
Tomorrow hills and ranges will part us,
the wide world coming between us again.[98]

As Horace says, "recepto/ dulce mihi furere est amico" (It's sheer joy to throw/ Sanity overboard/ When a dear friend's restored; *Odes,* II.7.27–28).[99] The following suggestions of Kim Yuk (1580–1658) adequately reiterate the same topos: friendship will sparkle under the beneficent workings of wine.

Be sure to invite me
When your good wine is brewed.
I shall certainly invite you
If flowers bloom in my arbor.
We shall discuss, then, how to live
A hundred years without worry.

Poems on the theme of "Bringing in the Wine" or "A Time to Drink" are another type. Korean examples, the most famous of which is that by Chŏng Ch'ŏl, are usually modeled on Li Po's poem of the same title, written to the tune of an old song "sung to the accompaniment of flutes and drums."

A Time To Drink

Let us drink a cup, and then another,
After drinking let us pluck a flower,
Let the flowers lie as we drink more.
When your body dies, it will be wrapped
In a mat and dragged along by a rope,
Or else, with last rites and painted carriages,
A thousand friends will follow you in tears.
And when you are laid away among the bracken,
Under tawny oaks and shivering poplars,
When the yellow sun shines and the moon rises,
And when the chilly winds mourn there,
Who, who will offer you a cup of wine?
Furthermore, when only a monkey whistles,
What good will it do you to regret, my dear,
The wine you forbore to drink while you were alive?

Here comes the wine, no standing cups!
I have a song to sing you,
Kindly turn your ears to me and listen.
It is nothing to feast on jade to the sound of bells and drums.
I ask only to be drunk for ever and never wake!
They lie forgotten, the sages of old;
Only the great drinkers have left us their names.
In time gone by, when the Prince of Ch'en feasted in the hall of
Peace and Joy,
At ten thousand a quart he never stinted the revellers.
Why must our host say he is short of money?
Send to the shop at once, keep the cups filled.
My five-flower horse,
My fur which cost a thousand,
Call the boy, send him out to change them for good wine,
And let me forget with you the sorrows of ten thousand ages![100]

Li Po wants to pawn his horse and furs at the tavern, another topos eagerly used by his emulators. Po Chü-i too exchanged his coat to pay for drinks:

> I remember how often in old days, when up for the examinations,
> I would pawn my coat to pay for drinks on the shores of the
> Serpentine.[101]

By mentioning Li Po in the following poem, Kim Ch'ŏn-t'aek (c. 1725–1776) pays tribute to the great Chinese drinker, but avers that he outdoes him:

> Having given my clothes to a boy,
> To have him pawn them at the tavern,
> And looking up to heaven,
> I question the moon.
> Who is Li Po, that ancient drunkard,
> What is he compared with me?

Kim questions the moon, the companion of the solitary drinker and recluse among other things, another reference to Li Po's famous poem:

> Amidst the flowers
> a jug of wine—
> I pour alone
> lacking companionship,
> So raising the cup
> I invite the moon,
> Then turn to my shadow
> which makes three of us.
> Because the moon
> does not know how to drink
> My shadow merely
> follows my body.
> The moon has brought the shadow
> to keep me company a while,
> The practice of mirth
> should keep pace with spring.
> I start a song
> and the moon begins to reel,
> I rise and dance
> and the shadow moves grotesquely.
> While I'm still conscious
> let's rejoice with one another,
> After I'm drunk
> let each one go his way.

Let us bind ourselves for ever
    for passionless journeyings.
Let us swear to meet again
    far in the Milky Way.[102]

The archetype of Korean drinkers is Li Po—and occasionally Liu Ling of the third century and Su Tung-p'o—a friend and confidant in wine and friendship poetry. Li Po was known as a great celebrator of the joys of wine and a great lover of the moon, and legend has it that he was drowned while trying to scoop up the reflected moon from the river. The solitary drinker is not alone, if he is with the moon or if he can conjure up the ghost of the Chinese poet. This was one way of making friends with the revered Chinese poet of the past. Chinese poets of later times could, if they wished, make a poetic pilgrimage to places associated with Li Po or any other poets of their tradition, but such possibilities were denied to most Korean poets. To them the only way of forming an affectionate bond with and feeling the enduring presence of the dead was by sharing the same experience in analogous situations. The poetic tradition was a community of friendship.

When you take a net on board,
Don't forget my wine jug.
The moon rises on the eastern ridge,
So let's push off the boat.
Keep on filling my cup, boy,
I am with Li Po tonight.

Yi Yu (c. 1675–1720)

After Li Po left the earth,
How desolate the hills and waters!
Only a slip of bright moon
Hangs in the blue void.
Now that Li Po is forever gone,
Why not play with me, O moon?

Yi Chŏng-bo (1693–1766)

Why is the moon invoked so often in East Asian poetry? At times the moon looks desolate and chilly because it reflects the landscape below in late autumn and winter. The sadness in poems of separation is partly caused by the lonely viewer who, when the north wind rattles the paper screen or blows snow in, imagines that his friend, even if many hundred miles away in the south, must suffer the same bleak weather. In other poems, the traveler often ascribes his melancholy nostalgia to the moon, which seems to intensify, even conspire to bring on, his forlorn state of mind. Especially the crescent moon, dawn moon, or misty moon will make him pace to and fro, sunk in reminiscence, or deny him sleep and dream. Worst of all, it seems to be utterly indifferent to the sorrow of man. If it seems to shed tears, it is because man wishes to narrow the gap between nature and man.[103]

In friendship poetry, however, the moon can be either sad or gay, depending on where the friend is. The speaker and friend share the same moon, but not at the same place. If the friend is restored, the bright moon is a symbol of happy reunion, communal joy, and undying affection. A party without the moon is unthinkable, and a third or fourth element, flowers of the season or a clear breeze, is often added. When, therefore, Yi Tŏk-hyŏng (1561–1613) asks the moon to pour down its light on a friend's wine cup, he has studied his poetry:

The moon hung in the sky, bright, full.
Since the dawn,
It has met wind and frost.
Alas, soon it will sink.
But no, wait, I say,
And shine on the gold cup of a drunken guest.[104]

The associated images of moon, wine, and friend are best summarized in the following poem by Yi Chŏng-bo:

If flowers bloom, we demand the moon.
If the moon lights up, we ask for wine;
And when we have all these at once,
Still there is something missing.
O, when can I drink a night away,
Enjoying moon and flowers and friend?

This recalls the Horatian ingredients of a banquet:

Huc vina et unguenta et nimium brevis
flores amoenae ferre iube rosae,
  dum res et aetas et sororum
    fila trium patiuntur atra.

(Come, bid them bring wine, perfume and beautiful
Rose-blooms that die too swiftly: be quick while the
  Dark threads the three grim Sisters weave still
    Hold and your years and the times allow it.)

Odes, III.3.13–16[105]

The only difference may be that girls are seldom asked to join in a feast in Korean poetry.

VI

Let me conclude with a poem by Yun Sŏn-do, whom we have met as the author of *The Angler's Calendar*. Addressed to his friend, the poem (1645) is a celebration of the unity of heart and music. Music is made sweeter by the beauty of the heart; the heart may have emotion but cannot express it without song. Song eternalizes the heart's desire, and heart and song are one. Such is the function of Yun's friend, whose name was Kwŏn Hae, on whom the poet bestowed the pen name Pan'gŭm, "Friend of the lute," for his mastery of the instrument.

> Heart wants to sing, but cannot sing alone;
> Heart wants to dance, but dancing must have music.
>   The lute shall play,
> For none but lute can strike the secret tone
>   My heart would sing
>   So heart and song are one;
>   Then lute shall play,
> For none but lute knows what is heart's desire
>   So heart may spring
>   Into the dance
>   And beat its rhythm out.
> Welcome, sweet lute, my dear, my dearest friend,
> There is no hurt thy music cannot mend.

Without doubt the poet had in mind a Chinese story about a master lutanist Po Ya and his good friend Chung Tzu-ch'i. A version in the *Lieh Tzu* goes:

> Po Ya strummed his lute, with his mind on climbing high mountains; and Chung Tzu-ch'i said:
>   "Good! Lofty, like Mount T'ai!"
> When his mind was on flowing waters, Chung Tzu-ch'i said:
>   "Good! Boundless, like the Yellow River and the Yangtze!"
> Whatever came into Po Ya's thoughts, Chung Tzu-ch'i always grasped it.
>
> Po Ya was roaming on the North side of Mount T'ai; he was caught in a sudden storm of rain, and took shelter under a cliff. Feeling sad, he took up his lute and strummed it; first he composed an air about the persistent rain, then he improvised the sound of crashing mountains. Whatever melody he played, Chung Tzu-ch'i never missed the direction of his thought.[106]

When Chung Tzu-ch'i died, Po Ya would play no more, for there was no one who knew the secret of his music. The phrase, "know the sound," is therefore a metonymy for an understanding friend who grasps another's inmost thoughts and to whom one can lay bare one's heart. This is the classical background in some friendship poems when they introduce yet another motif, the lute. The six-stringed Korean instrument is also called the Lute of the Black Crane, or simply the Black Lute, from the tradition that black cranes alighted dancing to the music of the lute. A poem by Kim Yŏng (fl. 1776–1800) enumerates four elements, snow, wine, music, and friend:

Snowflakes flutter—butterflies chase flowers;
Ants float—my wine is muddy.
I pluck the Black Lute,
A crane dances to my tune.
A dog barks at the wicker gate—
Boy, see if my friend has come.

One is tempted to read the last line as "Boy, my friend has come," for his music, which is enough to move the crane, must have produced reverberations in his friend, whatever the distance. The following anonymous poem offers another combination of associated images: chrysanthemums, wine, moon, music, and friend. Playing on the lute is the highest compliment to a friend, who truly "knows the sound":

I plant chrysanthemums outside the window
And brew wine under the plants.
Wine mellows, flowers open,
A friend comes, the moon rises.
Boy, tune my lute,
I'll enjoy the night out.

The friend's power, Yun Sŏn-do says, is analogous to the lute, whose song helps order experience and create a harmony equal to natural harmony. A friend on the path of wisdom, he rejects pretense and posturing and helps attain a sense of harmony in a world otherwise transitory. He is a paragon of friendship, embodiment of goodness and honesty, joy and consolation. Although ideal friendship, so often extolled in history and literature, is contradicted by experience, Yun Sŏn-do found in Kwŏn Hae a true friend, with whose companionship he was able to defy time by exploring to the fullest the hidden possibilities of the Korean language and by bequeathing to posterity his enduring verse. Thus Yun Sŏn-do has created an archetype of the friend.

We have seen, from send-off poems, poems of longing and of dream vision, and the function of wine and music in friendship poetry, that East Asian and Western writers seem to agree on the value of friendship and that East Asian poetry of friendship is often couched in the language of love, but with qualification. East Asian poets usually observe decorum and seldom overstep the boundary between love and friendship. Intense longing and dream vision approximate the language of love, but the native reader knows instantly if a given poem deals with one or the other. The major reason is the absence of anything approaching the Western courtly love convention. An English poet, who in his seventeen sonnets recommended his friend to marry, also sent pederastic poems to him. Indeed, "addressing love sonnets to a man is an all but predictable extreme of courtly love technique."[107]

Seasonal imagery plays an important role in poems of parting and longing, as does the theme of withdrawal. In such poems the "I will follow you to the end of the world" topos is usually absent, but the speaker, in an attempt to compliment his friend, sends him a painting of autumn sound, a handful of moonlight, or Nature itself, for which probably there is no Western counterpart. Equally absent in the West is the total identification of the friend with nature, although the topos of nature reversed is a commonplace.

Near Eastern and Western epics present moving examples of friendship, for example, Gilgamesh and Enkidu, Achilles and Patroclus, Aeneas and Pallas, Roland and Oliver. More friendship poems tend to take the form of elegies, for example, *Lycidas, Adonais, In Memoriam,* and *Thyrsis,* or Surrey's elegy on Wyatt, Spenser's on Sidney, and Carew's on Donne. Is it because the relations of friendship were "most acceptable as a poetic subject only when death has brought it to an end?"[108] Sociocultural differences may reflect the relative importance attached to romantic love and friendship in two cultures. Where romantic love is a primary literary concern, friendship tends to be eschewed, overshadowed, or takes different forms.

Whether friends celebrate a reunion with wine and music in an idyllic setting to reveal their true selves, to challenge frost and snow, or to explore the place of friendship in life and poetry, East Asian friendship is founded upon the affinity of intellect and sensibility. Dealings between man and man involved far less misunderstanding and suffering than those between man and woman, as so many paragons of love learned to their despair and destruction. The relative lack of tragic love is perhaps made up for by a great body of friendship poetry, which succeeded in offering an alternative model for revelation and fulfillment of self.

East Asian poetry offers little evidence for the mystical friendship of the divine, often expressed in such imagery as fire, water, darkness, wound, or sweetness. Buddhism inspired some meditative verse—occasionally the Buddha is addressed as the "true friend"—but it lacks the Western concern that love of friends leads man to love of God, that virtue and goodness—the basis of friendship—originate in God, that human friendship is a part of a greater friendship of man for God.[109] Most expressions of friendship in East Asia are earth-bound. The good of virtue is seen as the object of true friendship, but divine friendship is seldom a subject of poetic celebration. Lycidas "sunk low but mounted high/ Through the dear might of him that walkt the waves"; such optimism could not find expression in an East Asian elegy.

5 TIME

Swiftly, I sped, as in fearful pursuit,
Afraid Time would race on and leave me behind.

The days and months hurried on, never delaying;
Springs and autumns sped by in endless alternation . . .

For old age comes creeping and soon will be upon me,
And I fear I shall not leave behind an enduring name.[1]

Time falls away in shreds, changing always,
How can I tarry and stay?[2]

. . . the world's way is to drift the way the tide runs,
who can stay the same and not change with all the rest?[3]

THE OSTENSIBLE concerns of the "Li Sao" or "Encountering Sorrow" are the protestations of the purity of the slandered and exiled minister and his fabulous flights in search of the ideal prince who will recognize his worth. On a deeper level, the poem tells of the individual's consciousness of the flux of time, how time destroys everything man cherishes. As a poetic treatment of man pitted against the irreversible flow of time, the "Li Sao" marks the discovery of subjective time in Chinese poetry. Indeed the antagonist in the poem is not the corrupt court, but Time itself.

Time is the destroyer of beautiful things: "Orchids and iris have lost all their fragrance; Flag and melilotus have changed into straw."[4] It is also the destroyer of order and coherence, of the moral order in man. Like the speaker's fall from favor, such social favor and outward show as public honors and titles are subject to fortune. A voluntary surrender to externals, "the materialist and expedient life of external appearance,"[5] deceives our senses, falsifies our values.

But the Fragrant One refused to examine my true feelings;
He lent ear, instead, to slander, and raged against me.

But it grieves me to find the Fair One so inconstant . . .

What I do resent is the Fair One's waywardness:
Because he will never look to see what is in men's hearts.

The muddy, impure world, so undiscriminating,
Seeks always to hide beauty, out of jealousy.

For the world is impure and envious of the able,
And eager to hide men's good and make much of their ill.[6]

Calumniators and slanderers are "cunning artificers" who uphold a system of false values: "They gather up muck to stuff their perfume-bags with"[7]—their degenerate, perverse taste foreshadows an imminent disintegration of society. Such evidences of decadence, which foreshadow the end of the world, abound in the *Ch'u tz'u*. In the midst of such corruption the speaker exclaims, "How well I know that loyalty brings disaster;/ Yet I will endure: I cannot give it up"[8] and wants to "keep pure and spotless and die in righteousness."[9] At the close of the poem, the speaker may have gained a deeper sense of time, but he also realizes that an ideal political-moral order is a dream. The dramatic juxtaposition of the happy past and the gloomy present, the plight of a lonely, unhappy man caught by adverse fortune, the struggle of the wounded not to be carried away to oblivion by time's flow, enliven the tone of the poem but do not always help to maintain its balance. The poem leaves a number of unresolved contradictions: for instance, he says "I will no longer care that no one understands me,/ As long as I can keep the sweet fragrance of my mind"[10]; why, then, so much fuss? If he knows that virtue, unlike flowers, can withstand time, why so much despair? The mere fact that he has chosen to identify the power of time in sociopolitical terms seems to indicate his allegorical temper. He laments the changes of Fortune, the brittleness of worldly goods (the stuff of tragedy in Boethius and Chaucer's *Monk's Tale*), but has not discovered constancy in mutability.

The process of time increases disorder. Those who are prey to fluctuations of fortune have corrupt senses and perverse values and have ruined morals and manners. Images of a world without order and coherence abound in the *Ch'u tz'u,* reinforcing the speaker's disillusionment with the times.

White is changed to black,
The high cast down and the low made high;
The phoenix languishes in a cage,
While hens and ducks can gambol free;
Jewels and stones are mixed together,
And in the same measure meted.[11]

A broken nag is preferred to a fine steed[12]; orchid and iris are mixed with mugworts,[13] jade scepters with pottery shards.[14] "The pear tree withers among the tall grasses,/ The thorn bush is planted in the midst of the court."[15] They prize pebbles as jewels and call a jade disk a stone.[16] Indeed, "no one is left who can tell the difference."[17] These are all signs of approaching catastrophe, underscoring the relativity of human perception. The targets of moral indignation are corrupt, blind courtiers, held to be responsible for hastening the process of fortune, but seldom does the speaker say that the absence of greed and rejection of worldly temptations lead to felicity of mind. His criterion is social and moral, his doubts are not resolved, and he has not learned to espouse the sufficiency of virtue or the virtue of contemplative withdrawal.

Similar outbursts of a self-righteous man indulging in self-pity, lamenting a false world that fails to recognize the virtuous, recur throughout the *Ch'u tz'u*. The dominant mood of most of the complaints is elegiac, and the descriptions of autumn and winter enhance the speaker's mood and the setting. The length of such symbolic landscape varies, as does the transition from description to meditation, but its function is to help relate the speaker's state of mind to the proper setting for contemplation of mutability.

> When I think of the long nights of late autumn,
> My heart is tormented and full of grief.
> My springs and autumns are growing in number,
> And sadly I grieve for my hard lot.
> The seasons come and go and fulfill the year;
> Light and dark alternate: I scarce can keep abreast.
> The white sun reddens towards his setting;
> The bright moon pines and wastes away.
> All too quickly the year will be ended,
> And old age comes creeping on apace.
> My heart is distraught; its passion increases:
> I am disappointed, with nothing to hope for.
> My breast is bitter with grief and anguish,
> And sigh after long sigh I heave heavily.[18]

The rotation of the sun and moon and a rapid succession of the seasons remind the speaker of the onslaught of old age and death. The melancholy landscape is a mirror of mutability in nature and man; desolation and decay in nature mirror the plight of man in search of a place of stability in the corrupt world of politics and ethics. The speaker in the *Ch'u tz'u* often laments such a landscape, but nature's emblems do not always help him to attain a deeper knowledge of the workings of nature. Like Sackville's winter landscape ("the most central and inclusive of all the winter landscapes in Tudor poetry")[19] in his *Induction to Complaint of Henry, Duke of Buckingham,* the archetypal landscape in the *Ch'u tz'u* served as prototypes for later writers on the same theme.

A similar unresolved tension recurs, for example, in the following by Juan Chi (210–263):

Day and night
Revolve,
While my face wrinkles
And my spirit wanes,
But the sight of injustice
still pains me.[20]

One day, then another morning,
One dusk, then another dawn.
My complexion is not as normal,
My vital spirits ebb . . .
Facing my wine, I cannot speak,
Sick at heart, I carry bitterness inside.

In the first, injustice done him by chance seems to hasten his physical decay. The speaker has realistically assessed Time's power, but has not achieved peace of mind. In the second, the speaker introduces more details—wine makes him recall what is past and passing. Memory recalls past pleasures but intensifies keen disappointment in the harsh present. He thinks of becoming a farmer but laments that he might be without friends. Good deeds have brought him only sorrow, and the best course for him is to go underground, which might suggest a withdrawal to await an opportune time for emergence. The transition between the notational observation of the cycles of nature in the beginning of the poems and the ensuing meditation or lament has not been worked out well.

Contrarily, in "At the Year's End: A Reply to the Attendant Chang," T'ao Ch'ien develops more fully a parallel between the mutability in the world of nature and man.

In court and market we grieve for old friends;
The racing steed is moved by the Sad Fount.
With tomorrow's dawn today is no more,
Of this year's end what can I say?
The fresh complexion has lost its glow
And white hairs are become a multitude.
Duke Mu of Ch'in exaggerated—
An old man's strength is gone for good.

Toward evening a long wind rises,
Cold clouds engulf the western hill.
Chill, chill, the wind turns sharp,
In flocks the flying birds return.
Human life is seldom long,
And worst of all, is wrapped in suffering.
I often lack clear wine to drink
And have no way to make the present cheerful.
Success or failure do not trouble me,
Careworn, I adapt myself to change.
I press my breast lost in thought:
The turns of time provide more cause for sighs.[21]

The first line introduces the subject, which is said to refer to a saying, "In one lifetime court and market change," followed by the progress of nature, the coming of old age, a formulaic description of nature again (a long, chilly wind, cold clouds, the western hill, homing birds) and reflection: "Success or failure do not trouble me,/ Careworn, I adapt myself to change." A similar philosophic tone recurs in "Written on the First Day of the Fifth Month to Match a Poem by Secretary Tai" set in the summer:

Human life comes always to its end.
Accept your lot and wait until its' over,
To stay free, crook an elbow for a pillow.
Accord with change, whatever its ups and downs—
Follow your bent, no matter the height and depths.[22]

The acceptance of the constancy in change marks a refreshing advance over the outbursts of grief by victims of Time. The speaker advises adaptation to changing circumstances for moral and aesthetic grounds, not to be obstinate and unyielding, but to be pliable, flexible, and versatile ("I adapt myself to change," "Accord with change"). Ironically, T'ao Ch'ien and others like him who rejected the world of action and public time for various reasons were praised by history for the very mode of living they chose. The poet-speaker also accepts the finality of death here and elsewhere, for example in "The Return" ("So I manage to accept my lot until the ultimate homecoming./ Rejoicing in Heaven's command, what is there to doubt?"),[23] and his enlightened views on the subject are strengthened by the prestige of tradition, which told man how to counter change and decay.

I

Chinese classics taught how to view death, how to accept the process of time. Confucius declared that "death and life are the decree of

Heaven" (*Analects,* XII.5)[24] and went on to say that one who does not know about the living cannot know about the dead (XI.11).[25] That life and death are the same recurs elsewhere: "Who can look upon nonbeing as his head, on life as his back, and on death as his rumps? Who knows that life and death, existence and annihilation, are all a single body?" (*Chuang Tzu,* 6).[26] Life and death are the same story, that acceptable and unacceptable are on a single string (*Chuang Tzu,* 5).[27] Lung Shu says in the *Lieh Tzu* that he looks in the same way at life and death, riches and poverty.[28] Indeed, one who hates death is like a man who, "having left home in his youth, has forgotten the way back" (*Chuang Tzu,* 2).[29]

The sun going over the western ridge
Will rise again from the eastern sea.
The grass wilted in autumn
Will grow again in spring.
Dead, we never return;
Is that why life's so precious?

The speaker in the above poem by Kim Ch'ŏn-t'aek (c. 1728) affirms that the movement of nature is cyclical, that of man linear. He accepts the reality of time and goes on to say that therein lies the beauty and value of life, a twist that saves the poem from a repetition of the commonplace.

Fame and name are useless, and the perfect man of Taoism looks upon them as so many handcuffs and fetters (*Chuang Tzu,* 5).[30] Confucius also warned against accepting rank and wealth by wrong means and went on to say that such an idea is as remote from him as floating clouds (*Analects,* VII.15).[31] Grief and joy, happiness and misery, have no way to enter into one who "is content with the time and willing to follow along" (*Chuang Tzu,* 3);[32] if they visit man, it is because he called one or the other for himself (*Tso chuan,* Duke Hsiang 23).[33]

There is no crime greater than having too many desires;
There is no disaster greater than not being content;
There is no misfortune greater than being covetous.
Hence in being content, one will always have enough.[34]

Lao Tzu, 46

He who knows contentment is rich (*Lao Tzu,* 33)[35] and, as the Chou proverb has it, "A man may have no crime; that he keeps his jade is his crime" (*Tso chuan,* Duke Huan 10).[36]

The affairs of man, man-made institutions and societies, change through the assault of Time. The contrast between the unchanging heaven and earth and human affairs that change as policy and fortune change is the concern of the first poem by Yi Che-shin (1536–1584), while in the second by Hong Chŏk (1549–1591), false changes caused by expedience are expressed through the metaphors of snow and sand, which deceive man's perception.

Heaven and earth are unchanged,
So are sun and moon.
Heaven and earth, sun and moon,
Just as in sage rulers' times.
But why do affairs of men
Change from day to day?

Do you say yesterday's snow
Fell also on a sand bank?
Snow looks like sand,
And sand like snow.
So are affairs of the world,
They're false, they change.

The following anonymous Korean *sijo* singles out wealth and rank as transitory, but compares them ironically with the sun and moon, which are constant in their movements.

When day declines, the sun
Sets behind hills and waters.
The midmonth past,
The moon's corner's chipped.
Wealth and rank are like this.
They change, they're undone.

The law of retribution is that "what proceeds from you will return to you again" (*Mencius,* IB.12),[37] for Heaven shines down upon the earth below (*Book of Songs,* 207.1)[38] and "the net of heaven is cast wide. Though the mesh is not fine, yet nothing ever slips through" (*Lao Tzu,* 73).[39] Hence there is a recurrent warning to withdraw from the world at an appropriate time, for example, "To retire when the task is accomplished/ Is the way of Heaven" (*Lao Tzu,* 9).[40] Juan Chi, in one of the "Poems of My Heart," says:

Why, then, do the men in power,
Bent servilely, forget the place of return?
Why do they seek an empty name
And suffer sorrow till they are haggard?[41]

And Po Chü-i, in "The Waves Scouring the Sand," which elaborates the theme of mulberry fields changing into a sea, says at the end:

> But should imperial favor make you once more rich and grand,
> Please, Sir, never forget the waves scouring the sand![42]

The act of withdrawal as a show of moral protest or a search for contemplation and self-fulfillment I have discussed in Chapter Two. Here I will cite two poems that illustrate our immediate subject. The speaker in the first poem, by Kim Ch'ŏn-t'aek, is perplexed by those who are not awakened from illusion, clinging still to name and fame. In the second, by Yi Hyŏn-bo (1467–1555), the clear breeze and bright moon hovering over his cottage in the country beckon him to retire. The speaker here is wiser than those who know the virtue of withdrawal but cannot bring themselves to renounce the world. The fourth line, "What if I don't return?" registers his dilemma and implies resolution: he must and he will return, lest he disappoint the clear breeze and the bright moon.

> Return, return, they say,
> But who has bowed out?
> Everyman knows—does he?—
> Name and fame are floating clouds.
> No one's awakened from the dream,
> And that perturbs me.
>
> Return, return, they say,
> But none has returned.
> Fields and gardens are thick with weeds,
> What if I don't return?
> Clear breeze and bright moon wait,
> Going in and out of my grass hut.

Nondiscrimination is perhaps the most subtle way of withstanding the changes of Time according to the Taoist view.

Any thing is "other," any thing is "it." What is unseen from the other's standpoint, from his own standpoint the knower knows. Therefore it is said, "Other comes out from It, It too adapts to Other," the opinion that It and Other are born simultaneously. However, "at birth we are simultaneously dying" and at death we are simultaneously living, the admissible is simultaneously inadmissible and the inadmissible is simultaneously admissible, if adapting to the one "that's it" then adapting to the other "that's not," and if adapting to the one it is not, then adapting to the other it is. Therefore the sage does not take this course but illuminates all by the light of Heaven; his too is an adaptive "That's it."[43]

"Nothing in the world is bigger than the tip of an autumn hair, and Mount T'ai is small; no one lives longer than one cut off in childhood, and P'eng

Tsu died young; heaven and earth were born together with me, and the myriad things and I are one."[44]

Lady Li and Lady Mao were beautiful in the eyes of men; but when the fish saw them they plunged deep, when the birds saw them they flew high, when the deer saw them they broke into a run. Which of these four knows what is truly beautiful in the world?[45]

One who does not discriminate is not affected by life and death, benefit and harm, and the following *sijo* by Kim Su-jang (b. 1690) makes reference to the virtue of nondiscrimination:

They call black white
And white black.
Whether it's black or white,
None can tell which is right.
I'd rather close my ears and eyes,
Refuse to listen or see.

Or in a poem by Yi T'aek (1651–1719) about the roc and the small black birds, which owes its genesis to the beginning of the *Chuang Tzu:*

O roc, don't ridicule the small black birds:
You and the little birds both fly way up in the clouds,
You're a bird,
And they're birds.
Really, I can't see much difference between you!

High and low are relative concepts, tall trees are struck first, lowness is good and height is bad, as is behind the following by Kim Ch'ŏn-t'aek:

Standing in your lofty tower,
Don't laugh at this lowly place.
In the midst of thunder and storm,
Would you be surprised to slip?
We sit on level ground,
Who needs distinctions?

The Taoist symbol of water supremely illustrates the virtue of lowness: "The reason why the river and the sea are able to be king of the hundred valleys is that they excel in taking the lower position" (*Lao Tzu,* 66).[46]

Several parables in the *Chuang Tzu* illustrate how the useless has its use and how the useful are the first to suffer the vicissitudes of fortune: the beautiful markings of the tiger and the leopard—as do the tusks of the elephant (*Tso chuan,* Duke Hsiang 24)[47]—call out the hunters, "the nimbleness of the monkey and the ability of the dog to catch rats make them end up chained" (7);[48] "The straight-trunked tree is the first to be felled; the well of sweet water is the first to run dry" (20).[49] Indeed, "A man has to understand the useless before he can talk about the useful" (26).[50]

Dwellers at the vermillion gate,
Boast no four-horse carriage.
When a rabbit is caught,
We boil the hound.
We don't know honor and disgrace,
So what's there to fear?

The fourth line refers to Han Hsin's remarks to Liu Pang, the founder of the Han, when he ordered his guards to bind Han: "When the cunning hares are dead, the good dog is boiled; when the soaring birds are gone, men put away the good bow; when the enemy states have been defeated, the ministers who plotted their downfall are damned. The world is now at peace, and so it is fitting that I be boiled."[51] One who does not discriminate and knows the utility of inutility may not be frustrated by external reality, whose agent is Time. Therefore, "the sage keeps to the deed that consists in taking no action and practices the teaching that uses no words" (*Lao Tzu,* 2).[52] But the teaching that uses no words, the benefit of resorting to no action, are "beyond the understanding of all but a very few in the world" (*Lao Tzu,* 43).[53] Indeed, how many were able, like Master Kuang Ch'eng, to "enter the gate of the inexhaustible and wander in the limitless fields, to form a triad with the light of the sun and moon, to partake in the constancy of heaven and earth, mingling with what stands before him and leaving in darkness what is far from him" (*Chuang Tzu,* 11)?[54]

II

Every literature has gnomic utterances on life's mutability, the vicissitudes of fortune, or the transitoriness of human accomplishments. Admonitory sententiae on the fall of pride or the ineluctability of fate are a staple of epideictic rhetoric, the literature of praise and blame, not of our concern here. Poets also expressed their views on the subject in various contexts, as our discussion shows. Here let me cite some occasional reflections on human transience. Man's existence is compared to "dust scattered by a gust of wind" by T'ao Ch'ien ("Untitled Poems," I.3),[55] who also says "life is as brief as the startling lightning bolt" ("After Drinking Wine," III.8),[56] or "a conjurer's illusion,/That reverts in the end to empty nothing" ("Returning to the Farm to

Dwell," IV.15–16).[57] Man's brief existence between heaven and earth is "like the passing of a white colt glimpsed through a crack in the wall—whoosh!—and that's the end" (*Chuang Tzu,* 22),[58] and it is likened to a visit ("Human life is like a visit") in "Trees in Bloom" (I.5),[59] and repeated by the following anonymous Korean poem which echoes tradition by evoking key images:

> Heaven and earth are an inn,
> Our world is a traveler through ages.
> Life is a grain of millet
> On vast green seas.

(The poem ends with the *carpe diem,* which I will discuss later.) One reference is to Su Shih's rhymeprose, "The Red Cliff" (I), where the speaker says, "And what are you and I compared with him (Ts'ao Ts'ao)? Fishermen and woodcutters on the river's isles, with fish and shrimps and deer for mates, riding a boat, as shallow as a leaf, pouring each other drinks from bottlegourds; mayflies visiting between heaven and earth, infinitesimal grains on the vast sea, mourning the passing of our instant life."[60]

A comparison of life to dream is recurrent (especially in classical Japanese literature), as again in T'ao Ch'ien: "Born into the midst of dream-illusion/ Why should I submit to dusty bonds?" ("Twenty Poems After Drinking Wine," VIII.9–10),[61] which recalls early Greek observations that man is a shadow in a dream or an unsubstantial phantom. Or as in Li Po, "Life in the world is but a big dream" ("Waking from Drunkenness on a Spring Day"),[62] and Su Shih, "Man's life is like a dream" ("Recalling Antiquity at Red Cliff").[63] The second chapter of the *Chuang Tzu,* "Discussions on making all things equal," looms large in all these comparisons. "We drink wine in our dreams and weep at dawn, we shed tears in our dreams and at dawn go hunting. While we dream we do not know that we are dreaming, and in the middle of a dream interpret a dream within it; not until we wake do we know that we were dreaming. Only at the ultimate awakening shall we know that this is the ultimate dream."[64] This, like a parable on Chuang Tzu and the butterfly, illustrates the "relativity of all knowledge," but its striking imagery and argument must have suggested the material for later poetry, for example, by Li Po:

> Chuang Chou dreamt he was a butterfly,
> Awake, the butterfly became Chuang Chou.
> One body transforms in turn,
> Ten thousand things are truly in flux.[65]

And another by Yi Chŏng-bo:

> Chuang Tzu dreamt he was a butterfly,
> A butterfly dreamt it was Chuang Tzu.
> Is a butterfly Chuang Tzu,
> Or Chuang Tzu a butterfly?
> Old man of the lacquer garden,
> Whom should I ask?

The old man of the lacquer garden refers to Chuang Tzu from a tradition that he once served as an official in the lacquer garden in Meng (*Shih chi,* 63). The last two lines show the ingenuity of the poet: now that the philosopher who set the speaker to meditate on the reality of life is dead, to whom should he address himself?

Another image is that of dew, as in the following by Ch'in Chia:

> Man's life is like the morning dew:
> In this world he has many trials.[66]

Early Japanese elegies fondly evoke the same image:

> He left this dear and precious world
> As vanishes a drop of dew
> Long enough before his time . . .
>
> *MYS,* III.443–5

> My beloved brother, born of my own parents,
> A life fleeting as the morning dew . . .[67]
>
> *MYS,* IX.1804–6

Men pass away like dew on leaves (*SKKS,* 8.757, 834), more specifically, upon the sagebrush (*SKKS,* 8.769). And Issa (1763–1827) in a poem written shortly after the death of his daughter:

Tsuyu no yo wa	The world of dew
tsuyu no yo nagara	Is a world of dew, and yet,
sarinagara	And yet . . .[68]

The images of insubstantiality—we have encountered all except for the first three—are summarized in *The Diamond Sutra:*

> As stars, a fault of vision, as a lamp,
> A mock show, dew drops, or a bubble,
> A dream, a lightning flash, or cloud,
> So should one view what is conditioned.[69]

But, in spite of the poignancy it evokes, how different is the East Asian dew from a dewdrop celebrated in Marvell's "On a Drop of Dew." In one of "the subtlest and most lovely English irregular odes,"

Marvell established an analogy between the dewdrop and the soul, the first 18 lines describing the dewdrop within a rose as though it were a soul and another 18 the soul as though it were a dewdrop.

See how the Orient Dew,
Shed from the Bosom of the Morn
Into the blowing Roses,
Yet careless of its Mansion new;
For the clear Region where 'twas born
Round in its self incloses:
And in its little Globes Extent,
Frames as it can its native Element.
How it the purple flow'r does slight,
Scarce touching where it lyes,
But gazing back upon the Skies,
Shines with a mournful Light;
Like its own Tear,
Because so long divided from the Sphear.
Restless it roules and unsecure,
Trembling lest it grow impure:
Till the warm Sun pitty it's Pain,
And to the Skies exhale it back again.

The dewdrop scarcely touches "its Mansion new," trying to create within itself the "clear Region where 'twas born"; it mourns its separation from its proper sphere, "gazing back upon the skies"; restless, it trembles and waits to be exhaled by the sun.

So the Soul, that Drop, that Ray
Of the clear Fountain of Eternal Day,
Could it within the humane flow'r be seen,
Remembering still its former height,
Shuns the sweat leaves and blossoms green;
And, recollecting its own Light,
Does, in its pure and circling thoughts, express
The greater Heaven in an Heaven less.
In how coy a Figure wound,
Every way it turns away:
So the World excluding round,
Yet receiving in the Day.
Dark beneath, but bright above:
Here disdaining, there is Love.
How loose and easie hence to go:
How girt and ready to ascend.
Moving but on a point below,
It all about does upwards bend.

The soul also "shuns the sweet leaves and blossoms green," remembers its former height, recollects itself, and expresses "the greater Heaven" in the "Heaven less," its terrestrial life.

> Moving but on a point below,
> It all about does upwards bend.

Such is its movement within the body. The last four lines describe it as celestial dew that runs into the glories of the sun.[70]

III

One of the most moving images of mutability is the falling and dying flower. "He comes forth like a flower, and withers" (Job 14.2); "As for man, his days are like grass; he flourishes like a flower of the field; for the wind passes over it, and it is gone, and its place knows it no more" (Ps. 103.15–16); and "All flesh is grass, and all its beauty is like the flower of the field. The grass withers, the flower fades" (Isaiah 40.6). Delicate and beautiful, fragile and powerless, the fall of the flower is a poignant reminder of the triumph of time over beauty. Shakespeare's Sonnet 65:

> Since brass, nor stone, nor earth, nor boundless sea,
> But sad mortality o'er-sways their power,
> How with this rage shall beauty hold a plea,
> Whose action is no stronger than a flower?

Indeed, "what strong hand can hold his [Time's] swift foot back?/ Or who his spoil of beauty can forbid?" We have seen earlier the predominance of spring and autumn as poetic seasons and the symbolic use to which they were put to underscore the transience of natural beauty and the brevity of life.

> The glorious blossoms are hard to keep
> Decline and growth cannot be foretold.
> Yesterday's springtime lotus flower
> Today has become the seedpod of autumn . . .
> Sun and moon will still revolve
> But we leave never to shine again.[71]

> Do you not see the hibiscus, which seldom lasts a day?
> It lingers a moment, then falls and passes away.
> Those who are young and charming and indulge in extravagances
> Before long too will be buried.
> Once gone, there is no return.[72]

The first is by T'ao Ch'ien ("Untitled Poems," III), and the second is the tenth poem in "Tedious Ways" by Pao Chao (414–466). The burden of both poems, like that in another poem by Pao Chao ("Tedious Ways," 5), is that "we are different—/ Once gone, we never return."

> Time doth transfix the flourish set on youth
> And delves the parallels in beauty's brow,
> Feeds on the rarities of nature's truth,
> And nothing stands but for his scythe to mow.
>
> Sonnet 60

Seen from the flower's point of view, the falling flower will never blossom again. But natural time continues, while subjective, human time ceases with death, as T'ao Ch'ien affirms. Indeed, as Liu Yin (1249–1293) says, "The wind of Spring, wishing to admonish us here,/ Lets drop one red petal before our eyes."[73]

"The Fall of the Flowers" by Yen Yün (ninth century) poses the timeless question:

> Where does spring light return, slowly, slowly?
> Again I face the flowers and raise my cup.
> Daylong I ask the flowers, but the flowers don't reply:
> For whom do you fall, for whom do you blossom?[74]

A more humorous advertisement for the lost spring occurs in a lyric, "Pure Serene Music," by Huang T'ing-chien (1045–1105):

> All alone, without a trace,
> Where has spring gone?
> If anyone knows where spring has gone,
> Call it back to linger with us.
>
> Spring left no trace: who knows?
> You may ask the orioles:
> No one understands their hundred tunes,
> Wind-blown, flying over the roses.[75]

And in a lyric by Liu K'o-chuang (1187–1269):

> Fluttering like the light pinions of the butterflies,
> Scattering like blood-red drops—
> If the Lord of Heaven has no love for flowers,
> What do these charms and beauties mean?
>
> In the morning we see them richly deck the branches;
> In the evening we see the branches growing thin.
> If the Lord of Heaven really loves flowers,
> Why are they borne away by wind and rain?[76]

The Lord of Heaven (*t'ien-kung*) cannot be indifferent to flowers, the speaker says, for he fashioned them beautifully. But, if the heavenly lord cares for beautiful things, why do rain and wind destroy them? Nature gave birth to flowers, but cannot protect them from perishing. From the flower's point of view its fall is final, as from the man's point of view death is final. Change is the mode of existence of nature, but nature is also persistent like the movement of the waves; everything returns in cycles, except for man. The above three poems are artistically rewarding, because a link between the transience of seasons and the frailty of man remains implicit, as in Ki no Tomonori's poem.

Hisakata no	This perfectly still
Hikari nodokeki	Spring day bathed in the soft light
Haru no hi ni	From the spread-out sky,
Shizu kokoro naku	Why do the cherry blossoms
Hana no chiruramu.	So restlessly scatter down?[77]

Perishability, the Japanese believed, is "a necessary element in beauty," and "without it there could be no beauty." This explains why their favorite flower is the cherry blossom, which seems to scatter as soon as it has opened, and why it is the emblem of the samurai, "whose ideal was to drop dramatically, at the height of his strength and beauty, rather than to become an old soldier gradually fading away."[78] In the following by Yo Chŏng-bo the speaker develops the poem to the invitation to seize the day.

Yesterday a flower opened,
Today another opens.
Yesterday's flowers were gorgeous,
Today they wither already.
When flowers shrivel, man also ages;
Why not enjoy this life?

The flower as a symbol of impermanence is behind a number of allegorical poems which identify the ephemeral spring flowers with fools of time.

Do not grieve, little birds,
Over the falling blossoms:
They're not to blame, it's the wind
Who loosens and scatters the petals.
Spring is leaving us.
Don't hold it against her.

Song Sun (1493–1583)

What amuses you in the sound
Of blue rain on the clear stream,
O flowers and trees on the hill?
You shake and laugh, laugh and shake.
Take pleasure, then, while you may;
Only a few more days of the spring breezes.
Prince Pongnim (1619–1659)

The first is a lament on the purge of 1545. The wind that shakes and scatters the blossoms is a political upheaval, and little birds should not blame the passing spring enjoyed by possessors of fortune's gifts—fame, riches, honor, glory. In the second, the flowers and trees that, oblivious of an impending catastrophe, tremble and laugh are those who enjoy brief glory and will soon be snared by capricious fortune.

The following two lyrics written to the tune of "Song of Divination" (*Pu-suan tzu*) offer a different view. In the first lyric by Lu Yu (1125–1210), the lonely flower blossoming by the broken bridge "does not crave spring for herself alone." Other flowers are envious, because they do not understand the intent of its early blossoming and its tender loveliness, which is not to claim the joy and warmth of spring for itself alone but to announce to other flowers the miracle of nature. The wind and rain may despoil the flower, but "her fragrance will endure." It is not the flower, itself fragile, powerless, and passive, for it is aware of imminent destruction by time, but its special quality that is exempt from the ravages of time. The poem's resolution lies in the speaker's confidence in the flower's metaphorical action to combat transience and decay. The posthumous reputation of a gentleman, his virtue, grace, beauty, name, or ideal mode of life, will abide even in an age of change and uncertainties, and his name will awaken memories of him as subtle as fragrance. In the second lyric (1962), written to counter the first, Mao Tse-tung invests the flower—the plum blossom—with revolutionary significance. A leader of people's revolution, a harbinger of political spring, a new golden age of freedom and equality, it will mingle with other mountain flowers in celebration of a classless society.

By the broken bridge outside the post station,
Deserted, ownerless, a plum blossom.
Dusk already, she laments alone,
Still more suffering wind and rain.

With no thought to compete in springtime,
She leaves other blossoms to feel envy.
Scattered in the mud, ground to dust,
Only her fragrance will endure.

Wind and rain escorted Spring's departure,
Flying snow welcomes Spring's return.
On the ice-clad rock rising high and sheer,
A flower blooms sweet and fair.

Sweet and fair, she craves not Spring for herself alone,
To be the harbinger of Spring she is content.
When the mountain flowers are in full bloom,
She will smile mingling in their midst.[79]

Contrarily, one who has renounced worldly ambition and seeks virtue is often compared with the pine or the chrysanthemum. The pine, we have seen, recurs in the poetry of praise, emphasizing moral integrity and the nobility of fortitude. Although one view holds that height draws misfortune, the towering pinetree that withstands the ravages of time acquired a moral significance early in the tradition. It does not stand for pride or aspiration, but a knowledge that pride and greed are ephemeral in the world of temporality.

Don't mock a pine
Twisted and bent by the winds.
Flowers in the spring wind,
Can they keep their brilliance?
When wind blows and snow whirls,
You will call for me.

Prince Inp'yŏng (1622–1658)

The pine functions often as a symbol of constancy and permanence, a principle of order and continuity. Nature has provided the speaker with an emblem that negates death. On the other hand, An Min-yŏng (c. 1870–1880) singles out the chrysanthemum. Content to freeze rather than compromise its principles, it does not join the flowers of a fickle spring in their gaudy but transient show.

Speak, chrysanthemum, why do you shun
The orient breezes of the third moon?
"I had rather freeze in a cruel rain
Beside the hedge of dried sticks,
Than humble myself to join the parade:
Those flowers of a fickle spring."

The number of poems with such emblematic trees and flowers seem to mirror the concerns of a society that equated public service with honor and success and witnessed a pageant of ups and downs. While ambition and intemperance are questioned and the frailty of human enterprise observed, the mutability in nature and man did not give voice to the ascetic scorn of the world (*de contemptu mundi*) or the espousal of the other world. Life and the world are to be espoused, not to be held in contempt.

IV

The poetic contemplation of the past—historical sites, persons, or events—is one of the favorite themes of East Asian poetry. The Chinese, "the most historically minded of all ancient people," viewed the process of history as real and vital, as one that brings fundamental changes in man.[80] History, which embodies the past experiences of men and states, is a mirror that yields lessons for society and culture and teaches how virtue is rewarded and vice punished. History's regressive evolution, its cycles of flux and reflux, often encouraged a backward look into the past to seek parallels or contrasts for a fuller evaluation of the present. As proof by examples was a favorite method in historiography, so the evocations of the past in poetry were a device to underscore a parallel or a contrast between the speaker's situation and historic examples or to find consolation in history's iterative pattern. In the following poems, such specific places as the Jade Flower Palace, the Temple of Su Wu, and Chia Yi's house stimulate the speaker's historical memory and cause him to indulge in retrospection and meditation. Characteristically, such a reflection does not seem to offer the spectator a resolution of conflicting forces in man and history, or possibilities for the future.

The Jade Flower Palace, built in 646 by the second emperor of the T'ang, is the subject of the poem with the same title by Tu Fu. The season is typically the autumn, which seems to correlate best the poem's theme and mood with the contemplation of human transience as well as to function as a metaphor of the speaker's state of mind. The mindless stream, the soughing wind among the pines, gray rats scurrying on ancient tiles, dark chambers, decayed roads, all evoke a desolate, melancholy tone.

> The beautiful women have become brown earth,
> As have the powdered and painted burial figures.
> Formerly they accompanied the emperor's golden sedan-chair,
> Now only stone horses remain.[81]

The poem is not merely a lament for the architectural monument but for the vanity of earthly glory and the ineluctability of mortality. "The Temple of Su Wu" by Wen T'ing-yün (812–870) is a lament for Su Wu, a Han general who returned to China in 81 B.C. after nineteen years of captivity by the Huns.

Su Wu was overcome with grief before the Han messenger,
The old temple and tall trees both look dim.
On the horizon not a trace of goose but the Tartar moon,
The sheep returns on the hill, smoke from border grasses.
Upon return he found everything changed,
He left in his prime with a cap and sword.
At Mao-ling he was not ennobled,
In vain he looks at the autumn waves and lament passing waters.[82]

The first two lines establish a contrast between man's discontinuity and nature's continuity: Su Wu is gone, but the temple survives and the trees endure. The subject in the last line can be Su Wu, the speaker, or the reader who shares the general's sorrow as he contemplates the passing waters that seem to weep for the impermanence of human enterprise. "On Passing Chia Yi's House in Ch'ang-sha" by Liu Ch'ang-ch'ing is inspired by Chia Yi (201–169 B.C.) who, after his service under Emperor Wen of Han, was sent south to Ch'ang-sha in the Yangtze Valley as tutor to its king. He considered this an exile and, when he crossed the Hsiang River, composed "A Lament for Ch'ü Yüan," in whose fate he found a parallel to his own predicament.

For three years you spent your exile here,
Leaving behind myriad years of sorrow of the guest of Ch'u.
Among autumn grasses alone I seek your trace,
I only see the setting sun through cold woods.
Emperor Wen had the Way, but his favors were few,
Would the mindless Hsiang know your sorrow?
On desolate hills and waters where leaves fall,
Why did you, luckless sir, come to this world's end?[83]

The autumn evening, desolate waters, and taciturn mountains seem to link the speaker to two figures in Chinese history, and all three seem to share the same destiny. But the stress is nature's ironic indifference to the fate of man. The season of the time mirrors the speaker's state of mind, but mountains and waters do not. The river does not understand man. It is a mocking reminder that nothing abides, although Su Shih, on his boating trip on the Yangtze under Red Cliff, advises his friend to view it differently: "Have you really understood the water and the moon? The one streams past so swiftly yet is never gone; the other for ever waxes and wanes and yet finally has never grown or diminished. For if you look at the aspect which changes, heaven and earth cannot last for one blink: but if you look at the aspect which is changeless; the worlds within and outside you are both inexhaustible."[84] But, characteristically, poets viewed the aspect that changes—water's constant motion.

As the most moving topical trope, the river recurs in the poetry of *de casibus* and *ubi sunt.*

As a river flows endlessly east,
So is human life always grief.
Li Yü, Tune: "Night Crow Calling"

To know the sum of human suffering
Look at this river rolling eastward in the spring.
Li Yü, Tune: "The Beautiful Lady Yü"[85]

The phoenixes are gone, the terrace is empty, the river just flows.
Li Po, "Ascending Phoenix Terrace at Chin-ling"[86]

The nation shattered, hills and streams remain.
Tu Fu, "Spring Scene"[87]

Rivers and mountains keep their scenic beauty . . .
Meng Hao-jan, "Ascending Mount Hsien with Several Gentlemen"[88]

How sad the affairs of the Southern dynasty . . .
Only the Long River flows on.[89]
Liu Ch'ang-ch'ing, "Climbing in Autumn for a View from the Temple on the Terrace of General Wu"

The Great River flows to the east:
Its waves have washed away
All the men of untrammeled spirit of a thousand ages.[90]
Su Shih, "Recalling Antiquity at Red Cliff"

Some of these quotations are from the poetry of ascent, which is a type of *huai-ku* ("cherishing the past") poetry. A view from a high place gives a better vantage point to look down, which is symbolically looking into the past and the present. Both types of poetry imply the speaker's arriving at a certain point on a journey. The journey is subjective time, man's experience of change, and the road along which he journeys is historical, objective, impersonal time, "a space in which events occur." Recalling the past after a journey and contemplating the effects of time, the agent of change, therefore, implies complex relationships between these viewpoints of time, a skillful device of heightening the poetic effect.[91] Life is a river, timeless in its flow, transient as well as immutable. The river could furnish a perspective on life and the timeless process of transformation. But the speaker in the examples seldom crosses the river; there is no transcending time. Nor is there epiphany, existential or otherwise.

We may again consider "water" in Korean *sijo*.

Waters rushing down from Fairy Bridge
Flow past Purple Mist Grotto.
Five hundred years of royal works,
Only the sound of running waters.
What's the use, boy, to ponder
The dynasty's rise and fall?

Chŏng To-jŏn (d. 1398)

Mountains are same as yesterday,
But waters are gone without trace.
Flowing, rushing, night and day,
How can they leave a mark behind?
Waters have run on myriad years;
They still race, I don't know why.

Prince Nangwŏn (1580–1640)

Deep among green valley grasses,
A stream runs crying.
Where's the terrace of songs,
Where the hall of dancing?
Do you know, swallow,
Cutting the sunset water?

Anonymous

The Purple Mist Grotto and Fairy Bridge below Mount Pine near Kaesŏng, the former capital of the Koryŏ dynasty, are known for their beautiful valleys and running waters. Chŏng To-jŏn, who helped to overthrow Koryŏ and set up the house of Yi, is reminded of the vanquished dynasty he had served. The basic contrast is that between the shattered royal house, which is gone and silent, and the water's unending flow with its tinkling sound. Dynasties rise and fall, but the only constant thing seems to be the running water. The last two lines are casual and colloquial, alleviating the pervading melancholy in the first four lines. "I'll say no more," the speaker says, "man's efforts are futile." The second poem sets off the immutable mountain against the rushing water. Historical time races, sweeping away everything in its path. In the third poem, the stream is endowed with feeling. It seems to lament what time and the forces of nature have obliterated—the terrace of songs and the hall of dance, symbols of human glory. The poem, however, does not end with the *ubi sunt* formula. In the last line but one, the speaker shows his originality by addressing a darting swallow, which seems to cut the flow of time, albeit for a moment. Does the bird know what man does not?

This brings us to the *ubi sunt* theme, which is everywhere in East Asia and the West and which through its insistent query emphasizes the transitoriness of life, the fragility of beauty, or "the degeneracy of the current age by harking back to a glorious epoch."[92] Its use is as old as the Bible: "Where is he who counted, where is he who weighed the tribute? Where is he who counted the towers?" (Isaiah 33.18), or "Where is the wise man? Where is the scribe? Where is the debater of this age? Has not God made foolish the wisdom of the world?" (I Corinthians 20). In Old English, "The Wanderer":

> Where now is the warrior? Where is the war horse?
> Bestowal of treasure, and sharing of feast?[93]

In "Le Testament," 29, by Villon:

> Ou sont les gracieux gallans
> Que je suivoye ou temps jadis,
> Si bien chantans, si bien parlans,
> Si plaisans en faiz et en dis?
>
> Where are they now, those dear young folk
> I knew so well in days of old,
> They who so sweetly sang and spoke,
> In word and deed so gay and bold?[94]

Also in his "Ballade des dames du temps jadis":

> Tell me but where, beneath what skies
> Is lovely Roman Flora ta'en?
> Tell me where Archipiada lies,
> Or Thais (they were kin, these twain);
> Or Echo, answering again
> Across the river and the mere,
> Beauty of more than human strain?
> Where are the snows of yesteryear?[95]

Although such queries on the fragility of beauty, with the enumeration of archetypal beauties, is rare in East Asia, women are occasionally invoked in similar poems:

> Where are the singing and dancing girls?
> The mountain slope is full of graves.[96]
>
> Pao Chao, "Tedious Ways," 15

Where are they now, those bright eyes and white teeth? . . .
Humankind has feelings, so tears dampen my bosom,
But the lake waters and lake flowers go on for ever.
Tu Fu, "By the Lake"[97]

Where is she who came with me to enjoy the moon?
Yet the scene resembles that of a year ago.
Chao Ku (fl. 842), "Thinking of the Past in the Tower by the River"[98]

The Swallow Pavilion stands empty:
Where is the beautiful lady now?
Su Shih, Tune: "Joy of Eternal Union"[99]

Here, however, the emphasis is not so much on the perishability of feminine charms—Tu Fu's "bright eyes" and "white teeth" are hardly an ecphrasis of a feminine portrait—than on the *ubi sunt* theme itself. If woman is brought in, it is because she illustrates the brevity of human existence, another example of mutability.

Generally, however, the East Asian version of the *ubi sunt* is not always couched in the interrogative form, but implied by a subtle juxtaposition of the past glory and the present desolation or the indifference of nature to the ravages of time.

Kou-chien, king of Yüeh, came back from the broken land of Wu;
his brave men returned to their homes, all in robes of brocade.
Ladies in waiting like flowers filled his spring palace
where now only the partridges fly.
Li Po, "In Yüeh Viewing the Past"[100]

In the waterside palaces the thousands of doors are locked.
For whom have the willows and rushes put on their fresh
greenery?
Tu Fu, "By the Lake"[101]

Far behind gate on fretted gate the weedgrown court is still;
Curtained windows forlornly face the autumn emptiness.
The feathered banners are all gone, no footfall breaks the silence,
The sound of song and flute from marble pavilions
Long broken off and scattered with the wind.

The misty moon, all unaware of change in men's affairs,
Still shines in the dead of night on the inner palace.
Lotuses huddle in a forgotten pool;
Mutely mourning the fallen kingdom
The pure dew weeps upon the fragrant petals.
Lu Ch'ien-yi (fl. 931), Tune: "The Fairy by the River"[102]

His [Tu Mu's] Twenty-Four Bridges still exist,
Waves stir at midstream—the cold moon makes no
sound.
I pity the peonies beside the bridge,
For whom do they grow year after year?
Chiang K'uei (c. 1155–1229), Tune: "Yangchow man"[103]

On horseback I visit Kaesŏng,
The capital for five centuries.
Hills and waters are ever the same;
But could we list our heroes' names?
Kil Chae (1353–1419)

Sazanamiya	The capital of Shiga
Shiga no miyako wa	Of the rippling waves
Arenishio	Is now in ruins:
Mukashi nagara no	Wild cherry blossoms
Yamazakura kana.	Remain as before.
	Taira Tadanori (1144–1184)

Nani goto mo	In this world
Kawari nomi yuku	Where everything
Yo no naka ni	Only changes,
Onaji kage nite	The bright moon
Sumeru tsuki kana.	Shines with the same light.
	Saigyō (1118–1190)[104]

The partridges still fly, hills and waters are ever the same, the mountain cherries stay as before, and the moon goes on shining. Indeed, the true terror of Time's nature is its unchangeability.[105] Such questions as "for whom are the willows and rushes green" or "for whom are the flowers still blossoming" are another way of affirming indirectly the disparity between man and nature. The knowledge that nature frustrates the promise of man's continuity and immortality heightens pathos and invites action.

The contemplation of the mortality of man in various forms brings about varying responses. The speaker in "Song on Climbing Yu-chou Terrace" by Ch'en Tzu-ang (661–702), overwhelmed by his loneliness, sheds tears.

Behind me I do not see the ancient men,
before me I do not see the ones to come.
Thinking of the endlessness of heaven and earth,
alone in despair, my tears fall down.[106]

Ōtomo Yakamochi (*MYS,* XX.4465–7) thinks that the name will survive, and it must not be disgraced.

Beware, you leaders of our clan
Which bears a most illustrious name
In this wide land of Yamato!

Polish it like a double-edged sword,
Make it ever bright—the name
Borne through ages, clean and without spot![107]

Through the performance of a set of social virtues, men discharge their obligations to their community. Conformity to the norms of the clan is a guide to action, and fear of disgrace, important in a shame culture, is the emotional basis of virtue. Where personal relations are important and spheres of action are well defined, what people say is the basis of "the name/ Borne through ages." "Those who see will tell of it [the ancestral office of the clan] from mouth to mouth;/ Those who hear will hold it up as a mirror . . ./ Neglect it [the name of the clan] never, lest even a false word/ Should destroy this proud name of our fathers." The Ōtomo clan derives their status from loyal services rendered to their lords, and the inherited, collective honor must be vindicated by imitating the models. Whether the clan members should disdain death to preserve the honor by negating their social condition, reminiscent of Greek heroes, is not stated, however. The speaker cannot bring himself to substitute action for history. The honor bestowed by the political authority (altohugh it always claims to be moral authority as well) is not always the same as that conferred by historians, and the same person's action may be valued differently by different groups. Likewise, the notion of name and honor in a Confucian monarchy cannot be the same as that in a feudal society ruled by the warrior class. The relations among name, honor, and virtue are complex, but despite local and temporal variations, the sentiment similar to Yakamochi's often finds expression in East Asia.

Some, like the anonymous poet in the *Man'yōshū* (XVI.3849), espouse the path of Buddha:

Loathing both seas of Life and Death,
How deeply I long
For the upland of Nirvana,
Untouched by the tides of Change![108]

The speaker seeks final release from the self in Nirvana, while others longed for a rebirth on earth or, better, in the Western Paradise of Amitabha ("Infinite Light") either through meritorious deeds (making offerings, reciting scriptures, doing charities) —although others like Hui-neng [688–713], the founder of the Southern school of Meditation, encouraged his followers to take refuge in their own nature rather than in the Buddha—or simply by faith and prayer. Others, like T'ao Ch'ien, seek a life of harmony, contemplation, and anonymity, calmly accepting the human condition. Still others, like the Korean poet Ch'oe Ch'ung (984–1068), seek consolation in recalling the golden age when men lived in harmony and happiness. His is, however, a golden age not of plenty, sweetness, and sensuousness, but of virtue and piety.

My lasting regret is
I was not born in Fu Hsi's time.
Only a grass coat to cover,
Fruit and acorns to eat,
Men kept their true hearts—
And that stirs my envy.

A slight shift of emphasis in these poems brings about not only the *ubi sunt* but *carpe diem* as well.

Poem 115 in the *Book of Songs* advises that good things should be enjoyed during one's lifetime:

On the mountain is the thorn-elm;
On the low ground the white elm-tree.
You have long robes,
But do not sweep or trail them.
You have carriages and horses,
But do not gallop or race them.
When you are dead
Someone else will enjoy them.[109]

The advice to make the best use of time and remove all possibilities of later regrets occurs in such gloomy poems as "Encountering Sorrow":

Gather the flower of youth before it is too late,
While the fair season is still not yet over.
Beware lest the shrike sound his note before the equinox,
Causing all the flowers to lose their fine fragrance.[110]

The speaker's concern here is the impermanence of youth and of beauty, as in Pao Chao ("Tedious Ways," 11): "When do you see youthful years and flourishing power?/ Follow your bent and cherish your noble aims./ Enjoy your wine and meat, make merry together."[111] Or Yüan Mei (1716–1798) can say, with some difference, that, "If I can rejoice for a moment,/ Death at an early age would still be a long life" ("Miscellaneous Poems," 3).[112] We are urged to abandon the idle speculations about the future and make the most of time, indeed snatch the fleeing joys before they escape. Such is the message of Tu Ch'iu-niang's "Gold Thread Coat":

> I adjure you, sir, not to prize your coat of gold thread;
> I adjure you, sir, to prize the time of youth.
> When the flower opens and is ready for plucking, it should straightway be plucked;
> Do not delay until there is no flower, and pluck an empty twig.[113]

The speaker in this poem is a woman. But despite the appearance of the flower imagery, there is an interesting lack of any urge to sensual indulgence. Most East Asian invitations to seize the day are seldom from an amorous or religious impulse,[114] as I pointed out earlier in Chapter Three. Most poems are written by men, and the speaker is usually addressing his friend, an invitation to join in merrymaking of one kind or the other, to forget the thought of death after a meditation on the same topic.

A consideration of the brevity of life often leads to the suggestion of *carpe diem.*

> Prolong life—what a lie!
> Who ever saw a true elixir?
> Illustrious emperors' grand tombs . . .
> Evening mist and autumn grass.
> Life is a spring dream,
> So why not enjoy it?
>
> Anonymous

> Have you seen a man
> Who returned from death?
> None has told us he came back,
> No man has seen another return.
> Since I know this is so,
> I'll savor life's joys.
>
> Kim Kwang-uk (1580–1656)

> What is life, I consider,
> But dream, a piece of dream!
> All good things and bad,
> They're dreams within a dream.
> If this is so, all right—
> Why not enjoy this dreaming?
>
> Chu Ŭi-sik (c. 1675–1720)

Even illustrious emperors' grand tombs are nothing but evening mist and autumn grass. "The impartial soil/ Opens herself to take/ The pauper and the prince alike" (aequa tellus/ pauperi recluditur/ regumque pueris: Horace, *Odes,* II.18.32–34).[115] Futile talks of prolonging life by drugs or exercises are lies. Further, no man has returned from death—speculation on physical immortality is useless. No amount of rage at the tyranny of mortality will lead man anywhere. "Life's brief tenure forbids high hopes to be built in disproportion" (vitae summa brevis spem nos vetat incohare longam: Horace, *Odes,* I.4.15).[116] Life is as ephemeral as a spring dream. Why not, then, accept calmly the final homecoming and try to enjoy the allotted span of life?

Wine figures prominently in some poems partly because it liberates man from dark cares.

> When happy you should have your fun,
> Call in the neighbors to share the wine.
> The time of youth will not come again
> No one day will dawn twice over.
> Do your best when you get the chance,
> The years and months will wait for no man.[117]
>
> T'ao Ch'ien, "Untitled Poems," I

> I only wish a strong wine to fill my cup,
> And not grudge a hundred cash beside my bed.
> A single year's joy is far better
> Than a century's bitter toil.[118]
>
> Pao Chao, "Tedious Ways," 18

> Worldly affairs go by like a flowing stream.
> Our floating life, I reckon, is a dream.
> I'll often take the smooth path to the land of drunkenness,
> No other route is safe to travel on.[119]
>
> Li Yü, Tune: "Night Crow Calling"

> Every man must know
> That life is a dream.
> . . . You say you know it:
> I never met one who does really.
> Because we truly know it so,
> We'll drink and enjoy life.
>
> Song Chong-wŏn, dates unknown

> I've known a long time
> That life is a dream.
> Whether there's wine or not,
> I have a good time.

No laughter in the dusty world—
Let's enjoy then without end.

Kim Su-jang (b. 1690)

Life is a floating dream,
Why bother with honor and rank?
Wise and foolish, high and low,
Death levels them all.
A cup of wine while I'm living,
Isn't that true pleasure?

Kim Ch'ŏn-t'aek

Most of these occasional pieces show how the poets improvised on a traditional topic. The last three in particular are perhaps of the sour-grapes kind. The absence of gloom and almost a casual approach to the topic engenders a frank, relaxed, and easy tone. They throw off poses and let the wine take its effect. In fact, such poems are still sung and recited when friends get together to enjoy wine and laugh at the realm of fortune. The poets are in a way recommending a cooperation with time,[120] while, for example, Shakespeare in his sonnets will have none of it. But our examples evince a kind of reconciliation, which helps the poets to get drunk on poetry and forget all time. And they knew that their poetry is one way of combating the dominion of time.

East Asian images of time are mostly drawn from Nature, either to compare the transient nature of human existence with the cycle of the seasons or to drive home an ironic contrast between the linear human existence and the cyclical recurrence of nature. Of these perhaps the most common and most moving emblem is that of the dying flower, underscoring the ephemeral character of all existence.

Fortune, honor, beauty, youth
Are but blossom dying.[121]

The concept of time as transience also occurs through the images of an unstable state of active life ruled by time, the ruins of monuments, or the irreparable past, all of which seem to stress the destructive force of time. Time's relentless movement is represented by the evocative metaphor of the river, both as the context and condition of existence and its utter indifference to human enterprise. All this time imagery reflects East Asian man's perception of mortality in the world of temporality, whether it is ruled by the Confucian Heaven that controls cosmic order, human history, and personal events, or the Taoist's naturalistic way, or the Buddhist's karmic retribution.

Children, fame, history, and civilization are means of securing succession and transcending change. Children provide hope for the future, but the consolations they bring for continuity are usually taken for granted, except when famine, pestilence, or war frustrates such hope. The importance of history in East Asia is well-known—a ruling house endeavored to maintain and preserve its line, history honored restorers of order who reestablished continuity, recorded those who upheld the highest values of civilization, and transformed them into the exemplars of moral virtues for emulation. But anyone who resorts to violence for his selfish grandeur—villains of epideictic poetry—is doomed to perish in the chaos of his own making. The supreme public virtues, the five relations, are constantly preached and upheld in order to guard society and culture against disorder and insecurity. Family, society, and dynasty provide comforts and certainties and protect man from disruptive forces.[122] Man, who deliberately threatens or defies such continuities, is seldom glorified. Falls of great men are seen usually as the workings of fate, and human endeavor to break the limitations imposed by the world is not viewed as valid—and this partly accounts for the lack of tragic vision in East Asia. Whatever the setting, East Asian man remains within the order of history and relies on the ways of succession. These are the traditional—and Confucian—ways of response to time and mutability, but they are the major concerns of epideictic and moral poetry, not of poetry on time and change. Therefore, if virtue is thought to withstand time, such conviction is found more elsewhere. Also, as the *carpe diem* is seldom an invitation to love, so it is rarely a persuasion to virtue. The persistent mood is that of calm acceptance, but there is neither a contempt for the world nor the espousal of the other world. The meaning of existence is seldom sought beyond or outside time, and it is indeed "perverse"[123] to anticipate in East Asian poetry a dewdrop that bends upwards, as it is perverse to expect a poem to end as does *The Mutabilitie Cantos* (VIII.2):

> For all that moueth doth in change delight;
> But thence-forth all shall rest eternally
> With Him that is the God of Sabbaoth hight.
> O that great Sabbaoth God, graunt me that Sabaoth's sight.[124]

Nature offered moving metaphors not only of transience, but of permanence. Poets found consolation in contemplating the virtues of the pine and the chrysanthemum or the "four gentlemen"—the plum, the orchid, the bamboo, and the chrysanthemum—which figure persistently in East Asian poetry and painting. Armed with the Taoist philosophy of nondiscrimination, the utility of inutility, or of nonaction, poets were happiest when they contemplated harmony with nature in the country or enjoyed the good life with friends. They struggled to be indifferent to time, or perhaps to rise above fortune. Friends and wine can drive away dark cares, northern winds, frost, and snow. Man is not old, if he can still enjoy flowers, laugh with friends, and exchange cups.

> Who says I am old?
> Is an old man this way?
> Heart welcomes sweet flowers,
> Laughter floats over fragrant cups:
> But what can I do, what can I say?
> My hoary hair floats in the spring wind.

The speaker in this fifteenth-century Korean *sijo* faces the certainty of death—with some disquietude in the fifth line—but calmly sets aside its finality and horror. He is aware of the paradox of human existence, but his response is different from what one might expect in a Western poem. Take, for example, Horace's tenth ode in the fourth book: Ligurinus, who has suffered a rude metamorphosis, sees his changed face in the mirror and asks: "Why did I lack as a boy the purpose that I have today? Why to my present spirit do not my rosy cheeks return?"[125] Unlike Ligurinus who cannot recognize his old self in the mirror, the East Asian speaker does not need the mirror to tell him the passage of time or his transformation. He knows what he is; he has known the truth all along. The hoary hair flying in the spring wind magnificently reflects the human condition, as does his serene mood the traditional enlightened view. What counts is the quality of life, the moments of experience, how one accepts change and embraces death. And his poem has captured that moment and enables us to participate in the celebration of timebound man.

More important, the poets we have discussed transcend time by their acts of celebration and by their faith in poetry. "Literature is a glorious achievement that never grows old," said a Chinese emperor.[126] Liu Hsieh (465–522) thought that only the names of those capable of perpetrating their brilliance in words are "suspended on high like the sun and moon."[127] Tu Fu avowed that "true literature lasts a thousand ages."[128] They believed in the power of literature and in the continuity of poetic tradition. Artistic communion joins the dead and the living, master and student. When a poet contemplates and communicates with the tradition, he places himself in a vital relation to past and future. His fidelity to the art, his allegiance to the tradition, is an act of transcending imperious time. Indeed, the poetic contemplation of the past is a means of combating oblivion; the names and events of the past unsung will be forgotten. (The poetic recovery of the past, like *The Prelude,* is seldom attempted.) As poet succeeds poet and reaffirms the place of poetry in life, what he celebrates is the hope of poetry, a denial of mortality and change.

EPILOGUE

THE TASK I have set out to perform is identification and analysis of major poetic topics in East Asian poetry and a comparison of these with Western topics. The major difficulty of students of East Asian poetry would seem to stem from their inadequate understanding of principal topics and structural, thematic, and imagistic patterns of a genre. The functions of such a trope as the river, for example, which recurs in poems of all of my five subjects, vary from one to the other. The use of the river imagery in the *Songs of Flying Dragons* and praise poems from the *Man'yōshū* cannot be the same as that in poems on the fisherman as sage, poems of parting in love and friendship poetry, or poems on time.

Although emphasis on parallels is in the nature of topoi studies, I have shown, whenever occasion called for it and selections warranted it, differences among the three East Asian traditions. Within each chapter, the materials are chosen so as to imply differences while stressing the frequency of a given topos. Hyperbolical praise of a ruler begun in the *Book of Songs* and continued by Chinese and Korean poets is almost absent in the Japanese imperial anthologies. Even in China there is nothing that approaches the *Songs of Flying Dragons* in its sustained use of encomiastic topics. The creation in words of the ideal portrait of the Confucian soldier and statesman cannot be expected in a society where the civil service examination did not take root, where the emperor had a unique status, and where Confucian political and moral philosophy, in spite of the rise of Neo-Confucianism from the Tokugawa period, varied in emphasis from that in China and Korea.

The civil service examination system not only required of every candidate a knowledge of Chinese verse and prose but set a mode of life. From childhood each Korean aspirant for a public career was educated in and read more or less the same books, mostly in Chinese. From his early life, therefore, he learned that the arts of statesmanship and literature went hand in hand. The prevalence, authority, and prestige of written Chinese set the course of development in Korean literature. Although some wrote in both Chinese and Korean, the former was the usual means of expression and communication by the literati. The skillful use of written Chinese, the supreme cultural creation, was a status symbol, and its privileged position was seldom questioned.

The cultural consensus of the authority of Chinese was not shared by the Japanese. True, some wrote in Chinese, but the quantity and quality of their works fall short of those in Korea. A glance at representative collections of poetry written in Chinese by the Japanese,[1] starting from the *Kaifūsō* (751), the first of these collections, illustrates the mode of reception and imitation. The absence in these collections of such major Chinese topics as "not finding him in," several types of nature and friendship poetry, and Taoist concepts of nondiscrimination and the utility of inutility seems to indicate the differences in institutions, beliefs, tastes, and tempers of the times. If topics of Chinese origin did not find expression in poems written in Chinese, they would not affect poems in the vernacular, with restrictions imposed by its own poetics and brief form.

Also, certain topics of Chinese origin are better suited to poems written in Chinese than in the vernacular. Poems on the topos of "not finding him in," and such topics of friendship poetry as send-off poems, poems of parting and of longing,[2] and dream vision found fuller expression in poems written in Chinese than in Korean and Japanese. The speaker in propemptic poems either sends his friend off or himself takes leave of his friend on account of a new appointment, exile, withdrawal, or retirement, all characteristic patterns of life of a civil servant. Such image clusters as flowing water, a solitary boat, lonely clouds, the setting sun, a long wind, the willow tree, and a cup of wine, with emphasis on the distance of space, are magnificently explored, for example, by Li Po and Wang Wei in more than one tenth of their work. In their quotations and allusions ("intertextuality"), Korean emulators added a new dimension to the same images and situations, thereby gaining authority and linking the past to the present, the present to the future. Invitation to a friend is another topos of Chinese origin prominent in poems written in Chinese by Koreans. It at once evokes and recommends a leisurely and cultured style of life, and through the tone and stance the speaker reestablishes a contract between himself and the reader. And such poems gain resonance in a society where the moral, intellectual, and aesthetic values of friendship had a cultural force.

It is a commonplace that in Japan two main subjects are the seasons and love. The *Man'yō* poets, awed by the beauty and mystery of nature, sang of the purity and clearness of hills and waters. The compilers of the *Kokinshū* devoted the first six of its twenty books to the seasons, assigning two books each to spring and autumn. For all its concern with nature, however, certain types of nature poetry were less in vogue: poems of happy rural retirement reminiscent of the *beatus vir* in the West, the topoi of modest sufficiency, of the cultivation of the True, and of "Can you fathom my joy," so prominent in T'ao Ch'ien and later imitators, and finally the fisherman as sage,[3] all reflections of the comparative unimportance of what were vital philosophical, political, moral, and aesthetic concerns elsewhere. On the other hand, secular human love occupied the central position in classical Japanese poetry, with such features as an almost equal status of woman; the frequency of Buddhist-inspired motifs of the "darkness of the heart" and "the path of dreams," with emphasis on darkness, confusion, wandering, path, and dream; the relative importance attached to the woman's hair; and the recurrence of the dew imagery as sexual symbol, the last two present in China but far less frequent in Korea. The variety of combined topoi of love and seasonal imagery and rich amatory vocabulary are the strengths of Japanese love poetry, especially in comparison with Chinese and Korean counterparts produced by the literati, who viewed love in retrospect. But everywhere in East Asia poems on the present—fulfillment and ecstasy—are comparatively few, with a tendency to focus more on parting, desertion, separation, betrayal, and neglect.

The lack in Japan of common systems of poetic conventions prominent in China and Korea is not only a historical and cultural accident but also a literary and generic one. The predominant form in the imperial anthologies was the *waka* or *tanka,* consisting of thirty-one syllables. Although such techniques as allusive variation enlarged the dimensions of the *tanka,*[4] its brevity precludes the treatment of certain topics that require extended description and development. Eulogies that demand a biographical pattern of a hero, a chronological survey of his life, for which the compilers of the *Songs of Flying Dragons* invented a new form, country-house poems that celebrate a landscape at once ideal and real, combining nature and culture, retirement poetry that pits court against country, with relative merits of two modes of life and a catalogue of rural delights, or the extended praise of the beloved's body (*blason*), all these demand a form more adequate to contain the complexity of the subjects. For the treatment of such topics Korean poets turned to the more discursive *kasa* form, which, like the Chinese *fu,* can be extended to hundreds of lines. The

Korean form comparable to the *tanka* is the three-line *sijo,* elastic, resilient, mnemonic, and compact, but it has at least a dozen more syllables than the *tanka.* As in the Chinese *chüeh-chü* (broken-off lines), a quatrain of either five or seven syllables to a line, the emphatic syntactic break or turn occurs at the third line. While Korean poets had at their disposal two different forms, Chinese poets had, in addition to the *chüeh-chü* and *fu, ku-shih* (old-style verse), the eight-line *lü-shih* (regulated verse), with a variant *p'ai-lü* (regulated couplets), which is extended to more than eight lines. Some great Chinese poets were said to have excelled in one or the other—for example, Li Po in the heptasyllabic *chüeh-chü* and Tu Fu in the heptasyllabic *lü-shih.* Li Po also wrote some of his representative works in the pentasyllabic regulated verse. Thus Chinese poets were free to choose and work with a form most suited to their temperament, themes, and techniques.

Throughout the book I have also attempted to point out the differences between two poetic traditions. In spite of the existence in East Asia of heroic topoi analogous to Western epic topics, such as the description of the hero's weapon and horse, use of portents, epic games, and the conflation of the hero with his people, certain Western war topoi are absent. The Confucian heroic ethos seen as comprising *fortitudo et sapientia* prefers a cultural heroism, the stress falling on rites and arts. *Paci imponere morem,* a glory of Confucian rule, was accomplished at times with the sword or with emblem books on the Three Bonds,[5] but the elimination of *furor impius* was a persistent concern in East Asian praise poetry. In place of a hero with individual prowess, heroic pride, and his own sense of honor and worth, we have an icon, a paradigm of public virtues, light (fidelity, compassion, continuity) rather than darkness (tragic waste and woe). Because the heroic and the tragic are related, where one who subverts or tests the limits of culture is a villain, with the usual reward of the good and the punishment of the bad, there cannot be a tragic man.

The conventions of love poetry in two cultures present more striking differences. Such topics as courtship, the ladder of love, the religious *alba, carpe diem,* and *carpe florem,* so characteristic of the courtly love lyric and later in the Renaissance and seventeenth-century poetry in the West, are almost completely neglected. The social status of woman and the Confucian morality in which passion is disruptive and unworthy of serious concern in polite literature had a lasting impact on the development of love poetry in China and Korea. This also explains the relative absence of praise of the woman's body and elevation of the beloved's beauty as the manifestation of an inner perfection (hence no eternizing conceit). Seldom is love presented as ennobling, purifying, or educative, seldom as a mode of knowledge, spiritual development, or an analogue of divine love. Indeed, no East Asian lover builds an altar to a lady with his burning heart as a sacrifice.

On the other hand, moving love lyrics in China and Korea were produced by anonymous or women poets who celebrated the permanence of emotional truth. Unlike the ladies in Latin love elegies and the English sonnet sequences (Stella, Delia, Parthenope, Zepheria, Coelia, Chloris, Fidessa, Diana, Cynthia, Idea), in China and especially in Korea it was women who conferred lasting fame on themselves. A Confucian bias against passion and fulfillment is also reflected in the poverty of erotic imagery. The persistent tendency is a retrospective stance, with emphasis on parting, desertion, and neglect—topoi of dilemma, role-reversal, dream vision, and metamorphoses. Time and again the speaker drives home the disjunction between the peacefulness of nature and the turmoil in the heart, the harmony of nature and the disharmony of the lover's anguish and sorrow. Its emphasis on the incongruence between external nature and internal landscape notwithstanding, anything like the Western pastoral in its handling of the theme of love is rare. Its meditation as a dramatic situation and the resolution of passion and reason are ignored.

Nowhere is the fundamental difference between East Asia and the West so pronounced as in the views of nature and versions of nature poetry. Where the East Asian man is not separated from nature and yearns for ultimate harmony with it, the Western man lives in the imperfection of fallen nature, forever estranged from it. Torn between a desire to set himself above nature, seductive, dangerous and inferior, and to be involved in it, the Western man is beset by moral ambiguities.[6] Some, like the Romantics, wish to achieve an unmediated contact with it by means of expanded consciousness and the imagination, but they have learned that they cannot have both a separate self and nature. Some like Yeats repudiate nature ("Sailing to Byzantium") and seek permanence in a dimension beyond it.

Such an outlook not only affected the development of nature poetry in the West but resulted in the absence of some major topics so prominent in East Asia. One is the topos of "not finding him in," where the subject of praise is portrayed as having attained a complete harmony with nature and disappeared into it. This is the highest praise accorded a recluse in the tradition, fully supported by Buddhist-Taoist metaphysics. Another is the absence of some major topoi in retirement poetry, such as those of land as an emblem of values, modest sufficiency, cultivation of the True, the Taoist motif, "Can you fathom my joy?", mountains as positive images and values, and the fisherman as sage. A man who has not achieved identity with nature cannot send his absent friend hills and waters, a handful of moonlight, a painting of autumn sound. This is a third example. The prerequisite for the ideal Confucian gentleman to be a moral example was harmony with rituals and nature, and feeling for the beauties of nature was a significant attribute of civil servants aspiring to emulate the Confucian way. This is a fourth example.

The view of nature is related to the view of time and history. As in the Western pastoral, the speaker's commitment to nature demands a commitment to the finality of death. But the speaker in East Asian nature poetry joyfully accepts the terrors of discontinuity as "the ultimate homecoming." He accepts the process of time or tries to transcend it by such Taoist views as nondiscrimination, the utility of inutility, or nonaction. He would have shared the remarks of Achilles' ghost to Odysseus that he would rather be a slave to the poorest on earth than king of all dwellers in the underworld. As the falling and dying flower magnificently captures the transience of beauty and the mutability of life, so does the trope of river furnish a perspective on life and the timeless recurrences of nature. The speaker often seeks to find a parallel or contrast between his situation and historical recurrence by contemplating the past, the ruins of time. But the indulgence in the *ubi sunt* theme seldom allows him to combat transience and decay. Nor is *carpe diem* an invitation to an amorous or religious experience. In most cases, what is proposed is calm acceptance of the human condition rather than the espousal of the other world. It is with their faith in the power of poetry that East Asian poets transcend time to impose order on the flux by commemorating fleeting life in monuments more lasting than bronze. In addition to children and fame, it is with poetry and culture that they challenge the march of time.

I have said that the view of time is related to that of history. Though this is not the place to digress on the East Asian concept of history, we may say that where history is viewed as recurrence, not as development with a clear end, such a world view is bound to affect the development of narrative as well. A single-focus narrative structure makes a very late appearance;[7] so does the *Bildungsroman* focusing on the development of an individual—a single character—from beginning to end. The Aristotelian or neo-Aristotelian ideal of plot cannot be imposed on traditional narrative in East Asia, just as it cannot be applied to medieval Western narrative. It is nevertheless clear that the lack of a clearly defined goal in history is reflected not only in various forms of East Asian poetry but also in narrative.

Such is the scope of this book, with a sustained comparison of relevant materials drawn from two cultures. Most East Asian selections are from the premodern period; most Western selections come before the nineteenth century. When East Asia embarked on the modernization of language and the creation of new poetry in new stanzaic forms and free verse, it broke completely from the past, a subject for another study. My analysis of major poetic topoi in East Asia and the West has a heuristic value, and with a map of principal topoi and imagery in each preferred subject, students will, I hope, be able to read East Asian poetry rhetorically, with confidence and discrimination. In traditional East Asia, literature played a vital role in maintaining society and culture. In that society renovation was innovation, originality often posed as convention, and even in nature poetry, which seeks the liberation and expansion of self away from society, the speaker often assumes a universalized self, the "I" of universal reference. Conventionality was a mark of East Asian poetry, and there one seldom thought of the burden of the past or the anxiety of influence. Tradition meant all that was vital and alive for the community, a source of inspiration and a repository of techniques, which allowed poets to rediscover and validate the truth of art in the past to make it live in the present. But they knew, as we do, that the most important function of poetry is the development of the power of the imagination.

APPENDIXES

ABBREVIATIONS

NOTES

INDEX

APPENDIX I

Pak Il-lo

Hall of Solitary Bliss

Long ago I have heard of Mount Chaok
and the Hall of Solitary Bliss—
these cool and quiet places.
But I was a soldier then,
anxious, with a burning heart.
Danger lurked, our shores were violated.
I wielded a glistening spear
and rode fast my armored horse.
But I long for my teacher
even when my hair is grey.
Today I will start out at last
with bamboo stick, in straw sandals.
Like Wu-i mountains, the peaks
look graceful and the river winds like the I.
Such a place cannot be without host.
Sages and soldiers of Silla and Koryŏ,
how many of you have crossed the lovely pass?
Heaven created it, earth treasured it
and revealed its secrets to him.
They say, everything has its owner.
How true! Yi Ŏnjŏk is its true owner.

I push aside the tangled creepers
and open the Hall of Solitary Bliss,
an elegant, secluded room.
Its beauty is unmatched;
outside, straight and solemn,
a thousand bamboo surround the stream—
and here ten thousand books are on the walls.
Works of Yen Hui and Master Tseng
are on the left and of Tzu Yu

and Tzu Hsia on the right.
He revered the sages of the past
and wrote his poems.
In quiet nature he was so immersed
that he felt at home in all situations.
He called it Solitary Bliss,
a fine name for so elegant a life.
Ssu-ma Kuang had *his* garden of solitary bliss,
though could it match the beauty of this place?
I enter Yangjin hermitage—
to search for truth.
Winds caress me as I contemplate,
my mind becomes pure and bright:
How marvelous is T'oegye's brush stroke,
I see its matchless excellence.
On my walk to the Fish-Viewing-Terrace,
the rocks show the dear traces
of my teacher's stick and sandals.
The pine he planted has grown tall.
Greetings, tall tree in timeless air.
I feel as refreshed as when
I entered his fragrant study.
I think of the past—
high rocks and sheer cliffs
resemble a mica screen by Lung-mien.
In the lucid mirror of the pool—
like cool breeze in bright moonlight—
clouds and sky dazzle my eyes.
Hawk and fish were my teacher's friends.
He contemplated, sought the truth,
and carried on the ancient sages' task.
I cross the creek to ask
white gulls near the fishing place:
Birds, do you know when Yen Kuang returned to the Han house?
The evening smoke settles on the mossy strand.

Dressed for spring I climb to Yŏnggwi Terrace;
the world is beautiful, my spirits are high:
"Enjoy the breeze and go home singing"—
today I had the pleasures of Tseng Hsi.
A mild rain over the lotus pond
scatters pearls on jasper leaves.
Chou Tun-yi died many years ago;
but the views are still clear and marvelous;
And only the presence of my teacher abides.
Through the hovering mist

a winding stream's cataract
jumps a sheer red cliff.
Censer Peak is behind clouds. Mount Lu is here.
I can see Chungsim Terrace,
my rustic mind cleansed by freshness.
I sit alone on the terrace—
the hills are reflected in the pond;
the birds sing sadly from green shadows.
I linger, retracing the master's steps.
As always, Spring has come to T'agyŏng Terrace;
but men still wrestle in the dusty world
when they had better clean their hat-strings.

I climb Lion Rock to look at Mount Todŏk.
Like jade in its own brightness
my master's brilliance shone here recently.
Now the phoenix has left, the hills are bare;
a solitary cuckoo sighs at dusk.
The spring from Tohwa Cave,
day and night, carries fallen petals.
Is this Mount T'ient'ai? Is it Peach Blossom Spring?
Where is it? Where am I?
The footsteps of immortals are remote.
How ignorant I am, how far from wisdom;
enjoying the mountain, I forget to go home.
Leaning against a rock, I scan
hills and waters, far and near.
Ten thousand flowers weave a brocade,
their fragrance drifts on valley winds.
A distant temple gong echoes beyond clouds.
Even the pen of Fan Hsi-wen fails us;
so marvelous are the views, they stir the wanderer's heart.
I ramble everywhere and go home late
as the sun sets beyond western hills.

On my climb to the Hall of Solitary Bliss
I look around for traces of his presence.
And here he is, he welcomes me, indeed
"I see him in the soup and on the walls."
Looking to the stars and to the ground
I sigh and recall his deeds.
This is the table by the window where he sat
oblivious of the tangled world,
where he continued the tradition, opened a bright new path,
and gave us the treasures of his thought.
He was a happy gentleman, a light of the East.

Through filial piety and brotherly love,
through loyalty and sincerity for our king,
he became a Hou Chi and Chieh and hoped
to achieve the peace of Yao and Shun.
But times changed, loyalists were banished.
In high mountains and deep valleys
people who knew lamented.
For seven years he never saw the sun;
he had shut the door to search his heart;
he achieved virtue and the forthright way.
Right prevailed over evil in the end—
people claimed him of their own accord.
They erected a shrine in Kanggye,
the place of his exile, mean and cold,
and learned men hastened to revere him.

On Mount Chaok perches an academy.
Students pluck the lute and hum poetry
as though Chou Tun-yi and young scholars of Loyang
were gathered here once again—
I walk around Kuin Hall—
it holds the sacred Ch'ein Shrine
where Yi Ŏnjŏk never ceases to be worshiped.

Because we cannot honor him enough,
he is enshrined in the Confucian Temple—
what beautiful custom, what enduring norm!
Our civilization matches that of Han, T'ang, and Sung—
We are in Tzu-yang, in Yün-ku.
The water in Sesim Terrace is like my teacher's virtue,
his spirit lingers where the dragon reigns.
Wonderful are the workings of nature.

Overjoyed, yet unable to fathom the infinite landscape,
I linger for a month;
I try to open my mind to the Way;
I turn every page to read his work.
His every word is wisdom and reveals
the long tradition and patterns of thought
as bright as sun and moon,
a light illuminating the dark.

If his thoughts fill our hearts,
If we order our minds and pursue the Way,
if our words are loyal and our deeds faithful,
goodness will naturally follow then.

My friends, look toward this wise man,
great as Mount T'ai, remote as the polestar.
Heaven so high and earth so rich,
they, too, end and dissolve to dust.
Only the cool wind is eternal that blows
over the Hall of Solitary Bliss.

The texts of "spring" poems. For "Tzu-yeh Songs of the Four Seasons, Spring, 1 and 10," see *SS,* 74–75; for "Spring Thoughts" by Li Po, *ACL,* 225–226; for "Spring Thoughts" by Chia Chih see below. For Yakamochi (Uraura ni), *MYS,* 172; for Narihira (Yo no naka ni), *JCP,* 199; Ki no Tomonori (Hisakata no), *AJL,* 80; Shunzei (Kiku hito zo) *JCP,* 9; Teika (Haru no yo no), *JCP,* 262. For Yi Cho-nyŏn, Song Sun ("Do not grieve, little birds"), Prince Pongnim ("What amuses you"), Kim Yu-gi ("Don't boast of your new dresses"), and anonymous *sijo* ("In the wind that blew last night"), see *Poems from Korea* (Honolulu: University Press of Hawaii, 1974), 64, 79, 144, 146–47, 156.

The texts of "autumn" poems. For "Tzu-yeh Song: Autumn," see *ACV,* 101; for "An Autumn Night" by Hsieh T'iao, *ACV,* 163; for "The Autumn Wastes" by Tu Fu, Graham, *Poems of the Late T'ang,* 42; for "Early Autumn" by Hsü Hun see below; for "Autumn Evening" by Tu Mu see below; for "Garden" by Li Yü see Ch'en and Bullock, *Poems of Solitude* (London, 1960), 107. For Sone no Yoshitada (Nake ya nake), *JCP,* 179; anonymous (Kita e yuku), *JCP,* 212; Shunzei (Yū sareba), *JCP,* 17; Teika (Miwataseba), *JCP,* 307; Jakuren (Sabishisawa), *JCP,* 261; Teika (Tabibito no), *JCP,* 308; Saigyō (Kokoro naki), *AJL,* 195. For Wŏn Ch'ŏn-sŏk ("Rise and fall is a destiny turning"), Yi Chŏng ("Night comes to the autumn river"), Yun Sŏn-do, "Autumn Night" and "Dispelling Gloom," Yi Chŏng-bo ("The Milky Way climbs higher"), and Cho Myŏng-ni ("Wild geese have passed overhead"), see *Poems from Korea,* 71, 75, 130, 127, 147, 153.

Chia Chih (718–772)

Spring Thoughts

The grass is so green, the willows are so yellow,
Peach blossoms bloom in profusion, plum blossoms are so fragrant.
The eastern breeze does not blow away my sorrow,
The spring day, deliberately, provokes my endless grief.

Hsü Hun (c. 832)

Early Autumn

In a long night floats the clear zither,
The west wind rises from the green creepers.
The remaining fireflies settle on the jade dew,
An early wildgoose brushes the River of Heaven.
Tall trees in the dawn are still leafy,
Many distant hills stand clearer in the fine sky.
A single leaf's fall on south of the Huai—
I feel a ruffle on the Tung-t'ing Lake.

Tu Mu (803–852)

Autumn Evening

The silver candlelight shines cold on the painted screen,
Her small gauze fan strikes passing fireflies.
The night color of courtyard is chilly as water,
She sits gazing at the Herdboy and Weaver.

APPENDIX II

Korean Poetic Forms

Forms of Korean poetry are less known to the general reader than those of China and Japan, which have been competently discussed in recent books on the subject, some of which I mention in note 15 to the Introduction.

There are four major forms in Korean poetry. The extant twenty-five Old Korean poems, such as "Ode to Knight Kilbo" and "Song of Ch'ŏyong," are written in the *hyangga,* also known as *saenaennorae,* form, which spans the seventh to the tenth century. Of the three variants, the most polished and popular consisted of two stanzas of four lines plus a conclusion of two lines. Middle Korean poems, such as "Song of the Gong," "Song of P'yongyang," "Spring Overflows the Pavilion," "Will You Go?" and "Winter Night" (see Chapter Three), are in the *changga* form, characterized by the refrain recurring at intervals, bespeaking the folk and musical origin and oral transmission. Consisting of a meaningless onomatopoeia of drum sounds or nonsense jingles, the effect of the refrain is to help achieve a mood or tone in order to carry the tune and spirit of the poem. The refrain attests, therefore, to the association of verbal and musical rhythm in the *changga.*

The *sijo,* the most popular, elastic, and mnemonic poetic form of Korea, is a three-line verse (in translation I have used a six-line stanza) and dates from the fifteenth century. Each line consists of four syllable groups, a minor pause occurring at the end of the second, and a major at the end of the fourth. The emphatic syntactic division is usually introduced in the third line, in the form of a countertheme, paradox, resolution, judgment, and the like. It often presents a leap in logic and development, and the skillful poet achieves a pattern of thought within formal limits and a unity in variety. The introduction of a deliberate twist in phrasing or its meaning is often a test of the poet's originality. As the Shakespearean sonnet is said to conform to the pattern of propositio–ratio–confirmatio, confutatio, or exonoratio, so the *sijo* is often held to follow the pattern of theme–development–antitheme, but exceptions abound. The *sijo* was sung and orally transmitted until the texts were written down from the beginning of the eighteenth century. It is an oral art even today for both the lettered and unlettered, and even shoeshine boys learn the texts without their tunes, as observed by a recent missionary. The number of variants of a given poem—the text of most poems varies with each source and perhaps with each performance—betrays the oral nature. Variations range from changes in verbal endings, particles, or phrases to a whole line. Sometimes, the contents remain the same with minor changes. Sometimes, minor variations result in the alteration of the contents. Often a single poem has metamorphosed into two different poems, and more popular ones exist in a great number of variants, large and small. The lack of a fixed text, especially in the case of an anonymous poem, is an insoluble problem. Although we are not sure which ones are oral compositions, composed during performance, the singer had the freedom to alter phrases and lines, whenever his memory failed him or his creative urge prompted him.

The *kasa* originated as song words written to prevailing *kasa* tunes. It is characterized by the lack of stanzaic division and varying length, the tendency toward description and exposition, at times also lyricism, and the use of balanced parallel phrases, verbal and syntactical. Its norm is a group of two four-syllable words—or alternating groups of three and four syllables—which form a unit and are repeated in parallel form. Emerging as a new genre towards the middle of the fifteenth century, its earliest extant example is "Hymn to the Spring," a 45-line poem. The form was perfected in the subsequent centuries by Chŏng Ch'ŏl, the author of "Little Odes of Mount Star" (see Chapter One), Hŏ Nansŏrhŏn, and Pak Il-lo. The form's greatest exponent was Lady Hŏ Nansŏrhŏn, whose "A Woman's Sorrow," discussed in Chapter Three, is a dramatic narrative on the sorrow of unrequited love. Pak Il-lo combined erudition and lyricism, as in "In Praise of Poverty" and "The Hall of Solitary Bliss," both discussed in Chapters Two and One, respectively.

ABBREVIATIONS

ACL	Cyril Birch, ed., *Anthology of Chinese Literature,* I
ACV	John D. Frodsham, *An Anthology of Chinese Verse*
AJL	Donald Keene, ed., *Anthology of Japanese Literature,* I
APCC	Paul Demiéville, *Anthologie de la Poésie chinoise classique*
Ayling and Mackintosh, I	Alan Ayling and Duncan Mackintosh, *A Collection of Chinese Lyrics*
Ayling and Mackintosh, II	*A Further Collection of Chinese Lyrics*
ChL	Burton Watson, *Chinese Lyricism*
CP	Wai-lim Yip, *Chinese Poetry*
Hightower	James Robert Hightower, *The Poetry of T'ao Ch'ien*
JCP	Robert Brower and Earl Miner, *Japanese Court Poetry*
KKS	*Kokin waka shū,* in *Nihon koten bungaku taikei,* 8
Kotewall and Smith	Robert Kotewall and Norman L. Smith, *The Penguin Book of Chinese Verse*
LCL	Loeb Classical Library (Cambridge, Mass., 1912–)
MYS	*Man'yōshū,* in *Nihon koten bungaku taikei,* 4–7
PCLP	Arthur Waley, *The Poetry and Career of Li Po*
SBCP	Wing-tsit Chan, *A Scource Book in Chinese Philosophy*
SKKS	*Shin Kokin waka shū,* in *Nihon koten bungaku taikei,* 28
SPTK	Ssu-pu ts'ung-k'an edition
SS	Wu-chi Liu and Irving Yucheng Lo, eds., *Sunflower Splendor*
TFC	Arthur Waley, *Translations from the Chinese*
TJM	Witter Bynner, *The Jade Mountain*

NOTES

Introduction

1. For topoi in general and the criticism of Curtius' usage in his book, see Arthur R. Evans, Jr., "Ernst Robert Curtius," in *On Four Modern Humanists* (Princeton: Princeton University Press, 1970), pp. 85–145, esp. 117–118 n59.

2. Although recent critics of oral narrative poetry would deny that written works can be formulaic, I think both written and oral poetry can use formulas, as shown, for example, by Earl Miner, "Formulas: Japanese and Western Evidence Compared," *Proceedings of the Vth Congress of the International Comparative Literature Association* (Amsterdam: Swets & Zeitlinger, 1969), pp. 405–417, and Hans H. Frankel, "The Formulaic Language of the Chinese Ballad, 'Southeast Fly the Peacocks,'" *Bulletin of the Institute of History and Philology (CYYY)*, XXXIX (1969), 219–244.

3. C. H. Wang, *The Bell and the Drum: Shih Ching as Formulaic Poetry in an Oral Tradition* (Berkeley: University of California Press, 1974).

4. See Shim Chae-wan, *Kyobon yŏktae sijo chŏnsŏ* [Annotated Canon of Sijo] and a companion volume, *Sijo ŭi munhŏnjŏk yŏn'gu* [Bibliographical Study of Sijo] (Seoul: Sejong munhwasa, 1972), pp. 159–395.

5. Ōyane Bunjirō, *Tō Emmei kenkyū* (Tokyo: Waseda daigaku shuppanbu, 1967), pp. 365–417.

6. E. H. Gombrich, *Art and Illusion: A Study in the Psychology of Pictorial Representation* (London: Phaidon Press, 1959), pp. 61, 65.

7. Evans, pp. 139–142.

8. Peter Dronke, *Poetic Individuality in the Middle Ages* (Oxford: Clarendon Press, 1970), pp. 11–22.

9. Rosalie L. Colie, *The Resources of Kind: Genre-Theory in the Renaissance* (Berkeley: University of California Press, 1973), p. 119.

10. H. M. Richmond, *The School of Love: The Evolution of the Stuart Love Lyric* (Princeton: Princeton University Press, 1964), p. 280.

11. Claudio Guillén, *Literature as System: Essays toward the Theory of Literary History* (Princeton: Princeton University Press, 1971), p. 507.

12. Geoffrey H. Hartman, *The Fate of Reading* (Chicago: University of Chicago Press, 1975), p. xiii.

13. Frank Lentricchia, *Robert Frost: Modern Poetics and the Landscape of Self* (Durham: Duke University Press, 1975), p. 14.

14. Robert Magliola, "The Phenomenological Approach to Literature: Its Theory and Methodology," *Language and Style,* V, 2 (1972), 79–99.

15. For example, Hans H. Frankel, *The Flowering Plum and the Palace Lady: Interpretations of Chinese Poetry* (New Haven: Yale University Press, 1976), esp. pp. 212–217; Wai-lim Yip, *Chinese Poetry: Major Modes and Genres* (Berkeley: University of California Press, 1976); and *JCP.*

1. Praise

1. *Shang shu* (*SPTK*), 6, 7b (Bernhard Karlgren, *The Book of Documents* [Stockholm: The Museum of Far Eastern Antiquities, 1960], p. 29; Legge, III, 304).

2. Arthur Waley, *The Book of Songs* (London: George Allen and Unwin, 1954), pp. 256, 258; Karlgren, *The Book of Odes* (Stockholm: The Museum of Far Eastern Antiquities, 1950), pp. 194–195.

3. C. M. Bowra, *Heroic Poetry* (London: Macmillan, 1961), pp. 179–214, 265–266; David Maskell, *The Historical Epic in France 1500–1700* (Oxford: Oxford University Press, 1973), pp. 208 ff.

4. C. H. Wang, "Towards Defining a Chinese Heroism," *Journal of the American Oriental Society* (*JAOS*), XCV (1975), 25–35.

5. No. 235 (Waley, p. 250; Karlgren, p. 185 ["vigorous"]).

6. Nos. 285, 295 (Waley, pp. 232, 238).

7. No. 236.3 (Waley, p. 261; Karlgren, p. 188 ["careful and reverent"]).

8. No. 241.4 (Waley p. 257).

9. No. 268 (Waley, p. 227).

10. Waley, p. 263.

11. *SBCP,* p. 8.

12. No. 245.1 (Waley, p. 248).

13. No. 236.8 (Waley, p. 263; Karlgren, p. 188 ["he killed and smote the great Shang"]).

14. Waley, p. 232; Karlgren, p. 247.

15. No. 293 (Waley, p. 237; Karlgren, p. 252; see also Waley, p. 232n1).

16. *Ibid.*

17. No. 240.2–3 (Waley, p. 260).

18. No. 244.8 (Waley, p. 264).

19. Waley, p. 230.

20. Waley, p. 237.

21. Eric A. Havelock, *Preface to Plato* (Cambridge, Mass.: Harvard University Press, 1963), p. 87.

22. John M. Steadman, *Milton and the Renaissance Hero* (Oxford: Clarendon Press, 1967), pp. 10 ff, 162–163.

23. For the discussion of virtù see Leonardo Olschki, *Machiavelli the*

Scientist (Berkeley: The Gillick Press, 1945), pp. 35–40; Harry Levin, *The Overreacher* (Cambridge, Mass.: Harvard University Press, 1952), pp. 179–183; and Joseph A. Mazzeo, *Renaissance and Seventeenth-Century Studies* (New York: Columbia University Press, 1964), p. 94, n. 1, and p. 156.

24. Waley, pp. 252–254.

25. Waley, p. 261.

26. Waley, p. 251.

27. Waley, p. 234.

28. Same as 26; see also *SBCP,* p. 7.

29. Waley (no. 241), p. 251.

30. Wang, p. 34.

31. George deF. Lord, "The Odyssey and the Western World," *Sewanee Review,* LXII (1954), 420, 423.

32. Michael Wilding, "The Last of the Epics: The Rejection of the Heroic in *Paradise Lost* and *Hudibras,*" in *Restoration Literature,* ed. Harold Love (London: Methuen, 1972), p. 97.

33. Quoted in Eugene M. Waith, *Ideas of Greatness: Heroic Drama in England* (London: Routledge & Kegan Paul, 1971), p. 131.

34. George E. Dimock, Jr., "The Mistake of Aeneas," *Yale Review,* LXIV (Spring 1975), 334–365.

35. The six dragons invoked in the first canto include the four royal ancestors and the first and third monarchs of the new dynasty: Mockcho (d. 1274), Ikcho (dates unknown), Tojo (d. 1342), Hwanjo (1315–1361), Yi Sŏng-gye (1335–1408), and Yi Pang-wŏn (1367–1422).

36. O. B. Hardison, Jr., *The Enduring Monument: A Study of the Idea of Praise in Renaissance Literary Theory and Practice* (Chapel Hill: University of North Carolina Press, 1962), pp. 30, 74–76. See also Barbara K. Lewalski, *Donne's Anniversaries and the Poetry of Praise: The Creation of a Symbolic Mode* (Princeton: Princeton University Press, 1973), pp. 11–41, and A. Leigh Deneff, "Epideictic Rhetoric and the Renaissance Lyric," *The Journal of Medieval and Renaissance Studies,* III (1973), 203–231.

37. Bowra, *Heroic Poetry,* pp. 157–170, esp. 157.

38. When the ball bounced off the goal post and came back on the horse's left, Yi Sŏng-gye shook off the right stirrup and turned his body around in such a way that his right foot reached down almost to the ground. He hit the ball cleanly, then back astride his mount, he hit it again and scored. The compilers call it the "sideway block" technique.

39. Peter F. Fisher, "The Trials of the Epic Hero in Beowulf," *PMLA,* LXXIII (1958), 171–183.

40. *SBCP,* p. 78.

41. Cf. Joseph Campbell, *The Hero with a Thousand Faces* (New York: Pantheon Books, 1961), pp. 97 ff.

42. Samuel C. Chew, *The Virtues Reconciled* (Toronto: University of Toronto Press, 1947), pp. 119–122.

43. This is another topos in Confucian historical writing.

44. *Hsün Tzu* (*SPTK*), 10, 13b (Watson, p. 69).

45. *Mencius*, 4A.17 (Legge, II, 307).

46. From Michael C. J. Putnam. See n. 47 below.

47. Bowra, "Virgil and the Ideal of Rome," in *From Virgil to Milton* (London: Macmillan, 1945), pp. 33–85, esp. 60 ff; Viktor Pöschl, *Die Dichtkunst Virgils,* tr. Gerda Seligson (Ann Arbor: University of Michigan Press, 1962), pp. 34–60; Michael C. J. Putnam, *The Poetry of the Aeneid* (Cambridge, Mass.: Harvard University Press, 1965), p. 193; Brooks Otis, *Virgil: A Study in Civilized Poetry* (Oxford: Clarendon Press, 1963), pp. 313–314; Kenneth Quinn, *Virgil's Aeneid* (Ann Arbor: University of Michigan Press, 1968), p. 173.

48. *De Clementia,* 11 (Moses Hadas, tr., *The Stoic Philosophy of Seneca* [Gloucester: P. Smith, 1965], p. 151).

49. Ibid., 5 (Hadas, p. 144).

50. Ibid., 23–24 (Hadas, pp. 162–163).

51. *SBCP,* p. 47.

52. Horace's fourth Roman ode (III. 4. 37 ff) deals with the power of literature as a civilizing force. See Roger A. Hornsby, "Horace on Art and Politics (3.4)," *Classical Journal,* LVIII (1962), 97–104, and Steele Commager, *The Odes of Horace: A Critical Study* (New Haven: Yale University Press, 1962), pp. 194–209.

53. *Republic,* X, 581–582; VII, 529; Francis M. Cornford, *The Republic of Plato* (New York: Oxford University Press, 1959), pp. 308–309, 223.

54. "On Kingship" (Lester K. Born, *The Education of a Christian Prince* [New York: Columbia University Press, 1936], p. 89).

55. *SBCP,* pp. 98, 107.

56. *The Mean,* 31 (*SBCP,* p. 112).

57. *The Mean,* 20 (*SBCP,* p. 107).

58. Martha Andresen, " 'Ripeness is All': Sententiae and Commonplaces in King Lear," in *Some Facets of King Lear: Essays in Prismatic Criticism,* ed. Rosalie L. Colie and F. T. Flahiff (Toronto: University of Toronto Press, 1974), p. 152.

59. Ibid.

60. Ibid., p. 163.

61. *Book of Songs,* 237 (Waley, p. 248).

62. Quoted in Paul A. Jorgensen, *Shakespeare's Military World* (Berkeley: University of California Press, 1956), p. 186 (Fulke Greville's sonnet 108 to Caelica, lines 7–8).

63. Legge, II, 455.

64. Seneca, *De Clementia,* I. 2 (Hadas, p. 140).

65. Dio Chrysostom, "On Kingship," IV.44, tr. J. W. Cohoon, I (Loeb Classical Library, 1949), 189.

66. Legge, II, 201–204.

67. *Moralia,* I (LCL, 1949), 327.

68. "How to Tell a Flatterer from a Friend," 1 (*Moralia,* I.267), 8 (I.285), 12 (I.299), 23 (I.345), 2 (I.291).

69. Ibid., 20 (*Moralia,* I.327).

70. *Book of Songs,* 200 (Waley, pp. 315–316). Philip Wheelwright, *The Burning Fountain* (Bloomington: Indiana University Press, 1954), pp. 117–118, for the symbolism of "weaving."

71. *Book of Songs,* 198 (Karlgren, p. 148).

72. *Book of Songs,* 200 (Waley, p. 315).

73. "How to Tell a Flatterer from a Friend," 22 (*Moralia,* I.335).

74. Legge, II, 210.

75. *The Odes and Epodes* (LCL, 1964), pp. 303–305.

76. Earl R. Wasserman, *The Subtler Language: Critical Readings of Neoclassical and Romantic Poems* (Baltimore: Johns Hopkins University Press, 1959), p. 120. The following paragraph is based on his interpretation of the motif (see pp. 113 ff).

77. Howard Nemerov, *The Western Approaches* (Chicago: University of Chicago Press, 1975), p. 88.

78. Francis Fergusson, chap. 5, "Redeeming the Time: The Monarch as 'Figura,'" in *Trope and Allegory: Themes Common to Dante and Shakespeare* (Athens: University of Georgia Press, 1977), pp. 71–103.

79. Richmond Lattimore, *The Iliad of Homer* (Chicago: University of Chicago Press, 1951), p. 157; Robert Fitzgerald, "Generation of Leaves," *Perspectives USA,* no. 8 (1954), 68–85.

80. Ed. D. M. Brodie (Cambridge: Cambridge University Press, 1948). See also James Howell, *Dendrologia* (London, 1644), pp. 134–135, for the allegory of the oak.

81. Waley, p. 135 (no. 138). The pine is also used as a tree of praise in *KKS,* VII.356 and in *SKKS,* VII.720, 726–728, 739, 747.

82. Also in *A Little Primer of Tu Fu* (Oxford: Clarendon Press, 1967), pp. 156–164. For a verse translation see Arthur Cooper, *Li Po and Tu Fu* (Harmondsworth: Penguin Books, 1973), pp. 219–225. The discussion is based on Hawkes' reading. For more poems on Tu Fu's hero see, for example, "The Chancellor of Shu" (pp. 103–108), "The Eight Formations" (pp. 185–187), and "Thoughts on Ancient Site, 2" (pp. 178–180).

83. But see Alastair Fowler, "The 'Better Marks' of Jonson's *To Penshurst,*" *Review of English Studies,* XXIV (1973), 273, where he comments: "It is a family tree, commemorating a heritage of greatness, a tradition of patronage. . . . More remotely, the oaks's roots reach down, through mythology of feasting gods (10–12), to an earthly paradise of accessible fruit; to the golden age; to a cosmic past."

84. *Ben Jonson,* ed. C. H. Herford, Percy and Evelyn Simpson, VIII (Oxford: Clarendon Press, 1947), 93, and XI (1952), 33.

85. Martial, *Epigrams,* tr. Walter C. A. Ker (LCL, 1968), II, 118–119.

86. Waley, p. 88.

87. *SBCP,* p. 264.

88. Legge, II, 420.

89. *SBCP,* p. 87.

90. *SBCP,* p. 102.

91. *SBCP,* p. 105.

92. *Tso chuan,* Duke Chuang 14 (Legge, V, 92b). I have used the translation of Burton Watson, *Ssu-ma Ch'ien: Grand Historian of China* (New York: Columbia University Press, 1958), p. 15.

93. Galen A. Rowe, "The *Adynaton* as a Stylistic Device," *AJP,* LXXXVI (1965), 392, 395.

94. From Raymond H. Coon, "The Reversal of Nature as a Rhetorical Figure," *Indiana University Studies,* XV (1928), 3–20.

95. Lattimore, p. 442 (Achilles speaks to Hector).

96. *Virgil,* tr. H. Rushton Fairclough, II (LCL, 1969), 313.

97. Smith P. Bovie, *The Georgics* (Chicago: University of Chicago Press, 1956), p. 34 (The subject is the number of trees.)

98. William Berg, *Early Virgil* (London: Athlone Press, 1974), p. 45. See also *Eclogues,* VIII, 52–56 (p. 77) for another example.

99. John Warden, tr. *The Poems of Propertius* (Indianapolis: Bobbs-Merrill, 1972), p. 83.

100. Nos. 154.8 (Karlgren, p. 99; Waley, p. 167); 166.4 (Karlgren, p. 110; Waley, p. 176); 172.2 (Karlgren, p. 116; Waley, p. 179); 209.2 (Karlgren, p. 162; Waley, p. 210); 210.3, 6 (Karlgren, p. 64; Waley, p. 213). In his translations, Waley has failed to do justice to the formula phrases.

101. Nos. 213.2–3 (Karlgren, 167–168; Waley, p. 195); 216.1–4 (Karlgren, p. 169; Waley, p. 185); 247.1–7 (Karlgren, pp. 203–204; Waley, pp. 214–215).

102. No. 262.5–6 (Karlgren, p. 234; Waley, p. 132).

103. No. 300.4, lines 37–38 (Karlgren, p. 260; Waley, p. 272). See also 243.5–6 (Karlgren, p. 197; Waley, p. 265).

104. Nippon Gakujutsu Shinkōkai, *The Manyōshū* (New York: Columbia University Press, 1965), pp. 28, 192, 193, 271.

105. Waley, pp. 175–176 (no. 167).

106. The Japanese national anthem, "His Majesty's Reign," which is a slightly modified version of the anonymous poem in *KKS,* VII.343, goes: "May your reign/ Last for ages, myriad ages/ Till the tiny pebbles/ Grow into mighty rocks and/ Moss overgrows them."

107. Tr. Rolfe Humphries (Bloomington: Indiana University Press, 1967), p. 373.

108. *Metamorphoses,* XV.872 (Humphries, p. 392).

109. Horace, *Odes,* III.30 (*Exegi monumentum aere perennius*); *Metamorphoses,* XV.871–879; Shakespeare, Sonnet 55.

110. Charles Molesworth, "Property and Virtue: The Genre of the Country-House Poem in the Seventeenth Century," *Genre,* I (1968), 141–157.

111. John Chalker, *The English Georgic* (Baltimore: Johns Hopkins University Press, 1969), p. 178.

112. Compare the ending of this poem with that of Su Shih's "Red Cliff, II" (*ACL,* pp. 383–384; Burton Watson, *Su Tung-p'o* [New York: Columbia University Press, 1965], pp. 92–93).

113. *ACL,* p. 382.

114. For his biography see Burton Watson, *Records of the Grand Historian of China* (2 vols.; New York: Columbia University Press, 1961), I, 508–516.

115. Karlgren, p. 191; Waley (no. 201), pp. 213–214.

116. Compare Ben Jonson, "To Penshurst," lines 30–38, esp. 32–33 (Thou hast thy ponds, that pay thee tribute fish,/ Fat, aged carps, that runne into thy net); and Carew, "To Saxham," lines 21–28, esp. 27–28 (The scalie herd more pleasure tooke,/ Bath'd in thy dish, then in the brooke). Herford and Simpson, XI, 34, and Rhodes Dunlap, ed. *The Poems of Thomas Carew, with His Masque Coelum Britannicum* (Oxford: Clarendon Press, 1949), p. 28. For more on the motif of "the voluntary sacrifice of the animals," which is absent in East Asian examples, see William A. McClung, *The Country House in English Renaissance Poetry* (Berkeley: University of California Press, 1977), pp. 121 ff.

117. *SBCP,* p. 100.

118. Refers to a tradition that Shun longed for Yao for three years after his death and saw his image on the walls, whenever he sat, and in the soup, whenever he ate.

119. E. R. Hughes, *The Art of Letters* (New York: Pantheon Books, 1951), p. 103; Shih-hsiang Chen, *Essay on Literature Written by the Third-Century Chinese Poet Lu Chi* (Portland: Anthoensen Press, 1953), p. xxxvi (*ACL,* p. 210).

120. *ChL,* p. 116.

121. Also in *PCLP,* p. 47; *TFC,* p. 123.

122. Translated by the author.

123. Also in *ACV,* p. 94.

124. *ChL,* p. 119; *APCC,* p. 278.

125. Also in *PCLP,* pp. 11–12; *TJM,* p. 42; and *APCC,* p. 220. "Sage" is argot for "strained wine."

126. According to the *Po-wu chih,* when Chang Ch'ien "went in search of the sources of the Yellow River, he reached a place where he saw women weaving and a man giving his cow a drink by the river." When, later, Chang consulted the fortune-teller Yen Chün-p'ing about the location, Yen told him that on such and such a day a guest star invaded spheres of the constellations, the Weaving Maid (Vega and Lyra) and the Cowherd (Aquila), on both sides of the Milky Way (James J. Y. Liu, *The Poetry of Li Shang-yin* [Chicago: University of Chicago Press, 1969], p. 112). Hsü Shih or Hsü Fu who persuaded the First Emperor of Ch'in to send out an expedition, accompanied by thousands of youths and maidens, to search for the Isles (*Shih-chou chi,* la-b). In "Ballad of the White Tiger," Li Ho (791–817) satirizes the emperor (J. D. Frodsham, *The Poems of Li Ho* [Oxford: Clarendon Press, 1970], p. 266).

127. A. C. Graham, *The Book of Lieh-tzu* (London: John Murray, 1960), p. 97.

128. Cf. Howard R. Patch, *The Other World* (Cambridge, Mass.: Harvard University Press, 1950), pp. 1–26, for mythological origins, Oriental and

classical, of the earthly paradise; Harry Levin, *The Myth of the Golden Age in the Renaissance* (Bloomington: Indiana University Press, 1969) ; A. Bartlett Giamatti, *The Earthly Paradise and the Renaissance Epic* (Princeton: Princeton University Press, 1966), pp. 11–33; and Joseph Needham, *Science and Civilization in China,* II (Cambridge: Cambridge University Press, 1956), 127–130.

129. *TFC,* pp. 182–183; see also Ho Peng Yoke, Goh Thean Chye, and David Parker, "Po Chü-i's Poems on Immortality," *HJAS,* XXXIV (1974), 177–178.

130. I have omitted discussion of paradoxical encomia, poems on death, adultery, plague, inconstancy, and the like, but for their English examples see Henry K. Miller, "The Paradoxical Encomium with Special Reference to its Vogue in England, 1600–1800," *MP,* LIII (1956), 145–178.

2. Nature

1. Matsumoto Masaaki, *Shikyō shohen no seiritsu katei ni kansuru kenkyū* (Tokyo: Tōyō bunko, 1958) ; Shih-hsiang Chen, "The *Shih-ching:* Its Generic Significance in Chinese Literary History and Poetics," *CYYY,* XXXIX (1969), 371–414.

2. Karlgren, *The Book of Odes,* p. 6; Arthur Waley, *The Book of Songs,* p. 82.

3. Karlgren, p. 76; Waley (no. 152), p. 157.

4. Karlgren, p. 76; Waley (no. 94), p. 87.

5. Karlgren, p. 46; Waley (no. 150), p. 155.

6. Karlgren, p. 60; Waley (no. 263), p. 291.

7. Karlgren, p. 191; Waley (no. 249), p. 266.

8. Karlgren, pp. 65–66, 103; Waley (nos. 71 and 72), pp. 67–68.

9. Karlgren, p. 43; Waley (no. 44), p. 48.

10. Karlgren, pp. 20–21; Waley (no. 54), p. 54.

11. Karlgren, p. 24; Waley (no. 39), p. 45.

12. Karlgren, pp. 83–84; Waley (no. 34), p. 42.

13. Peter Dronke, *The Medieval Lyric* (London: Hutchinson, 1968), p. 194. For a discussion of concatenate motifs used for achieving type-scenes (a sequence of topoi) or themes in the *Book of Songs,* see C. H. Wang, *The Bell and the Drum: Shih Ching as Formulaic Poetry in an Oral Tradition,* pp. 98–125.

14. *ChL,* p. 28; Joseph Needham, *Science and Civilization in China,* III (Cambridge: Cambridge University Press, 1959), 276: Edward H. Schafer, "The Sky River," *JAOS,* XCIV (1974), 401–407.

15. *The Manyōshū* (New York, 1965), pp. 211–212, 54; *JCP,* p. 89.

16. Robert Scholes and Robert Kellogg, *The Nature of Narrative* (New York: Oxford University Press, 1966), p. 27.

17. Stephen Reckert, *Lyra Minima* (London: Eyre & Spottiswood, 1970), pp. 7–9.

18. Phillip Damon, *Modes of Analogy in Ancient and Medieval Verse,* in *University of California Publications in Classical Philology,* XV, no. 6 (1961), 305.

19. Waley, p. 164.

20. The twelve months of the tropical year were divided into twenty-four fortnights as early as the late Chou times (Needham, III, 404–405).

21. For "Encountering Sorrow" see David Hawkes, *Ch'u Tz'u: The Songs of the South* (Oxford: Clarendon Press, 1959), pp. 21–34; for "Shang-lin Park," Burton Watson, *Early Chinese Literature* (New York: Columbia University Press, 1962), pp. 273–284; for "Climbing the Tower," Watson, *Chinese Rhyme-Prose* (New York: Columbia University Press, 1971), pp. 52–54.

22. *Huai-nan Tzu (SPTK)*, 10.7b. For the *Carmina Burana* quotation see James J. Wilhelm, *The Cruelest Month: Spring, Nature, and Love in Classical and Medieval Lyrics* (New Haven: Yale University Press, 1965), p. 116.

23. Karlgren, p. 13; Waley (no. 63), p. 60; Karlgren, pp. 97–99; Waley (no. 159), pp. 164–167.

24. Hawkes, p. 92.

25. For a different interpretation see Yu-kung Kao and Tsu-lin Mei, "Syntax, Diction, and Imagery in T'ang Poetry," *HJAS,* XXXI (1971), 115.

26. R. G. M. Nisbet and Margaret Hubbard, *A Commentary on Horace: Odes, Book I* (Oxford: Clarendon Press, 1970), pp. 58–72; *The Odes and Epodes,* tr. C. E. Bennett (LCL, 1964), pp. 16–17.

27. *The Odes and Epodes,* pp. 310–313. See Niall Rudd, *Lines of Enquiry* (Cambridge: Cambridge University Press, 1976), pp. 189–199, for his commentary on different English versions of the ode. This poem is more hopeful than I.4, because it offers the solace that there is a continuity in nature's changes. Compare these odes with T'ao Ch'ien's "Trees in Bloom," I–II, and "The Ninth of the Ninth Month, 409" (Hightower, pp. 19, 119–120).

28. James J. Wilhelm, *The Cruelest Month,* p. 56, comments: "The juxtaposition of spring and winter . . . mirrors the many paradoxes concerning life and love that lie at the heart of the finest Greco-Roman lyric poetry. We find no happy spring songs in this domain, except as facts of the religious or romantic sensibility. Even when these landscapes do occur in the larger works, they are frequently flawed. The Greco-Roman religion was vitally concerned with reality; it had no consistent metaphysic with which to shroud the paradoxes of the physical world."

29. *The Odes and Epodes,* pp. 330–333.

30. Arthur W. Hoffman, "Chaucer's Prologue to Pilgrimage: The Two Voices," in *Chaucer: Modern Essays in Criticism,* ed. Edward Wagenknecht (New York: Oxford University Press, 1959), pp. 31–32.

31. Richard Schoeck and Jerome Taylor, eds., *Chaucer Criticism,* I (Notre Dame: University of Notre Dame Press, 1960), 17.

32. Edward H. Schafer, "The Idea of Created Nature in T'ang Literature," *Philosophy East and West,* XV (1965), 153–160.

33. "Poetry and the Poem: The Structure of Poetic Content," in *Literary Theory and Practice: Essays in Honor of William K. Wimsatt,* ed. Frank Brady, John Palmer, and Martin Price (New Haven: Yale University Press, 1973), p. 107.

34. Ibid., p. 102.

35. Ibid., p. 105.

36. Paul de Man, "Intentional Structure of the Romantic Image," in *Romanticism and Consciousness,* ed. Harold Bloom (New York: Norton, 1970), pp. 65–77, Bloom's introduction to Part One (p. 2), and his essay, "The Internalization of Quest Romance," pp. 3–24 (also in *The Ringers in the Tower: Studies in Romantic Tradition* [Chicago: University of Chicago Press, 1971], pp. 13–35).

37. Etienne Balazs, *Chinese Civilization and Bureaucracy* (New Haven: Yale University Press, 1964), pp. 197–254; Richard B. Mather, "The Controversy over Conformity and Naturalness during the Six Dynasties," *History of Religions,* IX (1969–70), 160–180.

38. Hightower, p. 268.

39. Waley, *The Analects of Confucius,* p. 126.

40. Wai-lim Yip, *Hiding the Universe* (New York: Grossman Publishers, 1972), p. 49 (also in *TJM,* p. 163).

41. Translated by the author (cf. *TJM,* pp. 173–174).

42. Ch'u Ta-kao, *Chinese Lyrics* (Cambridge: Cambridge University Press, 1937), pp. 28–29.

43. "Untitled Poems," VIII.2.

44. Also called "my many models in the past" or "heroic models" ("For My Cousin Ching-yuan," 14).

45. "Written in the Ninth Month," 11.

46. "In Early Spring," II, 10.

47. Ibid., I, 14.

48. "A Farewell to Yin Ching-jen," 18.

49. Cited in Maren-Sofie Røstvig, *The Happy Man,* I (New York: Humanities Press, 1962), 56.

50. Burton Watson, *Cold Mountain* (New York: Grove Press, 1962), p. 43.

51. Waley, p. 117.

52. *The Odes and Epodes,* p. 365.

53. Waley, p. 182.

54. "After Drinking Wine," XVI.7.

55. "For My Cousin Ching-yuan," 1.

56. "After Drinking Wine," XVI.8.

57. "Lines Written as I Passed through Ch'ü-o," 3, and "Untitled Poems," VIII.7.

58. "Untitled Poems," VIII.8.

59. Northrop Frye, *The Stubborn Structure* (Ithaca: Cornell University Press, 1970), p. 132.

60. Gaston Bachelard, *The Poetics of Space,* tr. Maria Jolas (New York: Orion Press, 1964), chap. 5.

61. For example, Alexander Pope, "Study and ease/ Together mixed" ("On Solitude," stanza 4) and "Successive study, Exercise and Ease" (*Windsor Forest,* 240).

62. "Climbing the east hill and whistle long/ Or composing verses beside the clear stream."

63. "Written at T'u-k'ou at Night," 19. For "the True" in T'ao's poetry see Fukunaga Mitsuji, "Tō Emmei no 'shin' ni tsuite," *Tōhō gakuhō,* XXXIII (Kyoto, 1963), 1–80; Ōyane Bunjirō, *Tō Emmei kenkyū,* pp. 229 ff.

64. Smith P. Bovie, *The Georgics,* p. 70.

65. *The Odes and Epodes,* p. 17.

66. *TFC,* p. 88 (Hightower, p. 44).

67. Preface to "Lament for Gentlemen Born Out of Their Time" (Hightower, p. 259).

68. "After Drinking Wine," XX.2.

69. "An Exhortation to Farmers," I.3–4.

70. "Written at T'u-k'ou at Night," 19–20.

71. "In Praise of Ancient Farmers," II.15–16, and "Held Up at Kueilin by Adverse Winds," II.9.

72. Cf. *Georgics,* II.524–525 (Bovie, p. 53): "Meanwhile sweet children hang on the farmer's kisses,/ His decent home preserves its purity."

73. Louis L. Martz, *The Wit of Love* (Notre Dame: University of Notre Dame Press, 1969), p. 186.

74. Martz, pp. 176–177.

75. For a consideration of a twelfth-century Japanese poet-monk Saigyō (1118–1190) who viewed nature as both "a soteric reality and the ultimate Buddhist absolute," see William R. LaFleur, "Saigyō and the Buddhist Value of Nature," *History of Religions,* XIII (1973), 93–128, 227–248.

76. "The Argument of Marvell's 'Garden,'" in *Seventeenth Century English Poetry,* ed. W. R. Keast (New York: Oxford University Press, 1962), p. 295. See also Dale Herron, "Marvell's 'Garden' and the Landscape of Poetry," *JEGP,* LXXIII (July 1974), 328–337.

77. Bovie, p. 90 (my italics).

78. *The Odes and Epodes,* pp. 366–367.

79. Herford and Simpson, VIII, 97.

80. John R. Cooper, *The Art of the Compleat Angler* (Durham: Duke University Press, 1968), p. 95.

81. Røstvig, *The Happy Man,* II, 234.

82. *The Correspondence of Henry David Thoreau,* ed. Walter Harding and Carl Bode (New York: New York University Press, 1958), p. 444 (in a letter to H.G.O. Blake, dated December 6, 1856); Maynard Mack says the same, in *The Garden and the City: Retirement and Politics in the Later*

Poetry of Pope, 1731–1743 (Toronto: University of Toronto Press, 1969), p. 85.

83. David Evett, " 'Paradise's Only Map': The *Topos* of the *Locus Amoenus* and the Structure of Marvell's *Upon Appleton House*," *PMLA*, LXXXV (1970), 504–513, esp. 505–507.

84. Watson, *The Complete Works of Chuang Tzu* (New York: Columbia University Press, 1968), pp. 105, 93–94.

85. Ibid., p. 211.

86. Graham, *The Book of Lieh-tzu*, pp. 102–103.

87. Graham, p. 34.

88. Harry Levin's phrase from *The Myth of the Golden Age in the Renaissance* (Bloomington: Indiana University Press, 1969), p. 117.

89. D. C. Lau, *Tao Te Ching* (Harmondsworth: Penguin Books, 1966), p. 142; Watson, *The Complete Works of Chuang Tzu*, p. 107.

90. *TJM*, pp. 166–167 ("A Song of Peach Blossom River").

91. "Twenty Poems After Drinking Wine," V.4 (*TFC*, p. 83).

92. Peter V. Marinelli, *Pastoral* (London: Methuen, 1971), p. 45.

93. Ibid., p. 47.

94. Laurence Lerner, *The Uses of Nostalgia: Studies in Pastoral Poetry* (New York: Schocken Books, 1972), p. 246.

95. *Mountain Gloom and Mountain Glory: The Development of the Aesthetics of the Infinite* (Ithaca: Cornell University Press, 1959), p. 3.

96. Paul Demiéville, "La Montagne dans L'Art littéraire chinois," *France-Asie*, XX (1965), 7–32.

97. China's five sacred mountains are: T'ai (east) where imperial sacrifices were offered; Heng (north); Hua (west); Sung (central); and Heng (south). Korea's sacred mountain is T'aebaek for the nation's foundation myth has it that a son of the supreme ruler of Heaven descended upon it.

98. Hawkes, p. 120.

99. Lois Fusek, "The 'Kao-T'ang Fu,' " *Monumenta Serica* (*MS*), XXX (1972–73), 417 (also in Arthur Waley, *The Temple and Other Poems* [London: George Allen and Unwin, 1923], p. 69).

100. Also in *ACV*, p. 94.

101. Watson, p. 301.

102. Ibid., p. 33.

103. Frodsham, *The Murmuring Stream* (Kuala Lumpur: University of Malaya Press, 1967).

104. Burton Watson, *Chinese Rhyme-Prose*, pp. 82–83.

105. *ACL*, p. 198 (Burton Watson, *Cold Mountain*, p. 100).

106. Giuseppe Billanovich, *Petrarca letterato*, I (Rome, 1947), 193–198, cited in Donald R. Howard, *The Three Temptations* (Princeton: Princeton University Press, 1966), p. 29.

107. Geoffrey Keynes, ed. *The Complete Writings of William Blake* (London: Oxford University Press, 1966), p. 550 (*Notebook*, no. 64).

108. Thomas Hutchinson, ed., *Shelley: Poetical Works* (London: Oxford University Press, 1967), p. 533.

109. H. W. Garrod, ed., *The Poetical Works of John Keats* (Oxford: Clarendon Press, 1939), p. 158. Also Wordsworth's contemplation on the top of Snowdon.

110. For example, "Sitting Alone on Mount Chin-t'ing" (*SS*, p. 110), "On the Mountain: Question and Answer" (*PCLP*, p. 45), and "A Dream Visit on Mount T'ien-mu" (*ChL*, pp. 151–512, and *TJM*, pp. 49–50). See also Elling O. Eide, "On Li Po," in *Perspectives on the T'ang*, ed. Arthur F. Wright and Denis Twitchett (New Haven: Yale University Press, 1973), pp. 367–403, for a discussion of Taoist mysticism and shamanistic elements in his poetry.

111. Hawkes, p. 91.

112. Yeats's "The Fisherman" (1914) and "The Tower" (st. 3; 1926) may be cited for comparison. The fishermen are "Yeats's aristocrats: indomitably searching for beauty and perfection, intent upon 'contact with the soil,' skilled in *sprezzatura*—the effortless flick of the wrist." See Daniel S. Harris, *Yeats: Coole Park and Ballylee* (Baltimore: Johns Hopkins University Press, 1974), p. 194.

113. Waley, p. 142.

114. Waley, p. 120.

115. For example, Harold E. Toliver, *Marvell's Ironic Vision* (New Haven: Yale University Press, 1965).

116. Karlgren, p. 172; Waley (no. 287), p. 322.

117. *Ch'ien Han shu* (K'ai-ming ed.), 24B, 0391b–c, and Nancy Lee Swan, *Han Shu 22: Food and Money in Ancient China* (Princeton: Princeton University Press, 1950), pp. 271–272, 317–321.

118. H. M. Richmond, "Rural Lyricism: A Renaissance Mutation of the Pastoral," *CL*, XVI (1964), 209.

119. Mack, *The Garden and the City*, p. 232.

120. Yeats, "Lapis Lazuli," in *The Collected Poems of W B. Yeats* (New York: Macmillan, 1961), p. 293.

121. J. R. Mulryne, "The 'Last Poems,'" in *An Honoured Guest: New Essays on W. B. Yeats*, ed. Denis Donoghue and J. R. Mulryne (London: Edward Arnold, 1965), p. 134.

122. Quoted in Mulryne, p. 134.

123. Ibid., p. 134.

124. Ibid., p. 135.

125. Geoffrey H. Hartman, in *Wordsworth's Poetry, 1787–1814* (New Haven: Yale University Press, 1964), p. 49, defines "apocalyptic": "an inner necessity to cast out nature, to extirpate everything apparently external to salvation, everything that might stand between the naked self and God, whatever risk in this to the self." Cf. James W. Miller, "English Romanticism and Chinese Nature Poetry," *CL*, XXIV (1972), 216–236, which is chap. 2 of his dissertation, "The Poetry of Meng Hao-jan," Princeton University, 1973.

126. *The Collected Poems of W. B. Yeats*, p. 192.

127. *An Honoured Guest*, p. 138.

128. Guillén, *Literature as System*, p. 307.

129. Charles W. Hieatt, "The Integrity of Pastoral: A Basis for Definition," *Genre,* V (1972), 5.

130. *The Stubborn Structure,* p. 131. See James McIntosh, *Thoreau as Romantic Naturalist: His Shifting Stance Toward Nature* (Ithaca: Cornell University Press, 1974), for how Thoreau admired and ridiculed his stint as a farmer (p. 254).

131. Cecil A. Moore, *Background of English Literature: 1700–1760* (Minneapolis: University of Minnesota Press, 1953), p. 100.

132. Joseph R. Levenson, *Confucian China and Its Modern Fate,* III (Berkeley: University of California Press, 1965), 110–126.

133. Waley, p. 161. This became the favorite "place" in the classics for Korean nature poetry.

3. Love

1. Shih-hsiang Chen, "The Cultural Essence of Chinese Literature," in *Interrelations of Cultures: Their Contributions to International Understanding* (Paris: Unesco, 1953), p. 64.

2. Maurice Valency, *In Praise of Love: An Introduction to the Love Poetry of the Renaissance* (New York: Macmillan, 1958), p. 52: "the social status of woman was in general not too far above that of the horse."

3. Karlgren, *The Book of Odes,* p. 237.

4. Waley, *The Book of Songs,* p. 35 (no. 24).

5. Hans H. Frankel, "Yüeh-fu Poetry," in *Studies in Chinese Literary Genres,* ed. Cyril Birch (Berkeley: University of California Press, 1974), pp. 79–81 (*APCC,* pp. 102–103; *CP,* pp. 128–129).

6. James J. Wilhelm, *Medieval Song* (New York: Dutton, 1971), no. 61, pp. 126–128.

7. William P. Jones, *The Pastourelle* (Cambridge, Mass.: Harvard University Press, 1931), pp. 44, 187–195.

8. Frankel, *The Flowering Plum and the Palace Lady,* p. 6 (also in Waley, p. 60, and *CP,* p. 53). For more on the imagery of the woman as a stricken hind and gazelle see Marcelle Thiebaux, *The Stag of Love* (Ithaca: Cornell University Press, 1974), p. 94n8, and for the man as the hunted and captured stag, p. 154n12.

9. *Poetry and Experience* (Boston: Riverside Press, 1961), pp. 60 ff. See also C. M. Bowra, *Greek Lyric Poetry* (Oxford: Clarendon Press, 1961), p. 133n2.

10. Translated by the author; also in Richard Rutt, *The Bamboo Grove* (Berkeley: University of California Press, 1971), no. 91.

11. Waley, no. 86, p. 80.

12. Waley, no. 83, p. 77. Poems 55, 106, 108, and 177 praise the physical and occasionally moral beauty (117) of man. Cf. Sappho, "An Absent Friend" ("A glorious goddess in her eyes/ Were you") and Catullus, 51 ("Ille mi par esse deo videtur"). For the former see *The Oxford Book of Greek Verse in*

Translation, ed. T. F. Higham and C. M. Bowra (Oxford: Clarendon Press, 1950), p. 207, and for the latter, *Catullus,* tr. Frank O. Copley (Ann Arbor: University of Michigan Press, 1957), p. 46.

13. James R. Hightower, "The *Fu* of T'ao Ch'ien," *HJAS,* XVII (1954), 172 ff.

14. Cf. Earl Miner, "Japanese and Western Images of Courtly Love," *YCGL,* XV (1966), 174–179. See also Eugene M. Waith, *Ideas of Greatness* (London: Routledge & Kegan Paul, 1971), pp. 1–34, for discussion of such chivalric virtues as prowess, loyalty, courtesy, largesse (giving of self), and so on, which did not find expression in East Asian love poetry.

15. Peter Dronke, *Medieval Latin and the Rise of European Love-Lyric* (2 vols.; Oxford: Clarendon Press, 1968), I, 46.

16. Dronke, I, 297. For more on the praise of love see *Medieval Song,* nos. 37, 67, 80, 82, 103, 104, 107–109, 116, 131, 147, 152, 160, 193, 211; Wyatt, "A face that should content me won'drous well"; Surrey, "Give place, ye lovers"; Sidney, *Astrophil and Stella,* 71; and Greville, *Caelica,* 40, the last four poets conveniently gathered in Robert M. Bender, ed. *Five Courtier Poets of the English Renaissance* (New York: Washington Square Press, 1974).

17. Richmond Lattimore, tr., *Greek Lyrics* (Chicago: University of Chicago Press, 1960), p. 39; also in the *Aeneid,* IV.1–2 (C. Day Lewis, *The Aeneid of Virgil* [New York: Oxford University Press, 1952], p. 81): "But now for some while the queen had been growing more grievously love-sick,/ Feeding the wound with her life-blood, the fire biting within her." Or in Izumi Shikibu: "My Human body/ I have given to love's flame,/ Burnign as surely/ As insects round a summer lamp,/ But with a fire that none can see" (Edwin A. Cranston, "The Dark Path: Images of Longing in Japanese Love Poetry," *HJAS,* XXXV [1975], 97).

18. Frederick Turner, *Shakespeare and the Nature of Time* (Oxford: Clarendon Press, 1971), p. 111.

19. Leonard Forster, *The Icy Fire: Five Studies in European Petrarchism* (Cambridge: Cambridge University Press, 1969), p. 17.

20. Nippon Gakujutsu Shinkōkai, *The Manyōshū,* p. 134.

21. In Japanese court poetry such images as the fires of love (*moyuru omoi*) or unquenchable longing (*kienu omoi*), the embers of desire, and love's dark, enticing flame are commonplace. The speaker in a poem by Ki no Tomonori (*KKS,* XII.562) attempts to contrast her internal fire with the ice of her lover's indifference: "When evening falls,/ Brighter than the firefly/ Is my burning:/ Can it be he does not see the glow,/ That he should keep his cold indifference?" Cranston, "The Dark Path," *HJAS,* XXXV (1975), 97.

22. A. C. Graham, *Poems of the Late T'ang* (Harmondsworth: Penguin Books, 1965), p. 67.

23. Bowra, p. 184.

24. Ibid.

25. Bowra, p. 188.

26. Bowra, p. 189.

27. Bowra, p. 290.

28. Rosalie L. Colie, *Shakespeare's Living Art* (Princeton: Princeton University Press, 1974), p. 138. For more on the definition of love see, for example, Wyatt, "Of Love"; Surrey, "Such wayward ways has love"; and Sidney, *Astrophil and Stella,* 16.

29. *The Manyōshū,* p. 107.

30. Tune: "Night Crow Calling" (*Wu yeh t'i*); Ayling and Mackintosh, I, 51.

31. *The Manyōshū,* p. 57.

32. *AJL,* p. 77.

33. Shih-shun Liu, *One Hundred and One Chinese Poems* (Hong Kong: Hong Kong University Press, 1967), p. 137.

34. Ch'u Ta-kao, p. 52.

35. Lisle C. John, *The Elizabethan Sonnet Sequences* (New York: Russell & Russell, 1964), pp. 97–99.

36. I have used the Wanp'an edition. Compare Rutt's version in Richard Rutt and Kim Chong-un, *Virtuous Women* (Seoul: Korean National Commission for Unesco, 1974), pp. 274–275.

37. The love of Duke Mu's daughter (Nung-yü) for the flute player (Hsiao-shih) appears in the *Lieh-hsien chuan* and is alluded to in a poem by Lu Chao-lin (635–684), for which see Frankel, *The Flowering Plum and the Palace Lady,* p. 131. The Old Man of the Moonlight is a matchmaker in Li Fu-yen's story, for which see *T'ang-jen hsiao-shuo,* ed. Wang P'i-chiang (Hong Kong: Chung-hua shu-chü, 1958), pp. 223–224. Hsing-chen and his eight fairies refer to a Korean romance, *A Nine Cloud Dream.* For Hsiang Yü's love for Lady Yü see Burton Watson, *Records of the Grand Historian of China* (New York: Columbia University Press, 1961), I, 70.

38. Tune: "Strangers in Saint's Coif" (Ayling and Mackintosh, I, 39).

39. Francis Cairns, *Generic Composition in Greek and Roman Poetry* (Edinburgh: University Press, 1972), p. 15.

40. Ayling and Mackintosh, I, 139.

41. Horace, in the third ode in the second book, asks more or less the same question: "For whom but us do silvery poplar and/ Tall pine conspire such welcome with shadowy/ Laced boughs? Why else should eager water/ Bustle and work in its zigzag channel?" (James Michie, *The Odes of Horace* [London: Rupert Hart-Davis, 1964], p. 97). Addressed to Delius, the poem is an invitation to seize the day, for soon we have to "book a one-way berth in Charon's/ Boat on the journey to endless exile" (Michie, p. 99). Hwang Chin-i's poem does not go as far as Horace's does, but the general line of thought and imagery is similar.

42. Dronke, I, 139–142. For more on ecstasy and fulfillment see, for example, *Catullus,* 51, 45; *Medieval Song,* no. 106; *Astrophil and Stella,* 81; Carew, "A Rapture"; Donne, "The Extasie" and "The Good-Morrow."

43. *TFC,* p. 35.

44. Translated by the author.

45. James J. Y. Liu, *Major Lyricists of the Northern Sung* (Princeton: Princeton University Press, 1974), pp. 56–57; also in *CP,* p. 425.

46. Also in *SS,* p. 112.

47. *ChL,* p. 95.

48. Ch'u Ta-kao, p. 39.

49. Dronke, I, 276–277.

50. Julius S. Held, "Flora, Goddess and Courtesan," in *Essays in Honor of Erwin Panofsky,* ed. Millard Meiss (New York: New York University Press, 1961), pp. 201–218. For the woman's role in Roman love poetry from Catullus to Ovid, see Georg Luck, "The Woman's Role in Latin Love poetry," in *Perspectives of Roman Poetry: A Classics Symposium,* ed. G. Karl Galinsky (Austin: University of Texas Press, 1974), pp. 15–31.

51. John Warden, tr., *The Poems of Propertius,* p. 49. See Joseph Kau, "*Delia*'s Gentle Lover and the Eternizing Conceit in Elizabethan Sonnets," *Anglia,* XCII (1974), 334–348.

52. Waley, no. 26, p. 37.

53. Waley, no. 27, p. 37.

54. Helen C. McCullough, *Tales of Ise* (Stanford: Stanford University Press, 1968), p. 80; also in *Eos,* ed. Arthur T. Hatto (London: Mouton, 1965), p. 119.

55. Translated by the author; cf. *Studies in Chinese Literature,* ed. J. L. Bishop (Cambridge, Mass.: Harvard University Press, 1965), p. 212; Ayling and Mackintosh, I, 13; *SS,* p. 211.

56. Translated by the author. For *alba* see Dronke, *The Medieval Lyric,* pp. 167–185; Forster, *passim; Eos;* and P. K. King, *Dawn Poetry in the Netherlands* (Amsterdam: Athenaeum-Polak & Van Gennep, 1971).

57. *The Manyōshū,* p. 86.

58. Jonathan Saville, *The Medieval Erotic Alba* (New York: Columbia University Press, 1974), p. 177.

59. Frank O. Copley, *Exclusus Amator: A Study in Latin Love Poetry* (Baltimore: American Philological Association, 1956), pp. 17, 33.

60. Waley, no. 35, p. 43.

61. Waley, no. 37, p. 44.

62. Waley, no. 45, p. 48.

63. Waley, no. 101, p. 93.

64. Waley, no. 109, p. 102.

65. Waley, no. 75, p. 71.

66. Waley, no. 53, p. 53 (cf. Propertius, II. 12. 7–8).

67. Cf. "The neuer-resting stone of care to roule,/ Still to complaine my griefes, and none relieue me" (Daniel, *Delia,* IX.7–8) from *Poems and a Defence of Ryme,* ed. Arthur C. Sprague (Cambridge, Mass.: Harvard University Press, 1930), p. 15.

68. Waley, no. 75, p. 71.

69. Waley, no. 108, p. 101.

70. *TFC,* p. 34.

71. James R. Hightower, "Yüan Chen and 'The Story of Ying-ying,'" *HJAS,* XXXIII (1973), 95.

72. *AJL,* p. 80.

73. *AJL,* p. 78.

74. Translated by Peter Whigham in *Arion,* IV (1965), 612.

75. W. T. H. Jackson, *The Anatomy of Love: The Tristan of Gottfried von Strassburg* (New York: Columbia University Press, 1971), pp. 124 ff, 182, 231 ff.

76. *The Manyōshū,* p. 283.

77. Helen Waddell, *Medieval Latin Lyrics* (London: Constable, 1944), pp. 156–157; see also Wilhelm, *Medieval Song,* p. 71. For more on this theme see, for example, Wyatt, "You that in love find luck and abundance"; Surrey, "The soote season" and "When summer took in hand the winter to assail"; Sidney, *Certain Sonnets,* 4, and *Astrophil and Stella,* Eighth Song; and Greville, *Caelica,* 75.

78. Waley, no. 41, p. 46.

79. Waley, no. 65, p. 62.

80. Waley, no. 108, p. 100.

81. Karlgren, pp. 149–150.

82. Frank O. Copley, tr., *Catullus: The Complete Poetry* (Ann Arbor: University of Michigan Press, 1957), p. 104. See also no. 76.

83. Bowra, p. 283.

84. Kotewall and Smith, p. 33; also in Liu, *Studies in Chinese Literary Genres,* p. 136.

85. Tr. H. E. Butler (LCL, 1967), pp. 258–259.

86. The examples are cited in Julius Walter Lever, *The Elizabethan Love Sonnet* (London: Methuen, 1956), pp. 147, 202–204: Ronsard (*Amours Diverses,* 4); Constable (*Diana,* I. 9); the elder Giles Fletcher (*Licia,* VI); and Shakespeare, Sonnet 24.

87. David Roy, "The Theme of the Neglected Wife in the Poetry of Ts'ao Chih," *JAS,* XIX (1959), 25–31.

88. Bowra, p. 192.

89. Cf. "Since you, sir, went away,/ My bright mirror is dim and untended" (Hsü Kan, "A Wife's Thought, III" [Kotewall and Smith, p. 7]); "When you are away, wherefore should I adorn myself? Never shall I think of taking even the boxwood comb out of my toilet case" (by a young woman of Harima, *MYS,* IX.1777 [*The Manyōshū,* p. 239]).

90. "Wind-blown dew drops on the moonlight verandah,/ The courtyard bleak and lonely in the dawn./ Who could endure such loneliness?/ Lying awake, I listen to the crickets' tears" (Li Ho, "Thoughts in Her Chamber," in Frodsham, *The Poems of Li Ho,* p. 168).

91. "Myriad leaves give a thousand sounds—all are lamentation./ So I choose the solitary pillow in search of dreams,/ But dreams come not, and the lamp is guttering out" (Ou-yang Hsiu, "To Fisherman's Pride," in Kotewall and Smith, p. 38).

92. See John T. Shawcross, "The Poet as Orator: One Phase of His Judicial Pose," in *The Rhetoric of Renaissance Poetry: From Wyatt to Milton,* ed. Thomas O. Sloan and Raymond B. Waddington (Berkeley: University of California Press, 1974), pp. 5–36.

93. *TFC,* p. 49 (*APCC,* p. 66). For the unending sorrow of separation by death see Po Chü-i's "A Song of Unending Sorrow" (*TJM,* pp. 94–99; *APCC,* pp. 297–302).

94. T. F. Higham and C. M. Bowra, ed., *The Oxford Book of Greek Verse in Translation,* p. 545.

95. *Virgil* (*LCL,* 1965), pp. 430–431.

96. Charles P. Segal, *Landscape in Ovid's Metamorphoses,* Hermes Einzelschriften, 23 (Wiesbaden: Steiner, 1969), pp. 15 ff; see also Thiebaux, p. 96.

97. "Allegory and Pastoral in *The Shepheardes Calender,*" *ELH,* XXXVI (1969), 95.

98. Gilbert Lawall, *Theocritus' Coan Pastorals* (Cambridge, Mass.: Harvard University Press, 1967), p. 101.

99. MacCaffrey, p. 100.

100. MacCaffrey, p. 105.

101. Turner, p. 102.

102. James J. Wilhelm, *The Cruelest Month,* p. 209, and *Medieval Song,* p. 114. We may recall Petrarch's laurel (Laura), so favored by the heavenly light ("Tanto onorate dal superno lume"), under whose shade the poet took shelter; and the juniper (Genèvre), the tree planted by his love in Ronsard's heart ("Des mains d'Amour la racine plantée"), for which see H. M. Richmond, *Renaissance Landscapes: English Lyric in a European Tradition* (The Hague: Mouton, 1973), pp. 60–61.

103. *The Cruelest Month,* pp. 12, 15 (Latin text).

104. A poem by Yi Chŏng-bo (1693–1766) has: "You're a goddess of Mount Wu/ Who changes into clouds and rain." This is a compliment to an attractive lady whose unpredictable coming and going will bring only longing and sickness.

105. *ACL,* p. 354.

106. *The Manyōshū,* p. 56.

107. H. J. Chaytor, *The Troubadours and England* (Cambridge: Cambridge University Press, 1923), p. 139.

108. Translated by the author.

109. *AJL,* p. 78.

110. *Senzaishū,* XIV.874, quoted in *JCP,* p. 308.

111. *AJL,* p. 94; cf. Daniel, *Delia,* 49.

112. Cf. Ou-yang Hsiu (1007–1072), "To Fisherman's Pride," which magnificently captures the woman's frustration and agony of loving ("the lamp is guttering out")—the light of her hope and the lamp by which she keeps awake. Kotewall and Smith, p. 38.

113. For the following three poems (*KKS,* XII.559; XIII.656; XII.574) see *HJAS,* XXXV (1975), 70, 69.

114. *MYS,* XII.3117–8 (p. 284).

115. Ibid., XII.2912 (p. 300).

116. I have used the *Kokinshū* versions as translated by Edwin A. Cranston.

117. Dronke, I, 10–11, 178–179.

118. Hightower, *HJAS,* XVII (1954), 195 ff.

119. Saville, pp. 221 ff.

120. *The Manyōshū,* pp. 61, 134, 281.

121. *The Cruelest Month,* p. 191. Such erotic union that negates the spatial distance and the barriers that keep the lover and the lady separated cannot, Jonathan Saville argues, actually take place in the static, timeless universe of the chanson. "It can only be wished for—or dreamed of. The dream is a frequent device in the *chanson* for indicating the intensity of the lover's desire, and the unreality of its fulfillment. The dream is a product of the pleasure principle, and it is contrasted with the acceptance of reality that must come when the dreamer awakes" (p. 234). The appearance of the dream motif in the Chinese poems on "Stilling the Passions" may be viewed in similar terms.

122. Sidney Lee, ed., *Elizabethan Sonnets* (Westminster: Constable, 1904) I, 207.

123. See Brooks Otis, *Ovid as an Epic Poet* (Cambridge: Cambridge University Press, 1966), pp. 231–277. In Po Chü-i's "A Song of Unending Sorrow," the vows exchanged between Emperor Hsüan-tsung of T'ang and his Precious Consort Yang are expressed similarly: "to fly in heaven, two birds with the wings of one,/ And to grow together on the earth, two branches of one tree."

124. For example, Martial, *Epigrams,* XI.21; Cavalcanti, "Guata, Manetto, quella scrignutuzza" (Look, Manny, at that little hunchback) in *Medieval Song,* p. 227; Suckling, "The Deformed Mistress"; and Baudelaire, "A une Mendiante rousse."

125. By Bernart de Ventadorn in *Medieval Song,* p. 141.

126. *Virgil* (LCL), I, 407.

127. See *Korean Literature: Topics and Themes* (Tucson: University of Arizona Press, 1965), pp. 15–17.

128. Cranston, "The Dark Path," 61.

129. Morton W. Bloomfield, *Essays and Explorations: Studies in Ideas, Language, and Literature* (Cambridge, Mass.: Harvard University Press, 1970), pp. 184, 196.

130. For a similar observation see A. J. Smith, "The Failure of Love: Love Lyrics after Donne," in *Metaphysical Poetry,* ed. Malcolm Bradbury and David Palmer (London: Edward Arnold, 1970), p. 68.

4. Friendship

1. *Madly Singing in the Mountains,* ed. Ivan Morris (New York: Harper & Row, 1970), p. 295.

2. Montaigne's "Of Friendship" is cited from *The Complete Essays of Montaigne* tr. Donald R. Frame (Stanford: Stanford University Press, 1958), p. 137.

3. For example, *I-wen lei-chü* (compiled in early 7th century; Shanghai:

Chung-hua shu-chü, 1965), chap. 21; *T'ai-p'ing yü-lan* (983 completed; Peking: Chung-hua shu-chü, 1960), chaps. 406–410; *Ts'e-fu yüan-kuei* (1013; Hong Kong: Chung-hua shu-chü, 1960), chaps. 881–882; and *Tai-p'ing kuang-chi* (978; Peking: Chung-hua shu-chü, 1959), chap. 235.

4. See Arthur F. Wright and Denis Twitchett, ed., *Confucian Personalities* (Stanford: Stanford University Press, 1962), pp. 24–39.

5. *The Doctrine of the Mean,* 20 (*SBCP,* p. 105): "The five are those governing the relationship between ruler and minister, between father and son, between husband and wife, between elder and younger brothers, and those in the intercourse between friends."

6. Frame, p. 138.

7. Waley, *The Book of Songs,* no. 195, p. 204.

8. Ibid.

9. Waley, *The Analects of Confucius,* pp. 85, 143.

10. Ibid., p. 195.

11. Ibid., p. 224.

12. Ibid., p. 205.

13. Ibid., pp. 114, 128.

14. Cicero, *De amicitia,* XVIII.65 (Frank O. Copley, *On Old Age and On Friendship* [Ann Arbor: University of Michigan Press, 1967], p. 74).

15. Waley, p. 170.

16. *De amicitia,* XXII.83 (Copley, p. 81).

17. See Rob Roy Purdy, "The Friendship Motif in Middle English Literature," *Vanderbilt Studies in the Humanities,* I (1951), 113–114, which cites relevant passages from the *Republic,* the *Phaedrus,* the *Lysis,* and *The Nicomachean Ethics.* For Cicero see *De amicitia,* VI.20 (Copley, p. 55); XIV.48 (Copley, p. 68); XXII.83–84 (Copley, p. 81); XXVII.100 (Copley, p. 88).

18. *Li chi* (Ssu-pu pei-yao ed.), 17, 9b–10a (Legge, *Li Ki* [Oxford: Clarendon Press, 1926], II, 348).

19. *De amicitia,* XXV.91 (Copley, p. 85). For poems on the dangers of flattery see, for example, *The Paradise of Dainty Devices (1576–1606),* ed. Hyder E. Rollins (Cambridge, Mass.: Harvard University Press, 1927), pp. 73, 105, 107–108.

20. Waley, p. 170.

21. Waley, p. 178.

22. Frame, p. 136.

23. *De amicitia,* XXIV.88 (Copley, p. 83).

24. Waley, p. 121.

25. Waley, p. 111.

26. *Po hu t'ung* (T'u-shu chi-ch'eng ed.), 3B.206; Tjan Tjoe Som, *Po Hu T'ung: Comprehensive Discussions in the White Tiger Hall* (2 vols.; Leiden: Brill, 1952), II, 473.

27. For stories in the *San-yen* collections see John L. Bishop, *The Colloquial Short Story in China* (Cambridge, Mass.: Harvard University Press, 1965), pp. 128–130, esp. nos. A7 and B1 and Bishop's translation of "Fang

Chu-ch'ing's Eternal Friendship" on pp. 88–97; see also Cyril Birch, *Stories from a Ming Collection* (Bloomington, Indiana University Press, 1959), pp. 121–149. For more on the tests of friendship, see John Conley, "The Doctrine of Friendship in *Everyman*," *Speculum*, XLIV (1969), 374–382.

28. *Chou i* (*SPTK*), 7.6a (Richard Wilhelm, *The I Ching or Book of Changes* [2 vols.; New York: Pantheon Books, 1950], I, 329). The worth and value of friendship are summarized in "Of friendship" by Nicholas Grimald, for which see *Tottel's Miscellany* (*1557–1587*), ed. Hyder E. Rollins (Cambridge, Mass.: Harvard University Press, 1965), I, 106. For an analysis of the poem see Laurence J. Mills, *One Soul in Bodies Twaine* (Bloomington: The Principia Press, 1937), pp. 113–114.

29. Frame, p. 142.

30. Also read as a love poem. *TFC*, p. 32; also Watson, *Early Chinese Literature*, p. 290, and *CP*, p. 101.

31. *Madly Singing in the Mountains*, p. 296.

32. *ChL*, p. 89.

33. Shih-shun Liu, *One Hundred and One Chinese Poems*, p. 55.

34. *SS*, p. 102 (also in *TJM*, p. 40, *APCC*, p. 237, and *CP*, p. 323).

35. *ChL*, p. 89.

36. William Hung, *Tu Fu* (Cambridge, Mass.: Harvard University Press, 1952), p. 153.

37. Kotewall and Smith, p. 8.

38. "A Farewell to Li Tuan" (translated by the author; also in *TJM*, p. 82).

39. *SS*, p. 94.

40. Hung, p. 278.

41. "To Fan Yeh," Kotewall and Smith, p. 9 (also in *APCC*, p. 169); see Hans H. Frankel, "The Plum Tree in Chinese Poetry," *Asiatische Studien*, VI (1952), 93–94.

42. *One Hundred and One Chinese Poems*, p. 55.

43. Ibid., p. 33. Cairns, *Generic Composition in Greek and Roman Poetry*, p. 9.

44. H. Rushton Fairclough, *Satires, Epistles and Ars Poetica* (LCL, 1966), pp. 315, 319, 361.

45. W. Milgate, ed., *The Satires, Epigrams and Verse Letters* (Oxford: Clarendon Press, 1967), pp. 71–73.

46. For example, Tu Fu, "Inviting Minister Li to Dismount and Keep on Drinking in the Moonlight" (Hung, p. 256; Liu, p. 29), and Wang Wei, "To See Yüan Erh Off as Envoy to An-hsi" (Wai-lim Yip, *Hiding the Universe*, 73).

47. Kenneth Quinn, *Latin Explorations: Critical Studies in Roman Literature* (New York: Humanities Press, 1963), pp. 239–273.

48. *The Odes and Epodes* (LCL, 1964), p. 361.

49. John Warden, tr., *The Poems of Propertius*, p. 104.

50. *TJM*, pp. 148–149, 170 (*ChL*, p. 118).

51. Also in Graham, *Poems of the Late T'ang*, p. 127.

52. Hung, p. 149; also in Hawkes, *A Little Primer of Tu Fu,* p. 102.

53. Hung, p. 51.

54. Hung, pp. 50, 36, 188.

55. Also in Yip, p. 79; *ACL,* p. 219.

56. Hans H. Frankel, "Poetry and Painting: Chinese and Western Views of Their Convertibility," *CL,* IX (1957), 289–307.

57. Watson, *The Complete Works of Chuang Tzu,* pp. 83–84, 86.

58. *ACL,* pp. 165–166.

59. *TFC,* p. 223.

60. *TFC,* p. 237.

61. *TFC,* p. 218.

62. *TFC,* p. 270.

63. Hung, pp. 133–134; Hawkes, pp. 92, 98; *TJM,* pp. 130–131; *SS,* pp. 128–129; *APCC,* p. 262; *CP,* pp. 391–392.

64. Arthur Waley, *The Life and Times of Po Chü-i* (London: George Allen and Unwin, 1949), p. 35.

65. *TFC,* p. 206.

66. Claudio Guillén, *Literature as System,* p. 246.

67. *TFC,* pp. 148–149.

68. Michie, *The Odes of Horace,* p. 245.

69. *Wordsworth's Prelude,* ed. Ernest de Selincourt and Helen Darbishire (Oxford: Clarendon Press, 1959), pp. 502–505.

70. *The Complete Poetical Works of Samuel Taylor Coleridge,* ed. Earnest H. Coleridge (2 vols.; Oxford: Clarendon Press, 1966), pp. 403, 408.

71. Guillén, p. 250.

72. Justus Buchler, *The Main of Light: The Concept of Poetry* (New York: Oxford University Press, 1974), p. 114.

73. Ibid., pp. 115–116.

74. Kotewall and Smith, p. 23.

75. "After Drinking Wine," VII.3 (Hightower, p. 133).

76. "The Double Ninth, in Retirement," 9 (Hightower, p. 27).

77. "After Drinking Wine," III.8 (Hightower, p. 127).

78. Hung, p. 177.

79. Hung, p. 176. Ōtomo Tabito's poem in the *MYS,* III.338–350, praises the attributes of wine in similar terms (*The Manyōshū,* pp. 117–118):

> Instead of wasting thoughts on unavailing things,
> It would seem wiser
> To drink a cup of raw saké . . .
>
> Far better, it seems, than uttering pompous words
> And looking wise,
> To drink saké and weep drunken tears.
>
> I know not how to name it, how to define it.
> Ten thousand times precious
> Is saké to me!

Grotesque! When I look upon a man
Who drinks no saké, looking wise,
How like an ape he is!

Even a treasure priceless in the world—
How could it surpass
A cup of raw saké?

If there were a gem shining in the darkness of night,
How could it excel
Saké that kills all care?

80. "Untitled Poems," I.8 (Hightower, p. 185).

81. Bowra, *Greek Lyric Poetry,* pp. 158–159.

82. Liu, p. 73; *TJM,* p. 92; and *ChL,* pp. 186–187.

83. *The Odes and Epodes,* p. 397; see Steele Commager, "The Function of Wine in Horace's Odes," *TAPA,* LXXXVIII (1957), 68–80.

84. Michie, p. 35.

85. Hung, p. 68.

86. *ACL,* pp. 232, 231; see also *SS,* p. 110.

87. "After Drinking Wine," XIV.10 (Hightower, p. 145).

88. Michie, p. 39.

89. Hung, p. 129; *SS,* p. 127; *APCC,* p. 267.

90. *TFC,* p. 314.

91. "Being Visited by a Friend during Illness" (*TFC,* p. 234).

92. Kotewall and Smith, p. 60.

93. *TFC,* p. 151.

94. *TFC,* p. 222.

95. Bowra, p. 161.

96. *The Life and Times of Po Chü-i,* p. 87.

97. Ibid., p. 124.

98. *ChL,* p. 164 (Hawkes, p. 72; Hung, p. 139; Liu, p. 43; *TJM,* pp. 128–129).

99. Michie, p. 107.

100. *ACL,* pp. 232–233 (also in *TJM,* p. 56, *PCLP,* pp. 46–47, *APCC,* p. 232).

101. *The Life and Times of Po Chü-i,* p. 182.

102. *ACL,* p. 230; *SS,* p. 109; *APCC,* p. 226.

103. Yoshikawa Kōjirō, "To Ho to tsuki," *Chūgoku bungaku hō,* XVII (1962), 38–44.

104. The anonymous *Man'yō* poem (VII.1295) echoes the same sentiment: "Above the height of Mikasa in Kasuga/ The boat of a moon appears;/ We, revellers, see it,/ Reflected in our wine-cups" (*The Manyōshū,* p. 291).

105. Michie, p. 99.

106. Graham, *The Book of Lieh-tzu,* pp. 109–110.

107. Stephen Booth, *An Essay on Shakespeare's Sonnet* (New Haven: Yale University Press, 1969), p. 180.

108. An observation made by Professor Leonard Nathan, University of California, Berkeley.

109. Leo M. Bond, "A Comparison between Human and Divine Friendship," *The Thomist,* III (1941), 59–94. Rob Roy Purdy, "The Friendship Motif in Middle English Literature," *Vanderbilt Studies in the Humanities,* I (1951), 113–141; Adele M. Fiske, R.S.C.J., "Alcuin and Mystical Friendship," *Studi Medievali,* III (1961) 551–575, and "St. Augustine and Friendship," *Monastic Studies,* II (1964), 127–135.

5. Time

1. David Hawkes, *Ch'u Tz'u: The Songs of the South* (Oxford: Clarendon Press, 1959), pp. 22, 24.

2. Shih-hsiang Chen, "The Genesis of Poetic Time," *CHHP,* X (1973), 36.

3. Hawkes, p. 33.

4. Hawkes, p. 32.

5. Frederick Turner, *Shakespeare and the Nature of Time* (Oxford: Clarendon Press, 1971), p. 16.

6. Hawkes, pp. 23, 24, 29, 30.

7. Hawkes, p. 31.

8. Hawkes, p. 23.

9. Hawkes, p. 25.

10. Ibid.

11. Hawkes, p. 70.

12. Hawkes, p. 95.

13. Hawkes, p. 96.

14. Hawkes, p. 137.

15. Hawkes, p. 166.

16. Hawkes, p. 175.

17. Hawkes, p. 172.

18. Hawkes, p. 97.

19. Alan T. Bradford, "Mirror of Mutability: Winter Landscape in Tudor Poetry," *English Literary Renaissance,* IV (1974), 13.

20. *ACL,* p. 180; also in Jerome Ch'en and Michael Bullock, *Poems of Solitude* (London: Abelard-Schuman, 1960), pp. 16, 18; Donald Holzman, *Poetry and Politics* (Cambridge: Cambridge University Press, 1976), pp. 131–132.

21. Hightower, pp. 89–90.

22. Hightower, p. 69.

23. Hightower, p. 270.

24. Waley, *The Analects of Confucius,* p. 163.

25. Waley, p. 155.

26. Watson, *The Complete Works of Chuang Tzu,* p. 84.

27. Watson, p. 72.
28. A. C. Graham, *The Book of Lieh-tzu,* p. 82.
29. Watson, p. 47.
30. Watson, p. 72.
31. Waley, p. 126.
32. Watson, p. 53.
33. Legge, V, 502b.
34. *Lao Tzu,* 46 (Lau, p. 107).
35. Lau, p. 92.
36. Legge, V, 55a.
37. Legge, II, 173.
38. Waley, *The Book of Songs,* p. 143.
39. Lau, p. 135.
40. Lau, p. 65.
41. Also in Ch'en and Bullock, p. 14; Holzman, pp. 117–118.
42. Ayling and Mackintosh, II, 21.
43. A. C. Graham, "Chuang-Tzu's Essay on Seeing Things as Equal," *History of Religions,* IX (1969–1970), 152–153.
44. Graham, p. 155.
45. Graham, p. 157.
46. Lau, p. 128.
47. Legge, V, 507b.
48. Watson, p. 94.
49. Watson, p. 213.
50. Watson, p. 299.
51. Watson, *Records of the Grand Historian of China,* I, 229.
52. Lau, p. 58.
53. Lau, p. 104.
54. Watson, p. 120.
55. Hightower, p. 185; also in one of the "Nineteen Old Poems of the Han": "Man lives out his little sojourn,/ Scudding by like a swirl of dust" (*ChL,* p. 24).
56. Hightower, p. 127.
57. Hightower, p. 53.
58. Watson, p. 240.
59. Hightower, p. 19. Cf. "This world is but a thoroughfare of woe/ And we are pilgrims passing to and fro" ("The Knight's Tale," 2847–8).
60. *ACL,* p. 382.
61. Hightower, p. 136.
62. *TFC,* p. 122; *APCC,* p. 244.
63. Liu, *Major Lyricists of the Northern Sung,* p. 140.
64. Graham, p. 158.
65. Also in *PCLP,* p. 44; Cooper, *Li Po and Tu Fu,* p. 141.
66. Also in Kotewall and Smith, p. 3; *ACV,* p. 2.
67. *The Manyōshū,* pp. 186, 235 (original texts on pp. 374, 416).

68. Also in Geoffrey Bownas and Anthony Thwaite, *The Penguin Book of Japanese Verse* (Harmondsworth: Penguin Books, 1964), p. 122.

69. Edward Conze, *Buddhist Wisdom Books* (London: George Allen and Unwin, 1958), p. 68; *Taishō Tripiṭaka,* VIII, 752b and 757a.

70. See, for example, Toliver, *Marvell's Ironic Vision,* p. 72–77; J. B. Leishmann, *The Art of Marvell's Poetry* (New York: Funk & Wagnalls, 1968), pp. 199–203; Joseph H. Summers, "Andrew Marvell: Private Taste and Public Judgment," in *Metaphysical Poetry,* ed. Malcolm Bradbury and David Palmer (London: Edward Arnold, 1970), p. 189.

71. "Untitled Poems," III (Hightower, p. 188).

72. Also in Ch'en and Bullock, p. 33; *ACV,* p. 148.

73. Kotewall and Smith, p. 54.

74. Ibid., p. 26.

75. Also in *CP,* p. 432; Ayling and Mackintosh, I, 127; *SS,* p. 358.

76. Ch'u Ta-kao, *Chinese Lyrics,* p. 50.

77. *AJL,* p. 80.

78. Donald Keene, *Landscapes and Portraits: Appreciations of Japanese Culture* (Tokyo: Kōdansha International, 1971), p. 24.

79. *Mao Tse-tung Poems* (Peking: Commercial Press, 1976), p. 86. Lines 3–4 of st. 1 should read: "On a hanging cliff a hundred fathoms of ice,/ Already there is a flowery branch of beauty." Also in *SS,* p. 519.

80. Joseph Needham, "Time and Knowledge in China and the West," *The Voices of Time,* ed. J. T. Fraser (London: Penguin Press, 1968), pp. 101, 116.

81. Hans H. Frankel, "The Contemplation of the Past in T'ang Poetry," in *Perspectives on the T'ang,* ed. Arthur F. Wright and Denis Twitchett (New Haven: Yale University Press, 1973), pp. 350–351. Tu Fu's favorite tragic hero is Chu-ko Liang, and for the interpretation of his "The Design of Eightfold Array" see Shih-hsiang Chen, "To Circumvent 'The Design of Eightfold Array,'" *CHHP,* VII (August 1968), 26–53.

82. Translated by the author.

83. Translated by the author.

84. *ACL,* p. 382.

85. *ACL,* p. 352 (also in *SS,* pp. 305–306).

86. Frankel, p. 353.

87. *CL,* p. 162 (also in Hawkes, *A Little Primer of Tu Fu,* p. 48; *TJM,* p. 119; Cooper, p. 171; Hung, *Tu Fu,* p. 105; *CP,* p. 260).

88. Frankel, p. 111.

89. Translated by the author.

90. Liu, p. 139 (also in Ayling and Mackintosh, I, 121, and *CP,* p. 428). For instance, *An Account of My Hut* (*Hōjōki*) by Kamo no Chōmei (1153–1216) begins with a comparison of human life to an endlessly flowing river: "The flow of the river is ceaseless and its water is never the same. The bubbles that float in the pools, now vanishing, now forming, are not of long duration: so in the world are man and his dwellings" (*AJL,* p. 197). The third stanza in "Coplas por la muerte de si padre" (Verses on the Death of

his Father) by Jorge Manrique (1440?–1479) uses the river imagery: "Our lives are the rivers that flow out into the sea, which is death." See J. M. Cohen, ed., *The Penguin Book of Spanish Verse* (Harmondsworth: Penguin Books, 1956), p. 41.

91. Turner, pp. 3–4.

92. Alex Preminger, ed., *Encyclopaedia of Poetry and Poetics* (Princeton: Princeton University Press, 1965), p. 876a.

93. Charles W. Kennedy, *An Anthology of Old English Poetry* (New York: Oxford University Press, 1960), p. 7.

94. Norman Cameron, *Poems of François Villon* (New York: Harcourt, Brace & World, 1966), p. 50.

95. Ibid., p. 53.

96. Also in Ch'en and Bullock, p. 37.

97. Also in Hawkes, *A Little Primer of Tu Fu,* p. 55; Hung, pp. 106–107; Cooper, pp. 178–179.

98. Also in Kotewall and Smith, p. 27; Frankel, p. 47.

99. Liu, p. 133.

100. *ChL,* pp. 145–146. Cf. "A Visit to the Terrace of the King of Yüeh" by Yang Wan-li (1127–1206), in *Heaven My Blanket, Earth My Pillow,* tr. Jonathan Chaves (New York: John Weatherhill, 1975), p. 92.

101. Hawkes, p. 55.

102. *ACL,* p. 345.

103. Shuen-fu Lin, *The Transformation of the Chinese Lyrical Tradition: Chiang K'uei and Southern Sung* Tz'u *Poetry* (Princeton: Princeton University Press, 1978), p. 73.

104. Also in Bownas and Thwaite, pp. 99, 101; the original in *Senzaishū,* I.66, and in the *Tale of the Heike,* XVI (Kitagawa and Tsuchida translation; Tokyo: Tokyo University Press, 1975, p. 439) and *Sankashū,* I:350.

105. Ricardo J. Quinones, *The Renaissance Discovery of Time* (Cambridge, Mass.: Harvard University Press, 1972), pp. 169, 429.

106. *ChL,* p. 115.

107. *The Manyōshū,* p. 179 (original on p. 391).

108. Ibid., p. 274 (original on p. 431).

109. Waley, *The Book of Songs,* no. 191, p. 200.

110. Hawkes, p. 32.

111. Also in Ch'en and Bullock, p. 34; *ACV,* p. 149.

112. Kotewall and Smith, p. 67.

113. Ibid., p. 24; for more see Wayne Schlepp, *San-ch'ü* (Madison: University of Wisconsin Press, 1970), p. 106.

114. Fredelle Bruser, "Comus and the Rose Song," *SP,* XLIV (1947), 625–644.

115. James Michie, *The Odes of Horace,* p. 131.

116. Ibid., p. 27.

117. Hightower, p. 185.

118. Also in Ch'en and Bullock, p. 38; *ACV,* p. 153.

119. Also in Ch'en and Bullock, p. 110.

120. The phrase is J. B. Leishman's, in *Themes and Variations in Shakespeare's Sonnets* (London: Hutchinson, 1961), p. 100.

121. Quoted in Hiram Haydn, *The Counter-Renaissance* (New York: Scribner, 1950), p. 363.

122. Quinones gives a fuller treatment of the subject.

123. *JCP,* p. 446.

124. S. P. Zitner, *The Mutabilitie Cantos* (London: Nelson, 1968), p. 118.

125. *The Odes and Epodes,* p. 325.

126. Quoted in Burton Watson, *Early Chinese Literature* (New York: Columbia University Press, 1962).

127. Vincent Yu-cheng Shih, *The Literary Mind and the Carving of Dragons* (Taipei: Chung Hwa Book Company, 1970), p. 131.

128. William Hung, *Tu Fu,* p. 248.

Epilogue

1. I have consulted the following: *Kaifūsō, Bunka shūrei shū* (818?), and *Honchō monzui* (1028?) by Fujiwara Akihira (989–1066); *Wankan rōei shū* (1018?) by Fujiwara Kintō (966–1041) and *Ryōjin hishō* (1179) by Emperor Goshirakawa (1127–92); and *Gozan bungakushū* and *Edo kanshi shū,* in *Nihon koten bungaku taikei,* LXIX (1964), LXXIII (1965), and LXXXIX (1966).

2. Japanese examples in the vernacular have not yet achieved definite structural, thematic, and imagistic patterns, as, for example, in *KKS,* VIII.

3. See *Edo kanshi shū,* pp. 194, 211, 227, 277, 294. Emperor Saga wrote five poems in Chinese on the fisherman after Chinese models, for which see *Keikokushū,* 14.536b (*Gunsho ruijū,* VIII [Tokyo, 1932], 125). In this connection I might mention that in the early period in Japan, when the *Man'yō* poets wrote, the Korean influence was very strong. Yamanoe Okura was a third-generation Korean-Japanese and also a reasonably skilled understander of Chinese. Some scholars think that perhaps as much as a third of the Japanese aristocracy in the eighth century was Korean. The lack of surviving documents makes it difficult to be certain, but close study of the evidence has made the Korean presence seem ever greater. I owe this information to my friend Earl Miner.

4. *JCP,* p. 437.

5. During the Yi dynasty.

6. McIntosh, *Thoreau as Romantic Naturalist,* p. 269; "The enemy to all those New Englanders was Nature," Allen Tate says in "Emily Dickinson," *Essays of Four Decades* (Chicago: The Swallow Press, 1968), p. 287.

7. Of course Japan had *The Tale of Genji,* a long courtly romance written about 1010, but I do not consider it a single-focus narrative work.

INDEX